当代中国名家双语阅读文库 | 丛书主编 | 杨昊成
当代中国名家双语阅读文库 | 丛书副主编 | 李钟涛

|卷|

FAN
XIAO
QING

南京师范大学出版社
NANJING NORMAL UNIVERSITY PRESS

图书在版编目（CIP）数据

当代中国名家双语阅读文库.范小青卷：汉英对照／杨昊成主编；范小青著. —— 南京：南京师范大学出版社，2018.3
 ISBN 978-7-5651-3579-8

Ⅰ.①当… Ⅱ.①杨… ②范… Ⅲ.①中国文学－当代文学－作品综合集－汉、英 Ⅳ.①I217.1

中国版本图书馆CIP数据核字（2017）第298517号

丛 书 名	当代中国名家双语阅读文库
丛书主编	杨昊成
书 　 名	当代中国名家双语阅读文库·范小青卷
著 　 者	范小青
译 　 者	Florence Woo，Helen Wang，Shelly Bryant，Edward Allen，Jesse Field
封面题字	杨昊成
策划编辑	郑海燕　王雅琼
责任编辑	李思思　郑海燕
出版发行	南京师范大学出版社
地 　 址	江苏省南京市玄武区后宰门西村9号（邮编：210016）
电 　 话	（025）83598919（总编办）　83598412（营销部） 83598297（邮购部）
网 　 址	http://www.njnup.com
电子信箱	nspzbb@163.com
照 　 排	南京理工大学资产经营有限公司
印 　 刷	江苏凤凰扬州鑫华印刷有限公司
开 　 本	880毫米×1230毫米　1/32
印 　 张	10.875
字 　 数	316千
版 　 次	2018年3月第1版　2018年3月第1次印刷
书 　 号	ISBN 978-7-5651-3579-8
定 　 价	38.00元
出 版 人	彭志斌

南京师大版图书若有印装问题请与销售商调换
版权所有　　侵犯必究

范小青

江苏苏州人，1955 年出生于上海松江一个知识分子家庭。1982 年毕业于苏州大学中文系，并留校担任文学理论教师。但她很快发现自己对写作更感兴趣，三年后改行从事专业写作。

范小青是一位勤奋而多产的作家，至今已出版超过十六部长篇小说、七部散文集以及大量的短篇小说。《裤裆巷风流记》《百日阳光》《城市表情》《女同志》《城乡简史》《瑞云》《鹰扬巷》等作品不仅获得了评论界的高度赞誉，而且受到老幼读者的广泛好评。如今范小青任江苏省作家协会主席，这已是她第三次担任此职了。

Fan Xiaoqing

A native of Suzhou, Jiangsu Province, was born into a family of intellectuals in Songjiang, Shanghai, in 1955. After graduating from the Chinese Department of Soochow University in 1982, she became a teacher of literary theories at her *alma mater*. But she soon came to find herself more interested in writing than in teaching, and switched to professional writing three years later.

Fan is a diligent and prolific writer; she has published over sixteen novels, seven collections of prose, and numerous short stories. *Romance from Kudang Alley*, *A Hundred Days of Sunshine*, *Urban Expressions*, *Women Comrades*, "City Living, Country living" "Rui Yun" "Ying Yang Alley" and others have not only won much critical accolade but are widely popular with readers young and old as well. Fan Xiaoqing is now on her third term in office as the Chair of Jiangsu Writers Association.

总　序

　　如今的大学生还读书吗？当然。可是他们又都读些什么呢？上网，看短信，深陷在微博、微信等网络平台那大海般的巨量信息中。他们看似阅读广泛，可他们所读和热爱阅读的东西，大都纯粹是垃圾。他们什么都懂一点，可懂的那点东西却缺少实质的深度与广度。他们整天手机不离手，对周围的一切置若罔闻。小小的一部机器已然进入教室，取代教科书，成为最吸引眼球、最引人注目的玩物，令教师们绝望地目瞪口呆。"反正教科书也充斥了不地道的文字"，我回忆起多年前曾就中国的大学教育问起过先师 Jessie Chambers，她就这么说过，当时令我大感意外。

Preface

Do college students read today? Certainly they do, but what do they read? Well, they surf the net, they read the text messages, and they get bogged down in an ocean of information from blogs or WeChat. They seem to be extensively read, but much they read and enjoy reading is nothing but sheer guff and hogwash. They know something about everything, but nothing they know seems to be of any substantial depth or width. Mobile phones not leaving their hands even for a moment, they are phubbing all those around them. The tiny machine makes its way to the classroom where it replaces the textbook as the most eye-catching and attention-drawing plaything to the hopeless stare of the teachers. "The textbook is full of corrupt stuff anyway," as I recall with astonishment what my late advisor Jessie Chambers said years ago when she was asked to give her opinion on China's college education.

所以，如今的大学生似乎更喜欢来自新媒体的碎片化阅读，严肃文学因此令人悲哀地受到轻视或藐视，被遗忘在图书馆的书架上，满是尘埃，仅成为少数书生的精神食粮。而论及英语学习，情况同样令人沮丧。中国学生不再阅读严肃文学，他们学到的是满口"kind of"的莫名其妙的一堆"废话"、网络用语、流行歌曲和夸张的耸肩行为。他们常常自以为英文流利，完全不知真正掌握一门外语必须建立在大量阅读各种优秀文学作品的基础之上。

说起课外阅读，我想起十一年前我和我太太在纽约看望她的表妹时所见到的情形。她表妹有一个儿子和一个女儿：儿子Franklin是宾夕法尼亚大学的本科生；女儿Shelly刚小学毕业。Shelly当时正激动地等待着毕业典礼的到来，次日我们全都参加了她的毕业典礼。出于好奇，我随手翻阅了Shelly所看的书。我看到她的书桌上散乱堆放着莎士比亚、弥尔顿、马克·吐温、海明威等人的书，当然还有一册《哈利·波特》。我问Shelly："你在读这些书？""看着玩。"小姑娘随口答道。一个小学生，课外在阅读莎士比亚、弥尔顿、马克·吐温、海明威！而且是"看着玩"！我们的大学生们在看什么书？多年来，这件事一直如铅块一样压在我的心头。

或者拿美国学生来比较不太合适？那好，咱们来看一下战时

So it is fragmented reading from the new media that college students seem to be enjoying today, and serious literature is woefully slighted or neglected, forgotten in the dust-covered shelves of the libraries, becoming the spiritual food for a minority of bookish souls. When it comes to English learning, the situation is no more encouraging. Chinese students do not read serious literature anymore; what they have learned is gibberish full of "kind of," or the internet jives and cants, some pop songs, and an exaggerated show of shrugs. They count themselves fluent in English, not knowing that a real command of the foreign tongue is built on an extensive reading of good literatures of all kinds.

Talking of extracurricular reading, I remember what I saw when my wife and I were visiting her cousin eleven years ago in New York. She has a son and a daughter; the boy, Franklin, was an undergraduate of the University of Pennsylvania, and the girl, Shelly, having just finished her elementary school, was awaiting with great excitement her commencement which we all attended the next day. I, out of curiosity, was flipping through Shelly's reading materials. I saw Shakespeare, Milton, Mark Twain, Hemingway, etc., lying helter-skelter on her reading table. There was a copy of *Harry Potter* of course. I asked Shelly, "You're reading these?" "For fun!" snapped the teenage girl. An elementary school pupil reading Shakespeare, Milton, Mark Twain, and Hemingway outside classroom! And for fun! What are our college students reading? This has been weighing upon me like a leaden slab over the years.

Maybe American students don't make a good comparison? Well, let's look at the contents of *Freshman Readings in English*

中国西南联大的本科生用的教材《大学一年级英文教本》的内容。注意了，这可是西南联大所有大一学生的必读教材，并非英文专业的学生所专有。该书由出生于夏威夷的哈佛大学教育硕士陈福田教授编写，总共遴选了43篇文章，几乎全都出自大家之手，具有浓郁的人文博雅气息，与时下风行大学课堂的所谓"实用英语""商务英语""法律英语""文秘英语"等教材内容大相径庭：《贫瘠的春天》（赛珍珠）、《负重的牲口》（毛姆）、《河之歌》（毛姆）、《妹妹的出生》（邓惜华）、《论烤猪》（查尔斯·兰姆）、《乐观看中国》（胡适）、《生活的目的》（林语堂）、《圣山》（高兹沃斯·洛斯·狄金森）、《花事记忆》（诺拉·沃恩）、《致青年》（安德烈·莫洛亚）、《一对啄木鸟》（佚名）、《红蚂蚁大战黑蚂蚁》（梭罗）、《论自由》（伍德罗·威尔逊）、《何为科学？》（里拉·雷姆森）、《对生活的持久满足》（查尔斯·艾略特）、《妄想的病人》（哲罗姆·K.哲罗姆）、《泄密的心》（埃德加·爱伦·坡）、《孤儿寡母》（华盛顿·欧文）、《呼噜王》（佚名）、《通识教育》（托马斯·亨利·赫胥黎）、《民主社会中教育之功用》（查尔斯·W.艾略特）、《教育的目的》（罗素）、《民主的力量》（沃尔特·李普曼）、《技术文明》（查尔斯·奥斯丁·比尔德）、《大学生的社会价值》（威廉·詹姆斯）、《自由与约束》（阿伯特·劳伦斯·洛维尔）、《民族生命力的解放》（伍德罗·威尔逊）、《习惯》

for undergraduate students of the National Southwestern Associated University in war-torn China. Mind you, this is for all the freshmen and not just the English concentrators. Compiled by Prof Chen Futian, a Hawaii-born Harvard ME, the *Readings* has a total of 43 essays, almost all written by master hands and smack of a strong spirit of liberal education, vastly different from the so-called "Practical English," "Business English," "Legal English," "Secretarial English," etc., so prevalent in college classrooms today: "Barren Spring" by Pearl S. Buck, "Beast of Burden" by W. Somerset Maugham, "Song of the River" by W. Somerset Maugham, "Birth of a Sister" by Tan Shih-hua, "A Dissertation upon Roast Pig" by Charles Lamb, "An Optimist Look at China" by Hu Shih, "The End of Life" by Lin Yutang, "A Sacred Mountain" by G. Lowes Dickinson, "Fragments from a Flower Diary" by Nora Waln, "A Word to Youth" by Andre Maurois, "A Pair of Woodpeckers" by an unknown author, "The Battle of the Red and the Black Ants" by Henry David Thoreau, "Liberty" by Woodrow Wilson, "What Is Science?" by Ira Remsen, "The Durable Satisfactions of Life" by Charles W. Eliot, "The Imaginary Invalid" by Jerome K. Jerome, "The Tell-Tale Heart" by Edgar Allan Poe, "The Widow and Her Son" by Washington Irving, "The Champion Snorer" by an unknown author, "A Liberal Education" by Thomas Henry Huxley, "The Function of Education in Democratic Society" by Charles W. Eliot, "What Shall We Educate for?" by Bertrand Russell, "The Strength of Democracy" by Walter Lippmann, "Technological Civilization" by Charles A. Beard, "The Social Value of the College-Bred" by William James, "Liberty and

(威廉·詹姆斯)、《经典之所以为经典》(阿诺德·本涅特)、《时代变迁》(约翰·高尔斯华绥)、《加利波利战役》(约翰·梅斯菲尔德)、《半英里》(T. O. 比奇克罗夫特)、《长长的阴影》(约翰·汉普森)、《萨梯跳舞的田野》(邓萨尼勋爵)、《人人想当别人》(塞缪尔·麦考德·克罗瑟斯)、《哲学家》(毛姆)、《俾斯麦》(埃米尔·路德维希)、《希特勒之谜》(斯蒂芬 H. 罗伯茨)、《英国外交政策》(约翰·根室)、《美国人对自由之热爱》(埃德蒙·伯克)、《什么是大学?》(约翰·亨利·纽曼)、《通识学院的理论》(亚历山大·米克尔约翰)、《英语学习的自我培养》(乔治·赫伯特·帕玛)。而这还仅仅是大学一年级学生的阅读材料。试想一下,经过四年对人文材料这种螺旋式不断上升的精研细读,学生们会变成什么样?

读者们可能会说,这毕竟是外国文学,我们是中国人。那么中国学生一定精通母语或对中国文学博识通览吧?根本不是这么回事!我惊愕地发现,如今有的中国大学生什么中国文学经典也没读过。我曾教授过一门名为"文学经典翻译"的课程,在我准备的中英文材料中,似乎没有一篇在学生的阅读名单中,唯一的例外也许是鲁迅的《孔乙己》,而那是在中学课本里的。大家都很熟悉例如"四大名著"的书名,但没多少人有耐心真正去阅读那些作品。道家和儒家经典如《道德经》

Discipline" by Abbot Lawrence Lowell, "The Liberation of a People's Vital Energies" by Woodrow Wilson, "Habit" by William James, "Why a Classic Is a Classic" by Arnold Bennett, "Evolution" by John Galsworthy, "Fighting in Gallipoli" by John Masefield, "The Half Mile" by T. O. Beachcroft, "The Long Shadow" by John Hampson, "The Field Where the Satyrs Danced" by Lord Dunsany, "Every Man's Natural Desire to Be Somebody Else" by Samuel McChord Crothers, "The Philosopher" by W. Somerset Maugham, "Bismarck" by Emil Ludwig, "The Riddle of Hitler" by Stephen H. Roberts, "British Foreign Policy" by John Gunther, "The American Love of Freedom" by Edmund Burke, "What Is a University?" by John Henry Newman, "Theory of the Liberal College" by Alexander Meiklejohn, "Self-Cultivation in English" by George Herbert Palmer. And these are only freshman readings. Just imagine what the students would be like after four years of intensive, spiral reading of arts and letters like these!

You would say that they are most of them foreign literatures and our students are Chinese, and as Chinese they must be well versed in their mother tongue or well read in Chinese literature. Not at all! I find to my dismay that Chinese college students haven't read anything of Chinese literary classics. I used to teach a course named "Translation of Literary Classics." Among all the English and Chinese materials I'd prepared, nothing seemed to have been on the students' reading list except perhaps Lu Xun's "Kong Yiji," which was in their middle school textbook. They're well acquainted with, say, the names of the "Four Literary Masterpieces," but not many of them have bothered to read any one of them. Taoist and

《庄子》《论语》《孟子》《大学》《中庸》等更是无从谈起,尽管这些都是往日每一位小学生的必读书目。他们声称,其中的教诲远离当今的现实生活,它们的语言表达方式对于现代读者来说显得十分晦涩难懂。

这样的情形真够令人丧气的,可也正是在如此灰暗的背景下,南京师范大学出版社推出了《当代中国名家双语阅读文库》,旨在挽回一部分"迷途的羔羊",希望他们能回到传统的纸质阅读的正常轨道上来。不过,本文库的目标读者并非只限于大学生,因为每一个对汉译英、比较文学和中西文化比较研究感兴趣的人,都可以从中获益匪浅。对于这个文库,至少有两点可以一说。首先,它是在"中国文化走出去"这个有利气候下诞生的,这句自上而下、而今被热捧的全国性口号,对于文库的出版意义重大。一个国家在世界经济中获得坚强地位后——正如中国强有力地向外部世界所展示的那样,就希望在诸如文化等其他各个方面全面出击,这是很正常的事。从历史上看,法语联盟、英国文化协会、歌德学院等都是这样,它们都是各自国家从事文化交流的重镇。虽说它们多半是民族自信和自豪的产物,但它们的存在似乎完全没有错。关键问题还是在于一个国家的文化如何走出去。有两股力量在做着这方面的工作:一是各级官员,二是诸如学者、作家、翻译家、编辑等专业人士。这两股力量有着同一个

Confucian classics such as *Daodejing* (Classics of the Way and Virtue), *Zhuangzi*, *The Analects*, *Mencius*, *The Great Learning*, *The Doctrine of the Golden Mean*, etc., must readings of any school kids of olden days, are even more out of the question. They claim that their teachings are far detached from real life and their way of linguistic expression is miserably esoteric to modern readers.

　　The situation is discouraging enough, but it is against this gloomy background that "A Bilingual Library of Contemporary Chinese Master Writers" is launched by Nanjing Normal University Press in hopes of bringing back some of the lost lambs to the normal track of conventional mode of paper book reading. However, our target readers are not limited to college students only, for any one who might be interested in Chinese-English translation, comparative literature, and comparative studies between Chinese and Western cultures may find their own rewards in reading the Library for which there are two points to say at the least. First, the present Library is born against the favorable climate of "Chinese culture going international" which, as a top-down, nationwide, and now largely canonized slogan, means a lot to its publication. It is all natural that when a country has won a stronghold in world economy, as China has now robustly shown to the outside world, it desires to go all out in other respects such as culture. It is historically true of such institutions as Alliance française, British Council, and Goethe-Institut, all important venues of their respective country's cultural interflow. Though probably a matter of national self-confidence and pride, there seems to be nothing wrong with that. The question remains how a country's culture is to go global. Two forces are at

目标，但不幸的是，在将自己的文化成就介绍到外部世界去的时候，他们所采取的策略和手段却不尽相同。前者很多都不通外语及外国文化，却想把自己认为的宝贝强行兜售给潜在的买家，殊不知文化交流很大程度上犹如贸易，是建立在平等交换及买家自愿选择的基础之上的，任何一厢情愿的强卖是注定要失败的。后者比前者要懂行得多，却在政治方向和经济资助上有赖于前者，因此常常陷入这样一种困境：他们想按自己认为的正确的道路前进，却不时遭遇令人厌恶的障碍，那就是来自前者的不受欢迎的指示或干扰。《中国文学》这份挣扎了整整五十年的官方杂志就是一个很好的教训。虽然《中国文学》在它的后半段有杨宪益这样多产又具有人格魅力的翻译家担任主编，但杨宪益一人显然无力抵御他那个时代的政治影响。《中国文学》有着明显的时代印记，这也解释了为什么这么多年它在海外一直不怎么为人所接受。

非常幸运的是，《当代中国名家双语阅读文库》得以坚持自己既定的标准，文库内收集的都是当今中国最负盛名的作家的代表作或得到人们高度认可的作品。数十年的意识形态斗争过去了，我们终于可以回归到文学创作的本体研究。所有收录在本文库的翻译作品，虽然它们对待文学的手法和角度有着天壤之别，却都道出了人性和人生的共性，那就是人类的喜、怒、哀、乐。这些

work: bureaucrats at all levels, and professionals such as researchers, writers, translators, editors, and publishers. The two forces have the same aim, but sadly, differing strategies and approaches in introducing their cultural achievements to the outside world. The former, largely ignorant of the foreign languages and their cultures, want very much to sell off what they deem it the precious stuff to the potential buyer, not knowing that cultural exchange is, to a great extent, like trade, and is built on the basis of equal give-and-take, and willing choice on the side of the buyer, and any one-sided forced selling is doomed to failure. The latter, though much more informed, is reliant on the former for political direction and financial support, and is thus left in a dilemma: they want to proceed with what they regard as the right path, but are now and then met with undesirable obstacles, those unwished-for directions or interferences from the former. *Chinese Literature*, an official-sponsored magazine which has struggled a whole of fifty years, is a good lesson. Though CL has as its chief editor prolific and charismatic translator Yang Xianyi in the second half of its fifty-year long life, Yang alone certainly would not have that strength to stay clear of the political influences of his day. CL bears the clear hallmark of the time, which explains its low acceptability overseas over the years.

Very luckily, the present Library is able to adhere to its set standard, and what is collected here is either the representative works or the highly recognized pieces of some of the most famous writers of contemporary China. After the elapse of dozens of years of ideological struggles, we are able to return at last to the

短篇,以其洗练的笔法、精巧的结构、典型的人物事件,成为当代中国文学宝库中极为重要的组成部分。为了更好更立体地呈现作家及其作品,除了少数例外,我们还为每个作家收录了一篇评论和一篇访谈。

其次,从事翻译的人都清楚,当目标语为母语时,译者们做得就要好一些。译者的母语是英语,从事汉译英就会得心应手得多,这是不争的事实。我还清楚地记得大约十二年前就《水浒传》的翻译给沙博理先生(Sidney Shapiro)打电话的情形。我生动地记得电话中沙博理先生对我说的话:"对我来说,翻译像《水浒传》这样的作品比将英文材料译成中文要容易得多。虽然早在1963年我就入了中国籍,但中文毕竟不是我的母语。"

本文库以拥有一支高超的职业翻译家队伍为豪,他们的母语是英语,又全都是双语或多种语言的使用者。这就完全不一样了。事实上,无论是《中国文学》还是几乎所有其他由中国人办的期刊杂志,都有着相同的问题:它们的译者大都是非母语使用者,其英语是作为第二语言习得的,无法跟母语是英语的职业翻译家相比。更为难得的是,这些译者对中文的掌握都是一流的,其中不少人是世界公认的汉学家或老牌的中国通。Denis Mair(梅丹理)、Nicky Harman(韩斌)、Natascha Bruce、Luisetta Mudie、Shelly Bryant(白雪莉)、Josh Stenberg(石峻山)、Helen Wang、 ontological study of literary creation, and all the works translated here speak of the commonality of human nature and human life, i. e. man's happiness, anger, sorrow, and joy, despite the vast different approaches and perspectives towards literature. With their succinct style, exquisite structure, and typical characters and events, these stories constitute an extremely important integral part of the treasure house of contemporary Chinese literature. For a better and more three-dimensional presentation of the authors and their works, we have also included a critique and an interview for each author with only a few exceptions.

Second, it is common knowledge among translators that they will do better when their target language is the mother tongue. It's an undeniable fact that translators whose mother tongue is English will be much more at home when it comes to Chinese-English translation. I recall with great amazement when about twelve years ago I called Sidney Shapiro about his translation of *Outlaws of the Marsh*. I remember very vividly what Mr Shapiro said to me on the phone: "Translating things like *Outlaws of the Marsh* is much easier for me than translating English materials into Chinese. After all Chinese is not my mother tongue though I became a Chinese citizen as early as 1963."

The present Library boasts a terrific pool of professional translators whose mother tongue is English and are all of them bilinguals or multilinguals. They are the same batch of translators working for *Chinese Arts and Letters*. This makes all the difference. In fact both *Chinese Literature* and almost all other journals and magazines run by the Chinese have the same problem: Many of their

Jeremy Tiang、Eric Abrahamsen、Michael Day、Simon Patton、Florence Woo 等,是我们最为尽职而宝贵的翻译家中的一部分。出自他们之手的译作,乍看之下可能并无特殊之处,实际却很是地道,读起来非常舒服,常令我们击节叹赏。这里我们给那些对汉译英有兴趣的读者略举几例,它们全都来自《中华人文》并且都已进入《当代中国名家双语阅读文库》。

"她有着凹凸有致的身材"译为"She has a figure of voluptuous curves"。还有一个高度口语化的专门词汇可以用来描述这样的女孩,即 zaftig,所以我们经常可以听到人们说:她是那种身材火辣、招蜂引蝶的女孩儿(She is a sort of zaftig, coquettish girl)。"包二奶"如今已是很常见的一个说法了,我们的译者将它译成"to keep a bit on the side","当小三"也就顺理成章地译作"to be sb's bit on the side";"bit"意为"水性杨花的女子","on the side"意思是"悄悄地""私下里",不过还带点幽默。如今许多年轻人喜欢用的"吃货"一词,在英文里也有相对应的说法,即"greedy guts"[注意是 guts 而非 gut,如 He is a greedy guts(他是个吃货)],虽然在已故陆谷孙教授主编的当今最为先进的《中华汉英大词典》中有诸如 foodie、glutton、gourmand、gastronaut、food aficionado 等其他译法。"恶搞"(to kuso)事实上来自日语,但已进入英语词汇,令"to parody""to lampoon""to snark"等稍显过时。"phubber"是

translators are non-native speakers or writers whose English is learned as a second language and not to be compared with those professional translators whose mother tongue is English and better still, whose command of the Chinese language is superb and many of whom are world recognized sinologists or old China hands. Denis Mair, Nicky Harman, Natascha Bruce, Luisetta Mudie, Shelly Bryant, Josh Stenberg, Helen Wang, Jeremy Tiang, Eric Abrahamsen, Michael Day, Simon Patton, Florence Woo, etc., are some of our most conscientious and treasured translators. What come out of their hands may seem to be, at first glance, nothing special, yet are so idiomatic and read so comfortable that we cannot but cry with admiration. Here are a pittance of examples for those interested in C-E translation, all picked from *CAL* and have made their way into the present Library:

"她有着凹凸有致的身材": She has a figure of voluptuous curves. And there is a special word, albeit highly colloquial, to describe that kind of girl, i.e. zaftig. So we constantly hear people say: She is a sort of zaftig, coquettish girl. "包二奶" is a very common term today, and *CAL* translator renders it into "to keep a bit on the side," and accordingly, "当小三" is "to be sb's bit on the side," "bit" meaning a loose woman, and "on the side" in secret or on the sly, but with a bit of humor. "吃货," enjoyed by many young people today, also has its English equivalent, "greedy guts," (Mind you, it's guts and not gut. For instance: He is a greedy guts.) aside from other renditions such as foodie, glutton, gourmand, gastronaut, food aficionado, as listed by the most advanced Chinese-English Dictionary chief-edited by the late Prof. Lu Gusun. And "phubbing"一词的逆构,据说是由澳大利亚的几个语言学家、词典编纂家和作家从"phone"和"snub"两个词合并创立的一个新词。这个新词用来描述那种不顾周围人事、一心看手机的人,和目前流行的中国词汇"低头族"完全一致。这个词只有五年的历史,尽管已被收入《澳大利亚国家词典》,其他绝大多数词典或工具书却尚未收入。简单而口语化的说法如"过了这村儿没这店儿"和"金窝银窝,不如自家狗窝",被高超地译成了简洁有力的"It's now or never",和至今为止最贴近原文的"Gold dish, silver dish, they cannot compare to your own dog's dish",它们分别是从平淡无奇的"last chance"和同样令人难忘却丢失了原意象的"East or west, home is best"中生出的天才的产物。

仅此一点——如果我可以这么说的话,就足以使本文库成为对于翻译感兴趣的读者的一个很好的阅读材料。读者们也许会对我的话抱有怀疑,但我绝不是自吹自擂。作为《中华人文》和本双语文库的主编,我对这两份出版物中的每一篇文章的每一个字都仔细拜读、研究过,所以我对本文库的鼓吹不是基于初步的印象,而是肺腑之言。事实上,编辑这些材料对我自己而言,也是一个了解两种语言以及全面提升自己的极好机会。

文学评论家吴义勤、学者及翻译家许钧、作家苏童都从他们各自不同的视角出发,对本文库的出版表示了强有力的支持。三

"恶搞" actually has a Japanese term "to kuso," which has already entered into the English language, making "to parody," "to lampoon," "to snark" seem somewhat outdated. "Phubber," the reverse formation of "phubbing," which is said to be a new coinage by some Australian linguists, lexicographers, and authors from "phone" and "snub," a neologism to describe the habit of snubbing people around you in favor of a mobile phone, is exactly the same as the popular Chinese term "低头族." It only has a history of five years, and though already in the *Australian National Dictionary*, most other dictionaries or thesauruses have not yet included it. And such simple and oral sayings as "过了这村儿没这店儿" and "金窝银窝,不如自家狗窝" are masterfully translated into a pithy "It's now or never," and the most faithful to date "Gold dish, silver dish, they cannot compare to your own dog's dish" respectively, both genius outgrowths from the prosaic "last chance," and the equally memorable yet the image-not-there clause "East or west, home is best."

This alone, if I may say so, is a good reason why the Library is a good read for all those who are interested in translation. Readers may take my word *cum grano salis*, but I'm not blowing my own trumpet, for as the editor in chief of both *Chinese Arts and Letters* and this bilingual library, I've read and studied each and every word of all the pieces printed in both publications and my boost for the Library is not just prima facie but from the bottom of my heart. In fact, editing them turns out to be a great opportunity for myself to learn about the two languages and uplift me in an all-around way.

As far as I know, literary critic Wu Yiqin, academic and translator Xu Jun, and writer Su Tong have all voiced their strong

位都是他们各自领域的重要人物，他们的意见更增加了本文库的权威性。

《当代中国名家双语阅读文库》是开放性的，它会不断地出下去。它以五位作家为一辑，每位作家为一卷，每卷包括五个短篇并附有一篇评论和一篇访谈，其中个别卷会略有变化。为了本文库的出版，各方面的人员做出了很多努力或给予了很大支持，其中包括我们杰出的翻译家、作家、评论家，《中华人文》和南京师范大学出版社的领导、编辑等，可以说这是一次令人快乐又组织有序的大合唱。

是为序。

杨昊成

2017 年 12 月 16 日

support for this Library, each speaking from their different perspectives. The three are all towering figures in their own fields and their opinions add to the authority of the Library.

This Library is meant to be open-ended, though set to be on a five-author basis which includes five short stories together with a critique and an interview for each author with slight variations. For the publication of the Library, various people have contributed their efforts and lent their support, including our terrific translators, authors, critics, editors from *CAL* and Nanjing Normal University Press, and the Press's leadership so you may say it's a joyful and well-orchestrated *tutti*.

And this is my preface.

Yang Haocheng

December 16, 2017

目录

城乡简史 026
鹰扬巷 082
生于黄昏或清晨 100
我们都在服务区 158
梦幻快递 222

附录
|评论
　　转型前后——阅读范小青/王　尧 278
|访谈
　　写作于我,更多的是享受过程中的创造、宁静和自由
　　　　——范小青访谈录/杨昊成 304

Contents

City Living, Country Living   027

Ying Yang Alley   083

Born in an Unknown Hour   101

We're All in the Service Area   159

The Hallucinated Courier   223

Appendices

|Critique

   Before and after Transition: Reading Fan Xiaoqing
   / Wang Yao   279

|Interview

   "It Is More the Creativity, Peace and Freedom in the
   Process of Writing that I Enjoy": An Interview
   with Fan Xiaoqing / Yang Haocheng   305

城乡简史

自清喜欢买书。买书是好事情，可是到后来就渐渐地有了许多不便之处，主要是家里的书越来越多。本来书是人买来的，人是书的主人，结果书太多了，事情就反过来了，书挤占了人的空间，人在书的缝隙中艰难栖息，人成了书的奴隶。在书的世界里，人越来越渺小，越来越压抑，最后人要夺回自己的地位，就得对书下手了。怎么下手？当然是把书处理掉一部分，让它还出位置来。这位置本来是人的。

City Living, Country Living

Translated by Florence Woo

Ziqing loved buying books. That in and of itself wasn't necessarily a bad thing, but over time it caused problems—the most serious of which was that there simply came to be too many books in the house. Originally, man was the master over books, as they were his acquisition. But eventually, as books grew more and more numerous, their roles reversed: books crowded into man's living space, and man had to beg for a dwelling place in their midst. Man thus became a slave to his books. In the world of books, man became more and more insignificant, more and more oppressed. So, when man wished to take back his rightful place, he must rise up against his books. How, then, did he do that? Why? Get rid of some of them, of course, and force them to relinquish the space that

自清的家属特别兴奋,她等了许多年终于等到了这一天,对于家里摆满了的书,她早就欲除它们而后快。在自清的决心将下未下、犹犹豫豫的这些日子里,她没有少费口舌,也没有少花心思,总之是变着法子说尽书的坏话。家里的其他大小事情,一概是她做主的,但唯一在书的问题上,自清不肯让步,所以她也只能以理服他,再以事实说话。她拿出一些毛料的衣服给他看,毛料衣服上有一些被虫子蛀的洞,这些虫子,就是从书里爬出来的,是银灰色的,大约有一厘米长短,细细的身子,滑起来又快又溜,像一道道细小的闪电,它们不怕樟脑,也不怕敌杀死,什么也不怕,有时候还成群结队大摇大摆地在地板上经过,好像是展示实力。后来自清的家属还看到报纸上有一个说法,一个家庭如果书太多,家庭里的人常年呼吸在书的空气里,对小孩子的身体不好,容易患呼吸道疾病,自清认为这种说法没有科学性,但也不敢拿孩子的身体来开玩笑。就这样,日积月累,家属的说服工作,终于见到了成效,自清说,好吧,该处理的,就处理掉,屋里也实在放不下了。

originally belonged to him.

 Ziqing's better half was extremely excited. She had waited many long years for this day; for all these years she had been wishing to rid the house of all the books. In the days when Ziqing was wavering between "should I" and "should I not", she spared no effort and left no method untried to depict the books as the common enemy.

 While she was normally the mistress of everything in the house, Ziqing would not yield on the book issue. Her only recourse was to present logical arguments and back them up with facts. She showed Ziqing some pieces of woollen clothing in which were little holes chewed through by worms. These worms couldn't have come from anywhere but the books. They were grey in colour, about a centimetre long, and had slender bodies. They glided around, swift and slick, like little bolts of lightning. Camphor had no effect on them, and they seemed immune to household pesticides too—or anything else for that matter. Sometimes they even strutted across the floor in packs, as if in a show of strength. Ziqing's better half also read something in the newspapers saying that, if there are too many books in a house, its inhabitants would breathe in the book-air day after day, which is bad for the health of children; it makes them contract respiratory illnesses more easily. Even though Ziqing didn't believe that this argument had any scientific grounds, he didn't dare to risk the health of his child either.

 So, in this fashion, Ziqing's better half presented more and more arguments for her case, and they finally produced a cumulative effect. Ziqing said, "Fine, I'll get rid of what needs getting rid of. The house is indeed getting too full."

处理书的方法有许多种，卖掉，送给亲戚朋友，甚至扔掉。但扔掉是舍不得的，其中有许多书，自清当年是费了许多心思和精力才弄到手的。比如有一本薄薄的书，他是特意坐火车跑到浙江的一个小镇上去觅来的。这本书印数很少，又不是什么畅销书，专业性比较强，这么多年下来，自清从来没有在别的地方看到过它，现在它也和其他要被处理的书躺在了一起。自清看到了，又舍不得，又随手捡了回来。他的家属说，你这本也要捡回来那本也要捡回来，最后是一本也处理不掉的，家属的话说得不错，自清又将它丢回去，但心里有依依惜别隐隐疼痛的感觉。这些书曾经是他的宝贝，是他的精神支柱，一些年过去了，他竟要将它们扔掉？自清下不了这样的手。家属说，你舍不得扔掉，那就卖吧，多少也值一点钱。可是卖旧书是三钱不值两钱的，说是卖，几乎就是送，尤其现在新书的书价一翻再翻，卖旧书却仍然按斤论两，更显出旧书的贱，再加上收旧货的人可能还会克扣分量，还会用不标准的秤砣来坑蒙欺骗。一想到这些书像被捆扎了前往屠宰场的猪一样，而且还是被堵住了嘴不许嚎叫的猪，自清心里就有说

There are many ways to get rid of books: selling them, giving them to family and friends, or even plain throwing them out. But he couldn't get himself to throw them out. Much of his collection was obtained through a great deal of perseverance and effort. For example, there was this one slim volume that Ziqing had to take the train to a small town in Zhejiang Province to dig up. There weren't very many copies of this book in print. Its topic was a bit esoteric and the volume was not a best-seller by any means. Ziqing had not seen it anywhere else since. And now it lay amongst the other books to be gotten rid of. The sight of that pained Ziqing, and he ended up picking it up and putting it back on the shelf again.

His better half said, "If you keep taking this one back and taking that one back, you'll end up not getting rid of a single book at all." Right she was. He threw it back, but the pain of parting still gnawed at his heart. These books had once been his beloved, his moral support, his anchor. To toss them out just after a few years? He could not make himself do it. His better half suggested, "If you can't bring yourself to throw them out, then sell them. At least you could get a bit of money back."

However, old books were not worth much on the market. Selling them practically meant giving them away. While new books were listed for more and more money, old books were still sold by weight, a testimony to their worthlessness. On top of that, junk collectors were likely to give short weight or cheat people with non-standard scales. When Ziqing pictured in his head his old books bundled up like a pig tied up to be sent to the slaughterhouse—a pig that is muzzled and not allowed to cry—he felt overwhelmingly wretched inside.

不出的难过。算了算了，他说，卖它干什么，还是送送人吧。可是谁要这些书呢，自清的小舅子说，我一张光盘就抵你十个书屋了，我要书干什么？也有一个和他一样喜欢书的人，看着也眼馋，家里也有地方，他倒是想要了，但他的老婆跟自清的家属不和，说，我们家不见得穷得要拣人家丢掉的破烂。结果自清忍痛割爱的这些书，竟然没个去处。

正好这时候，政府发动大家向贫困地区的学校捐赠书籍或其他物资，自清清理出来的书，正好有了去处，捆扎了几麻袋，专门雇了一辆人力车，拖到扶贫办公室去，领回了一张荣誉证书。

时隔不久，自清发现他的一本账本不见了。自清有记账的习惯，从很早的时候就开始了，许多年坚持下来，每年都有一本账本，记着家里的各项收入和开支。本来记账也不是一件很特别的事，许多家庭里都会有一个人负责记账，也是长年累月坚持不变的。但自清的记账可能和其他人家还有所不同，别人记账，无非就是这个月里买了什么东西，用了多少钱，再细致一点的，写上具体的日期就算是比较认真的记法了。总之，家庭记账一般就是

"Forget it," he said, "what's the point of selling them? I might as well give them away." But who would want these books? His brother-in-law said, "Nowadays you can put ten times the number of books you have in a single DVD, so what use would I have for your books?" Then there was another fellow who was as much of a bibliophile as Ziqing was. He coveted the books, and even had space for them at home. He would have gladly taken them off Ziqing's hands but for his wife, who didn't get along with Ziqing's better half. She said, "We're not so poor that we have to take another family's rubbish."

After all that, all those books that Ziqing was so reluctant to part with were still without a new home.

Right at that time, the government launched a campaign to collect donations in the form of books and other household goods, for schools in disadvantaged areas. Finally Ziqing's books had somewhere to go. He bundled them up in a few large hemp cloth sacks, and hired a rickshaw to carry them to the donation office. In return he received a Certificate of Honour.

Not long after, Ziqing realized that one of his ledger books was missing. He had been in the habit of keeping a household ledger for a long time and had persisted through the years. He kept a separate volume for each year, documenting each item of household income and expense.

To be fair, bookkeeping isn't anything particularly remarkable; in many families there would be a designated bookkeeper who would keep the household account year after year. However, Ziqing's ledgers might be a bit unlike most people's. Most people's accounts

单纯地记下家庭的收入和开销,但自清的账本,有时候会超出账本的内容,也超出了单纯记账的意义,基本上像是一本日记了,他不仅像大家一样记下购买的东西和价钱,记下日期,还会详细写下购买这件东西的前因后果,时代背景,周边的环境,当时的心情,甚至去那个商店,是怎么去的,走去的,还是坐公交车,或者是打的,都要记一笔,天气怎么样,也是要写清楚的,淋没淋着雨,晒没晒着太阳,路上有没有堵车,都有记载,甚至在购物时发生的一些与他无关、与他购物也无关的别人的小故事,他也会记下来。比如某年某月某日的一次,他记下了这样的内容:下午5时25分,在鱼龙菜场买鱼,两条鲫鱼已经过秤,被扔进他的菜篮子,这时候一个巨大的霹雷临空而降突然炸响,吓得鱼贩子夺路而逃,也不要收鱼钱了,一直等到雷雨过后,鱼贩子不知从哪里冒了出来,自清再将鱼钱付清,以为鱼贩子会感动,却不料鱼贩子说,你这个人,顶真得来。好像他们两个人的角色是倒过来的,好像自清是鱼贩子,而鱼贩子是自清。这样的账本早已经离题万里了,但自清不会忘记本来的宗旨,最后记下:购买鲫

are usually no more than a record of what they have bought each month and how much they have spent on it; those who include the actual dates of the purchases are already numbered among the meticulous. Ziqing's ledgers, on the other hand, often went beyond accounting, and beyond the immediate purpose of keeping book. His were practically diaries. On top of writing down the items purchased, their cost, and the date of purchase, he often included details about the reason for the purchase, the background information on the item, the shopping environment, his mood at the time, how he got to the store—did he walk there? Take the bus? Take a taxi?—he would record all that. And the weather had to be recorded clearly too. Did he get soaked in the rain? Or got too warm in the sun? Or got stuck in traffic on his way?—he would put all these down as well.

He would also often record some vignettes of things that happened during shopping, things that had nothing to do with him or his purchase. For example, one day he recorded the following—5∶25 pm, he was buying fish at Dragon Market. Two crucian carp had already been weighed and thrown into his shopping basket. At that time, a sudden thunderclap exploded in the skies, scaring the fishmonger into fleeing and hiding somewhere without first collecting the payment for the fish. Ziqing remained on the spot and waited for the storm to pass. The fishmonger emerged from somewhere. Ziqing paid him for the fish, thinking that he'd be thankful; instead, the fishmonger said, "Aren't you a goody-two-shoes, man!" It was as if their roles had been reversed, as if Ziqing was the fishmonger, and the fishmonger was Ziqing. Such an account had already

鱼两条,重六两,单价,5元/斤,总价,3元。这样的账本,有点喧宾夺主的意思,记账的内容少,账外的内容多。当然也有单纯记账的,只是写下,某年某月某日某时在某某街某某杂货店购买塑料脸盆一只,蓝底绿花,荷花。价格:1元3角5分。

但是自清的账本,虽然内容多一些杂一些,却又是比较随意的,想多记就多记一点,想少写就少写一点,心情好又有时间就多记几笔,情绪不高时间不够就简单一点,也有简单到只有自己能够看得懂的,比如,手:175元。这是记的缴纳的手机费,换一个人,哪怕是他的家属,恐怕也是看不懂的。甚至还有过了几年后连他自己都看不懂的内容,比如,南吃:97元。这个"南吃",其实和许许多多的账本上的许许多多内容一样,过了这一年,就沉睡下去了,也许永远也不会再见世面的,但偏偏自清有个习惯,过一段时间,他会把老账本再翻出来看看,并没有什么目的,也没有什么意义,甚至谈不上是忆旧什么的,只是看看而已。当他看到"南吃"两个字的时候,就停顿下来,想回忆起隐藏在这两个字背后的历史,但是这一小片历史躲藏起来了,就躲

deviated far from the original intent of bookkeeping. But Ziqing always remembered the main point of keeping his ledger—he added at the end: "Bought two crucian carp, 6 *liang*[①] in weight. Price: 5 *yuan* per *jin*[②]. Total cost: 3 *yuan*." Such an entry, mostly recounting non-accounting-related information, seemed to overshadow the principal function of bookkeeping. Of course there were also other entries that were more focused on bookkeeping, such as the ones that read, "On such and such a day at such and such a time, at such and such a general store on such and such a street, bought a plastic washbasin. Blue with green lotus design. Price: 1.35 *yuan*."

That said, even though Ziqing's ledgers had a bit more content and were a bit more disorganized than the general household account, he mostly let his mood dictate how much or how little to write. When the mood struck him and time allowed, he might include a bit more details; when his spirits were low and time was tight, he would be a bit more terse. And sometimes he was concise to the point that no one but himself could understand what he wrote, such as "Mob: 175 *yuan*", which was really an entry for the amount of his mobile phone bill. No one else, not even his better half, could have guessed its meaning.

There were even entries that Ziqing himself could not decipher anymore after a few years. Take, for instance, "N. eat: 97 *yuan*". The phrase "N. eat", like many other words and phrases in the ledgers, should have been laid to rest after the year was over, and never brought to light again. However, Ziqing was in the habit of

---

① Editor's note: liang, a unit of weight, 1 liang=50 grams.
② Editor's note: jin, a unit of weight, 1 jin=500 grams.

藏在"南吃"两个字的背后,怎么也不肯出来。自清就根据这两个字的含义去推理,南吃,吃,一般说来肯定和吃东西有关,那么这个南呢,是指在本城的南某饭店吃饭?这本账本是五年前的账本,自清就沿着这条线去搜索,五年前,本城有哪些南某饭店,他自己可能去过其中的哪些?但这一条路没有走通,现在的饭店开得快也关得快,五年前的饭店现在已经没有人记得清楚了,再说了,自清一般出去吃饭都是别人请他,他自己掏钱请人吃饭的次数并不多,所以自清基本上否定了这一种可能性。那么"南吃"两字是不是指的在带有南字的外地城乡吃饭,比如南京,比如南浔,比如南方,比如南亚,比如南非,等等。采取排除法,很快又否定了这些可能性,因为自清根本就没有去过那些地方,他只去过一个叫南塘湾的乡镇,也是别人请他去的,不可能让他买单吃饭。自清的思路阻塞了,他的儿子说,大概是你自己写了错别字,是难吃吧?这也是一条思路,可能有一天吃了一顿很难吃的饭,所以记下了?但无论怎么想,都只能是推测和猜想,已经没有任何的记忆更没有任何的实物来证明"南吃"到底是什么,这

digging up old ledgers and going over them again. He didn't have any particular purpose or reason to do so; it wasn't even out of nostalgia. He simply wanted to go over them again.

When he got to the "N. eat" entry, he paused and tried to recall the history behind that phrase. However, this little piece of history had concealed itself behind the phrase "N. eat" and refused to come out. So Ziqing tried to reconstruct the logic behind the phrase. Well, "N. eat" had the word "eat" in it, so most likely it had something to do with eating. And "N."? Perhaps it referred to dining out at a restaurant whose name started with an "N"? This ledger was from five years ago. Ziqing pointed his memory in that direction: which restaurants were there in town five years ago that had a name starting with "N"? And which of these would he have gone to? But this train of thought went nowhere. Restaurants these days come and go all the time, and it's impossible to recall what restaurants there were five years ago anymore. Besides, most of the time when Ziqing dined out, someone else paid for the meal. He rarely treated others to dinner. So this possibility had to be ruled out. Then, perhaps "N. eat" referred to eating out in a geographical location that started with an "N"? Could it be Nanjing, Nanxun, Nanning, or Nanchang? By the process of elimination, Ziqing ruled out this possibility as well, because he had never been to any of those places. The only N-place he had been to was a small town called Nantangwan, but he went there as a guest and they wouldn't have let him pay for dinner anyway. Ziqing was completely stumped.

His son said, "Perhaps you didn't write clearly enough, and it's actually 'Neat'?" Well, this was possible too. Perhaps one day he

90多块钱，到底是用在了什么地方。好在这样的事情并不多，总的说来，自清的记账还是认真负责的。

自清的账本里有许多账目以外的内容，但说到底，就算是这样的账本，也并没有什么重大的意义，甚至也没有什么实际的作用。自清的初衷，也许是想用记账的形式来约束自己的开销花费，因为早些年大家的经济都比较拮据，总是要想尽一切办法节约用钱，记账就是办法之一，许多人家都这么办。而实际上是起不到多大的作用的，该花的账照记，该花的钱还是照花，不会因为这笔钱花了要记账，就不花它了。所以，很多年过去了，该花的钱也花了，甚至不该花的也花了不少，账本一本一本地叠起来，倒也壮观，唯一的用处就是在自清有闲心的时候，会随手抽出其中一本，看到是某某年的，他的思绪便飞回这个某某年，但是他已经记不清某某年的许多情形了，这时候，账本就帮助他回忆，从账本上的内容，他可以想起当年的一些事情。比如有一次他拿了1986年的账本出来，他先回想1986年是一个什么样的年头，但脑子里已经没有具体的印象了，账本上写着，1986年2月，支出部分。2月3日支出：16元

bought something that was neat, and recorded it that way? It didn't matter, though. All these were mere speculations. There were no other memories, no other physical evidence, that could reveal the true meaning of "N. eat" and where the 97 *yuan* was spent. Fortunately, this didn't happen frequently. All things considered, Ziqing was pretty serious and responsible with his bookkeeping.

While Ziqing's ledgers were crammed with information, they weren't very meaningful at all, nor did they have any practical use. Ziqing's original intent was probably to use bookkeeping to curb his own spending. In earlier years, when the economy was not that good, everyone tried to save money through every possible means. One of the most popular ways was through bookkeeping. In reality, though, it made nary a difference. Whatever had to go in the books went in the books, and whatever money had to be spent was spent. It wasn't as if people stopped spending a certain amount of money just because they had to record it afterward.

Therefore, after all these years, the money that had to be spent was spent, and even the money that shouldn't have been spent was also spent. The stack of ledgers grew taller and taller into a monument. They only served one use: when Ziqing had nothing better to do, on a whim he would pick one out at random. Seeing the year on the cover of the ledger, he would let his mind drift back to that year. But he wouldn't remember exactly what that year was like. This was where the ledger came in; its contents could help him recall some of the things that happened back then. Once he picked the 1986 volume. He first tried to remember what it was like back in 1986, but mostly he drew a blank. Then, he looked in the ledger, in

2角（酒，2元；肉皮，1元；韭菜，8角；点心，1元；蜜枣，1元3角；油面筋，4角；素鸡，8角；花生，5角；盆子，8元4角）。在收入部分记着：1月9日，自清月工资：64元。

当年的账本还记得比较简单，光是记账，但只是看看这样的账，当年的许多事情就慢慢地回来了，所以，当自清打开旧账本的时候，总是一种淡淡的个人化的享受。

如果一定要找出一点实际的作用，在自清想来，也就是对下一代进行一点传统教育，跟小孩子说，你看看，从前我们是怎么过日子的，你看看，从前我们过个年，就花这一点钱。但对自清的孩子来说，似乎接受不了这样的教育，他几乎没有钱的概念，就更没有节约用钱的想法，你跟他讲过去的事情，他虽然点着头，但是目光迷离，你就知道他根本没有听进去。

自清开始的时候可能是因为经济条件差，收入低，为了控制支出才想到记账的，后来条件好起来，而且越来越好，自清夫妻俩的工作都不错，家庭年收入节节攀升，孩子虽然在上高中，但一路过来学习都很好，肯定属于那种替父母扒分的孩子，以后读

which was recorded:

"February '86, Expenses:

Expenses on 3 Feb: 16.2 *yuan* (cooking wine: 2 *yuan*; pork skin: 1 *yuan*; chives: 0.8 *yuan*; snacks: 1 *yuan*; honey dates: 1.3 *yuan*; fried gluten: 0.4 *yuan*; mock chicken(steamed bean curd rolls): 0.8 *yuan*; peanuts: 0.5 *yuan*; washbasin: 8.4 *yuan*)"

In the "Income" column, it was recorded:

"9 Jan: Ziqing's monthly salary: 64 *yuan*."

Back in those days, his ledgers were a bit simpler, and were purely about record keeping. Nonetheless, whenever he looked at those records, many things that happened in the past slowly came back to him. Therefore, every time Ziqing opened up an old ledger, it was a modest, personal kind of enjoyment.

If pressed to point out a practical use for the ledgers, Ziqing would say that they could be used for some good old-fashioned education for his offspring. He could say, "See here? This is how we used to live in the old days. Look, in the old days, this is all the money we got to spend for New Year's." However, Ziqing's son seemed unable to accept this kind of education. He had little concept of money, let alone the concept of saving it. Whenever you told him about the good old days, he would nod. But, from the unfocused look in his eyes, you could tell that none of what you said sank in.

At first, Ziqing started bookkeeping because his income was low and his financial situation unstable; he used the ledger as a way to control his expenses. Then, things started looking up for him. Both he and his wife had good jobs, and their household income climbed ever higher. Even though their son was still in senior high

大学或者出国学习之类都不用父母支付大笔的费用，家里新房子也有了，还买了一辆车，由家属开着，条件真的不错，完全没有必要再记账。更何况，这些账本既没有什么实际的用处，却又一年一年地多起来，也是占地方的，自清也曾想停止记账这一种习惯，但也只是想想而已，他做不到，别说做不到不记账，就算只是想一想，也觉得不行。一想到从此以后就再也没有账本了，心里就立刻会觉得空荡荡的，好像丢失了什么，好像无依无靠了，自清知道，这是习惯成自然。习惯，真是一种很厉害的力量。

那就继续记账吧。于是日子就这样一年一年地过去了，账本又一本一本地增加出来，每年年终的那一天，自清就将这一年的账本加入到无数个年头汇聚起来的账本中，按年份将它们排好，放在书橱里下层的柜子里，这是不要公示于外人的，是自己的东西。不像那些买来的书，是放在书橱的玻璃门里面的格子上，是可以给任何人看的，还是一种无言无声的炫耀。大家看了会说，哇，老蒋，十大藏书家，名不虚传。

现在自清打开书橱下面的柜门，就发现少了一本账本，少的

school, he had been a great student all along and certainly one that would not become a burden on his parents. He wouldn't need a lot of money from his parents even when he was to go to university or study abroad in the future. On top of that, they had already bought a house, and a car as well—Ziqing's better half drove it. They were really quite well off, and there was no need for bookkeeping. Furthermore, those ledgers had no practical use anyway; all they did was to accumulate through the years and take up space. Ziqing had actually played with the idea of quitting this habit, but that idea never passed the thinking stage. He just couldn't do it. The mere thought of it seemed wrong to him, let alone actually quitting. As soon as he imagined a life without ledgers, he would immediately feel an emptiness gnaw at his heart, as if he had lost something, as if he had become vulnerable. Ziqing knew that it was because old habits were hard to break. Habits are truly a powerful force.

So he kept keeping his ledgers, the years kept going by, and the collection of ledgers kept growing larger. On the last day of every year, Ziqing would add the past year's ledger to the ranks of the numerous ledgers of years past, organize them by year, and tuck them into the cabinet on the bottom of the bookcase. These were not for public viewing. These were for him and him alone, unlike the books which he bought. Those were placed on the shelves inside the glass doors of the bookcase, displayed for everyone to see, in a tacit form of bragging. When visitors saw them, they invariably exclaimed, "Wow, Old Jiang! No wonder they say you're a legendary book collector! The tales are true!"

But this day, when Ziqing opened the bottom door of his bookcase,

就是最新的一本账本。年刚刚过去，新账本才刚刚开始使用，去年的那本还揣着温度的鲜活的账本就不见了。自清找了又找，想了又想，最后他想到会不会是夹在旧书里捐给了贫困地区。

如果是捐给了贫困地区，这本账本最后就和其他书籍一样，到了某个贫困乡村的学校里，学校是将这些捐赠的书统一放在学校，还是分到每个学生手上，这个自清是不知道的。但是自清想，这本账本对贫困地区的孩子来说，是没有用处的，它又不是书，又没有任何的教育作用，也没有什么知识可以让人家学的，更没有乐趣可言，人家拿去了也不一定要看，何况自清记账的方式比较特别，写的字又是比较潦草的字，乡下的小孩子不一定看得懂，就算他们看得懂，对他们也没有意义，因为与他们的生活和人生根本是不搭界的。最后他们很可能就随手扔掉了那本账本。

但是对于自清来说，事情就不一样了，少了这本账本，自清的生活并不受影响，但他的心里却一阵一阵地空荡起来，就觉得心脏那里少了一块什么，像得了心脏病的感觉，整天心慌慌意乱乱。开始家属和亲友还都以为他心脏出了毛病，去医院看了，医

he found that a ledger had disappeared—the most recent one. They had just celebrated New Year's and just started a new ledger. But last year's ledger, still warm and breathing with memories, had already gone missing. Ziqing searched the house over and racked his brains. Finally, he came to the conclusion that it was likely put among the old books and donated to disadvantaged regions.

If it was indeed donated to a disadvantaged area, that ledger would end up like the other books, in a school in some poor village. Would the school keep all the books at the school, or would they distribute them among the students? Ziqing had no way of knowing. But then, he also thought, the ledger was completely useless to the children of impoverished areas. It was not a real book and was not educational at all, containing no knowledge that would benefit anyone. It was not even entertaining to boot. No one would read it. Besides, Ziqing had his special way of bookkeeping, and his handwriting was messier than most. The country children might not be able to decipher it. And even if they could read it, the contents wouldn't mean anything to them, because they would not intersect with anything that they might have experienced in their lives. At the end they might simply toss the ledger out.

But this was no simple matter to Ziqing. Without this ledger, life around him went on as usual, but he began to feel waves of emptiness inside, as if a part of his heart was torn out. He felt as if he had some kind of heart disease—his heart raced randomly, and his mind wouldn't focus. His better half and his friends all thought there was something wrong with his heart, and told him to get a check-up at the hospital. The doctor said that his heart was fine,

生说，心脏没有病，但是心脏不舒服是真的，不是自清的臆想，是心因性反应。心因性反应虽然不是器质性病变，但是人到中年，有些情绪性的东西，如果不加以控制和调节，也可能转变成具体的真实的病灶。

自清坐不住了，他要找回那本丢失的账本，把心里的缺口填上。自清第二天就到扶贫办公室去，他希望书还没有送走，但是书已经送走了。幸好办公室工作细致，造有花名册，记有捐书人的单位和名字，但因为捐赠物物多量大，不仅有书，还有衣物和其他物品，光造出来的花名册就堆了半房间。办公室的同志问自清误捐了什么重要的东西，自清没有敢说实话，因为工作人员都很忙，如果知道是找一本家庭的记账本，他们会觉得自清没事找事，给他们添麻烦。所以自清含糊地说，是一本重要的笔记本，记着很重要的内容。工作人员耐心地从无数的花名册中替他寻找，最后总算找到了蒋自清的名字。自清还希望能有更细致的记录，就是每个捐赠者捐赠物品的细目，如果有这个细目，如果能够记下每一本书的书名，自清就能知道账本在不在这里，但工作人员

but nevertheless the discomfort in his heart was real and not imagined. It was psychogenic. While it was not a disease of organic origins, according to the doctor, emotional problems at middle age could often morph into a physical illness if not controlled and treated.

Ziqing couldn't sit still anymore. He wanted to find that lost ledger and make his heart whole again. The next day, he went to the donations office, hoping that the books were still there. Unfortunately, they had already been sent off. Luckily for him, though, the office was careful and had kept a registry of each donor's name and workplace. However, as there were many donated items—besides books, there were also clothing and other household goods—the compiled registries filled half the room. The comrades at the office asked Ziqing if he had donated something important by mistake. Ziqing didn't dare to tell the truth; he knew that the staff were all busy, and if they found out that he was just looking for a family account book, they would feel that he was just making a fuss about nothing of consequence. So, Ziqing said vaguely that it was an important notebook with critical information in it.

The staff patiently sifted through the mountains of registries, and eventually found the name "Jiang Ziqing". Ziqing was actually hoping that the records were more detailed and the donations itemized; if they had itemized and recorded the title of each book, Ziqing could find out right away if the ledger was amongst them. However, the staff told him that this was impossible. Actually, even if they hadn't told him, he would have realized the impossibility of it—when he found his own name on the registry and saw the line "donated 125 books" under the "Remarks" section, he knew that

告诉他,这是不可能的,其实就算他们不说,自清也已经认识到这一点。也就是说,自清在花名册上找到自己的名字,名字后面的备注里写着"捐书一百五十二册",就是这件事情的结局了。至于自清的书,最后到了哪里,因为没有记录,没人能说清楚。但是大方向是知道的,那一批捐赠物资,运往了甘肃省;还有一点也是可以肯定的,自清的书和其他许许多多的捐赠物品一样,被捆扎在麻袋里,塞上火车,然后,从火车上被拖下来,又上了汽车,也许还会转上其他运输工具,最后到了乡间的某个小学或中学里,在这个过程中,它们的命运是不可知,是不确定的,麻袋与麻袋堆在一起,并没有谁规定这一袋往这边走那一袋往那边走,搬运过程中的偶然性,就是它们的命运,最后它们到了哪里,只是那一头的人知道,这一头的人,似乎永远是不能知道的。

其实这中间是有一条必然之路的,虽然分拖麻袋的时候会有各种可能性,但每一个麻袋毕竟是有它的去向的,自清的麻袋也一定是走在它自己的路上,路并没有走到头。如果自清能够沿着这条路再往前走,他会走到一个叫小王庄的地方。这个地方在甘

was the end of it. As for the final destination of the books, no one could tell him exactly where it was either, since it was not recorded. They did, however, know the general direction that it went. That shipment of donations went to Gansu Province. Another point was certain: Ziqing's books, along with all the other donations, were tied up in hemp cloth sacks and stuffed into a train carriage, after which they were dragged off the train and thrown onto a lorry. They might have been transferred to yet other vehicles, but at the end they would arrive at some school in a rural area. Their fate in this process could not be predicted or ascertained. The sacks sat in piles, one on top of another, and there was no rule or law that dictated where each sack should go. Chance, during the transfer process, was their fate. As for their final destination—that could only be known to the recipient. Those on *this* side of the process, it seemed, could never know.

In reality, though, there was a path of certainty running through all this. Even though all sorts of possibilities manifested themselves during the distribution of the sacks, each sack had its own destiny. Ziqing's sack was also on its own path of destiny, and it was not one with a dead end. If Ziqing could follow this path and keep going forward, he would end up at a place called Wang Village, in the far west of remote Gansu Province. There, a pupil at the village primary school called Wang Xiaocai would receive Ziqing's ledger and bring it home.

Wang Cai could read a few words, having managed half way through primary school. In the village he numbered among the well-

肃省西部,后来小王庄小学一个叫王小才的学生,拿到了自清的账本,带回家去了。

王才认得几个字,也就小学那点水平,但在村子里也算是高学历了,他这一茬年龄的男人,大多数不认得字,王才就特别光荣,所以他更要督促王小才好好念书。王才对别人说,我们老王家,要通过王小才的念书,改变命运。

捐赠的书到达学校的那一天,并没有分发下来,王小才回来告诉王才,说学校来了许多书。王才说,放在学校里,到最后肯定都不知去向,还不如分给大家回家看,小孩可以看,大人也可以看。人家说,你家大人可以看,我们家大人都不识字,看什么看。但是最后校长的想法跟王才的想法是一致的,他说,以前捐来的那些书,到现在一本也没有了,与其这样,还不如分给你们大家带回去,如果愿意多看几本书,你们就互相交换着看吧。至于这些书应该怎么分,校长也是有办法的,将每本书贴上标号,然后学生抽号,抽到哪本就带走哪本,结果王小才抽到了自清的

educated. Most men of his generation were illiterate. Wang Cai felt especially proud of himself, and because of that, he made his son study especially hard. He often told others, "I want Xiaocai to have an education and change the future of the old Wang family."

There had originally been no plans to distribute the donated books when they first arrived at the school. Wang Xiaocai came home that day and told his father that a lot of books had come to the school.

Wang Cai said, "If you leave them at the school, they'll just get lost somewhere anyhow. They might as well give them away, so everyone can take something home and read. The kids can read them, and the grown-ups can too."

Someone else pointed out, "You have a grown-up who could read in your family, but ours are all illiterate, so what's the point?"

But at the end the school principal felt the same way as Wang Cai did. He said, "The donated books we got in the past have all gone missing. Instead of having that happen again, we might as well give them out to everyone to bring home. Whoever wants to read a few more books can trade with other students." As for how the books should be distributed, the principal had that worked out too. He had a numbered tag stuck onto each book, and had the students each pick a number and take the book that corresponded to that number.

Wang Xiaocai picked the number for Ziqing's ledger. The ledger's cover was wrapped in stiff black paper, and nobody realized then that it wasn't a book—until Wang Xiaocai took it home happily and gave it to his father.

Wang Cai flipped it open. "This ain't right," he said, "This ain't no book."

那本账本。账本是黑色的硬纸封皮,谁也没有发现这不是一本书,一直到王小才高高兴兴地把账本带回家去,交给王才的时候,王才翻开来一看,说,错了,这不是书。王才拿着账本到学校去找校长,校长说,虽然这不是一本书,但它是作为书捐赠来的,我们也把它当作书分发下去的,你们不要,就退回来,换一本是不可能的,因为学校已经没有可以和你们交换的书了,除非你找到别的学生和他们的家长愿意跟你们换的,你们可以自由处理。但是谁会要一本账本呢,书是有标价的,几块,十几块,甚至有更厚更贵重的书,书上的字都是印出来的,可账本是一个人用钢笔写出来的,连个标价都没有,没人要。王才最后闹到乡的教育办,教育办也不好处理,最后拿出他们办公室自留的一本《浅论乡村小学教育》,王才这才心满意足回家去。

那本账本本来王才是放在乡教育办的,但教育办的同志说,这东西我们也没有用,放在这里算什么,你还是拿走吧。王才说,那你们不是亏了么,等于白送我一本书了。教育办的同志说,我们的工作都是为了学生,只要学生喜欢,你尽管拿去就是。王才

Wang Cai took the ledger back to the principal. The principal said, "Even though this isn't a book, it was donated to us as one. And so we distributed it among the books. You can't say you don't want it and trade it in for another one, because the school has no more books to trade with you. Maybe you can find another student whose parents are willing to trade? You're free to do with it as you wish."

But who would want a ledger? Normal books have prices printed on them—they could be a few *yuan*, ten *yuan*, or even thicker and therefore more expensive. The words in a book were printed, but ledgers were written by hand in ink, and didn't even have a price tag. No one wanted it. Wang Cai complained his way to the village Education Bureau, but they didn't know what to do about the matter either. At the end, they gave the one book they had kept for their own office, *On Education in Rural Primary Schools*, to placate Wang Cai, who then returned home fully satisfied.

At first Wang Cai wanted to leave the ledger with the village Education Bureau. But the comrade at the bureau said, "We don't have a use for such a thing either. We don't want it here. Just take it back with you."

Wang Cai said, "Then wouldn't I have shortchanged you? It'd be like you gave me a book for free."

The comrade at the bureau said, "All that we do here is for the good of the students. As long as the student likes it, go ahead and take it." And it was only then that Wang Cai went home, with both the book and the ledger.

However, neither Wang Cai nor his son could understand anything in the book from the Education Bureau. It was all about

这才将书和账本一起带了回来。

可这本教育办的书王才和王小才是看不懂的,它里边谈的都是些理论问题,比如说,乡村小学教育的出路,说是先要搞清楚基础教育的问题,但什么是基础教育问题,王才和王小才都不知道,所以王才和王小才不具备看这本书的先决条件。虽然看不懂,但王才并不泄气,他对王小才说,放着,好好地放着,总有你看得懂的一天。丢开了《浅论乡村小学教育》,就剩下那本账本了。王才本来是觉得占了便宜的,还觉得有点对不住乡教育办,但现在心情沮丧起来,觉得还是吃了亏,拿了一本看不懂的书,再加上一本没有用的城里人记的账本,两本加起来,也不及隔壁老徐家那本合算,老徐家的孩子小徐,手气真好,一摸就摸到一本大作家写的人生之旅,跟着人家走南闯北,等于免费周游了一趟世界。王才生气之下,把自清的账本提过来,把王小才也提过来,说,你看看,你看看,你什么臭手,什么霉运?王小才知道自己犯了错,垂落着脑袋,但他的眼睛却斜着看那本被翻开的账本,他看到了一个他认得出来但却不知其意的词:香薰精油。王小才

theoretical issues. Take, for example, this sentence: "The future of education in rural primary schools is dependent on figuring out the problems of China's compulsory education in the first place." But what did those problems actually refer to? Neither Wang Cai nor his son had any idea. In other words, they lacked the fundamental prerequisites for benefiting from this tome. Nonetheless, Wang Cai was not one to give up. He said to Xiaocai, "Keep it. Keep it well. The day will come when you can understand it."

Having put *On Education* aside, they were left with only the ledger. Originally, Wang Cai had felt he got a great deal, and felt a bit sorry for having taken advantage of the village Education Bureau. But now he felt utterly dejected and believed that he had got a rotten deal. He ended up with a book that he couldn't read, plus a useless ledger of a townsperson. Even if you put the two together, it was still not as good of a deal as what the Xus next doors had got. What good luck their son had! He picked a travelogue by a famous author, which meant he got to follow along on his adventures and travel around the world for free. Wang Cai got upset. He brought Ziqing's ledger before him, and then he dragged Wang Xiaocai over and said, "Look at this, look at this. What kind of dastardly rotten luck do you call this?" Wang Xiaocai, knowing that he was guilty, hung his head low. From the corner of his eye, though, he took a glance at the open ledger, and saw a phrase which he could read but whose meaning was alien to him: "essential oil".

Wang Xiaocai asked, "What does 'essential oil' mean?"

Wang Cai, stumped, looked at where those words were on the ledger. And he saw that phrase as well: "essential oil".

说,什么叫香薰精油?王才愣了一愣,也朝账本那地方看了一眼,他也看到了那个词:香薰精油。

王才就沿着这个"香薰精油"看下去了,他无论如何也想不到,他这一看,就对这本账本产生了强烈的兴趣,因为账本上的内容,对他来说,实在太离奇,实在太神奇。

我们先跟着王才看一看这一页账本上的内容,这是2004年的某一天中的某一笔开支:午饭后毓秀说她皮肤干燥,去美容院做测试,美容院推荐了一款香薰精油,7毫升,价格:679元。毓秀有美容院的白金卡,打七折,为475元。拿回来一看,是拇指大的一瓶东西,应该是洗过脸后滴几滴出来按在脸上,能保湿,滋润皮肤。大家都说,现在两种人的钱好骗,女人和小人,看起来是不假。

王才看了三遍,也没太弄清楚这件事情,他和王小才商榷,说,你说这是个什么东西。王小才说,是香薰精油。王才说,我知道是香薰精油。他竖起拇指,又说,这么大个东西,475块钱?它是人民币吗?王小才说,475块钱,你和妈妈种一年地也种不出来。

And so Wang Cai started reading from where "essential oil" was written. He would never have guessed that the one look he took would ignite in him such an interest in the ledger. The contents of the volume were simply too inconceivable, too incredible to him.

First, let us, too, take a look at the contents on that page on the ledger that Wang Cai saw. This was an expense recorded one day in the year 2004:

"After lunch, Yuxiu said her skin was dry, so she went to the beauty parlour to have it looked at. The beauty parlour recommended a type of essential oil. Price: 679 *yuan* for 7 ml. Yuxiu had a platinum card with the beauty parlour, which gave her a 30% discount, making the total 475 *yuan*. She took it home, opened up the box and took a look, and it was just a bottle the size of a thumb. Apparently you apply a few drops on your face after washing your face, and it would lock in the moisture and condition the skin. Everyone says that these days it's easiest to swindle money from two kinds of people—women and children. I can't agree more."

Wang Cai read the entry thrice and yet he could make neither head nor tail of this business. He discussed this with Xiaocai, "What kind of thing do you think this is?"

"It's essential oil," replied Xiaocai.

Wang Cai said, "I can read it's essential oil." He stuck out a thumb and continued, "It's just the size of this, and 475 *yuan*? It is made of money or something?"

Wang Xiaocai responded, "You and Ma couldn't farm 475 *yuan* out of the land working all year."

Wang Cai got upset. "Xiaocai, you saying your ma and your

王才生气了,说,王小才,你是嫌你娘老子没有本事?王小才说,不是的,我是说这东西太贵了,我们用不起。王才说,呸你的,你还用不起呢,你有条件看到这四个字,就算你福分了。王小才说,我想看看475块的大拇指。王才还要继续批评王小才,王才的老婆来喊他们吃饭了。她先喂了猪,身上还围着喂猪的围裙,手里拿着猪用的勺子,就来喊他们吃饭,她对王才和王小才有意见,她一个人忙着猪又忙着人,他们父子俩却在这里瞎白话。王才说,你不懂的,我们不是在瞎白话,我们在研究城里人的生活。

王才叫王小才去向校长借了一本字典,但是字典里没有"香薰精油",只有香蕉香肠香瓜香菇这些东西,王才咽了一口口水,生气地说,别念了,什么字典,连香薰精油也没有。王小才说,校长说,这是今年的最新版本。王才说,贼日的,城里人过的什么日子啊,城里人过的日子连字典上都没有。王小才说,我好好念书,以后上初中,再上高中,再上大学,大学毕业,我就接你们到城里去住。王才说,那要等到哪一年。王小才掰了掰手指头,说,我今年五年级,还有十一年。王才说,还要我等十一年啊,

pop are no good?"

Wang Xiaocai replied, "No, I'm just saying that this stuff is too expensive. It's not meant for us folks."

"Not meant for us folks?" Wang Cai said, "Damn right, you're lucky enough to even be able to set your eyes on these words."

Wang Xiaocai said, "I want to see a 475 *yuan* thumb."

Wang Cai was just about to set his son straight some more while his wife came over to tell them to go to dinner. She had been feeding the pigs, and when she came to announce dinner she still had around her the apron she wore for feeding pigs, and in one hand she was holding the ladle for scooping swill. She took issue with Wang Cai and Xiaocai—she had been busy taking care of the pigs and the family on her own all this while, and they were just standing around shooting the breeze. Wang Cai said, "You wouldn't understand. We ain't shooting the breeze. We're studying how city folk live."

Wang Cai told his son to borrow a dictionary from the principal. However, the phrase "essential oil" was not listed there—they could find definitions for "essential" and "oil", but none of the definitions added up to anything meaningful.

Wang Cai swallowed and said angrily, "Enough of that! What kind of dictionary is it? It doesn't even have essential oil."

Wang Xiaocai said, "The principal told me this is this year's newest edition."

"Son of a * itch, what kind of life do city folk live?" exclaimed Wang Cai, "They have stuff that's not even in the dictionary!"

Wang Xiaocai said, "I'm gonna study hard and get into middle school, then high school, then university, and when I graduate from

到那时候,香薰精油都变成臭薰精油了。王小才说,那我就更好好地念书,跳级。王才说,你跳级,你跳得起来吗,你跳得了级,我也念得了大学了。其实王才对王小才一直抱有很大希望的,王小才至少到五年级的时候,还没有辜负王才的希望,王才也一直是以王小才为荣的,但是因为出现了这本账本,将王才的心弄乱了,他看着站在他面前拖着两条鼻涕的王小才,忽然就觉得,这小子靠不上,要靠自己。

王才决定举家迁往城里去生活,也就是现在大家说的进城打工,只是别人家更多的是先由男人一个人出去,混得好了,再回来带妻子儿子。也有的人,混得好了,就不回来了,甚至在城里另外有了妻子儿子。也有的人,混得不好,自己就回来了。但王才与他们不同,他不是去试水探路的,他就是去城里生活的,他决定要做城里人了。

说起来也太不可思议,就是因为账本上的那四个字"香薰精油",王才想,贼日的,我枉做了半辈子的人,连什么叫"香薰精

university I'm gonna bring you to the city."

Wang Cai asked, "How many years away is that?"

Wang Xiaocai counted on his fingers, and replied, "I'm in fifth grade this year, so there are 11 years to go."

Wang Cai said, "I've got to wait 11 years? The essential oil's gonna be rancid by then!"

"Then I'll study even harder and skip grades," offered Wang Xiaocai.

"Skip grades? With what you've got?" Wang Cai retorted, "If you can skip grades, I am university material!"

Actually, Wang Cai had placed great hope on Xiaocai all along. At the very least, Wang Xiaocai had made it to fifth grade without showing any signs that the hope was misplaced, and Wang Cai was very proud of his son. However, the appearance of this ledger put his thoughts in disarray. He looked at the boy standing in front of him, face covered with snot. He suddenly thought, "I can't count on this kid. I can only count on myself."

Wang Cai decided to take his family to go to live in the city. This is what we call "migrant labour" these days. The only difference is, in most other families, the man moves to the city first, and only after making a decent living there would he come back to fetch his wife and children. There were others who settled in nicely out there and never came back, some of them even getting themselves a new wife and new children in the city. And yet there were others who couldn't make it out there and returned home for good. But Wang Cai was different. He wasn't going out there to test

油"都不知道,我要到城里去看一看"香薰精油"。王才的老婆不同意王才的决定,她觉得王才发疯了。但是在乡下老婆是做不了男人的主的,别说男人要带她进城,就是男人要带她进牢房下地狱,她也不好多说什么。王小才的态度呢,一直很暧昧,他只觉得心里慌慌的,乱乱的,最后他发出的声音像老鼠那样吱吱吱的,他说,我不要去,我不要去。可是王才不会听他的意见,没有他说话的余地。

王才说走就走,第二天他家的门上就上了一把大铁锁,还贴了一张纸条,欠谁谁谁3块钱,欠谁谁谁5块钱,都不会赖的,有朝一日衣锦还乡时一定如数加倍奉还,至于谁谁谁欠王才的几块钱,就一笔勾销,算是王才离开家乡送给乡亲们的一点心意。王才贴纸头的时候,王小才说,如数加倍是什么意思?王才说,如数就是欠多少还多少,加倍呢,就是欠多少再加倍多还一点。王小才说,那到底是欠多少还多少还是加倍地还呢。王才说,你不懂的,你看看人家的账本,你就会懂一点事了。其实王小才还应该捉出王才的另一些错误,比如他将一笔勾销的"销"写成了

the waters. He left expressly to live in the city, to become city folk.

As unbelievable as it sounds, that was all because of the words "essential oil" in the ledger. Wang Cai thought to himself, "Son of a * itch, I've lived half my life for nothing. I don't even know what 'essential oil' is. I have to go to the city to see this 'essential oil' for myself."

Wang Cai's wife objected to Wang Cai's decision. She thought Wang Cai had gone mad. However, in the country, wives had no say over anything their men decided on. Even if her man wasn't taking her into the city, but instead into prison or even down to Hell, she could not have protested. And as for Wang Xiaocai, he remained ambivalent. He could only feel confusion and bewilderment in his mind. At the end, he managed to let out a little mouse-like squeak, "I don't wanna go, I don't wanna go." But Wang Cai wouldn't listen to him. Wang Xiaocai was not in a position to speak.

Wang Cai left as soon as he made up his mind. The next day, a large padlock was hung at his front door together with a note to the effect of: "I owe so-and-so 3 *yuan*, and so-and-so 5 *yuan*, and I will honour all that. When I've made my fortune and return, I will repay double the amounts in full. As for those who owe me, I'll let bye gones be bye gones, as my parting gift to my fellow villagers."

As Wang Cai pasted the note on his door, Wang Xiaocai asked, "What does 'double the amounts in full' mean?"

Wang Cai replied, "'In full' means you pay the original amount you owe, and 'double' means you pay more than the original amount, twice as much."

Wang Xiaocai continued to ask, "Then does it mean you'll repay

"消",但王小才没有这个水平,他连"一笔勾消"这四个字还是第一次见到。

除了衣服之外,王才一家没有带多余的东西,他们家也没有什么多余的东西,只有自清的那本账本,王才是要随身带着的。现在王才每天都要看账本,他看得很慢,因为里边有些字他不认得,也有一些字是认得的,但意思搞不懂,就像香薰精油,王才到现在还不知道它是什么。

在车上王才看到这么一段:"周日,快过年了,街上的人都行色匆匆,但精神振奋,面带喜气。下午去花鸟市场,虽天寒地冻,仍有很多人。在诸多的种类中,一眼就看中了蝴蝶兰,开价800元,还到600元,买回来,毓秀和蒋小冬都喜欢。搁在客厅的沙发茶几上,活如几只蝴蝶在飞舞,将一个家舞得生动起来。"

后来王才在车上睡着了,他做了一个梦,梦见一只蝴蝶对他说,王才,王才,你快起来。王才急了,说,蝴蝶不会说话的,蝴蝶不会说话的,你不是蝴蝶。蝴蝶就笑起来,王才给吓醒了,醒来后好半天心还在乱跳,最后他忍不住问王小才,你说蝴蝶会

just the original amount or twice that?"

Wang Cai answered, "You are too young to understand. But if you read more of that ledger, you'll eventually get it."

Actually, Wang Xiaocai should have picked out other errors that his father made, such as writing "bygones" as "bye gones". But Wang Xiaocai was not at that good either. He had never even heard of the phrase "let bygones be bygones".

Apart from their clothes, Wang Cai's family didn't bring anything else with them—not that there was anything else in their house. The only exception was Ziqing's ledger, which Wang Cai felt obliged to carry on his person, since he had to read it every day. He read it slowly, as some words in the book were unfamiliar to him. There were also some phrases with words that he did recognize, but whose meaning eluded him. Take "essential oil" for example—Wang Cai still hadn't figured out what that could be.

While on the bus, Wang Cai got to this passage:

"Sunday. It's almost New Year's. People on the streets were walking hurriedly but in good spirits, and joy was evident on their faces. In the afternoon I went to the Flowers and Birds Market. Even though it was frigid outside, the place was quite crowded. Among the plethora of wares, it was the phalaenopsis orchid alone that caught my eye. The asking price was 800 *yuan*, but I talked them down to 600. I brought it home and both Yuxiu and Xiaodong loved it. When I placed it on the coffee table next to the sofa in the living room, it looked like a couple of butterflies flittering about, bringing vitality into the house with their dancing."

After a while, Wang Cai fell asleep in the bus. He had a

说话吗？王小才想了想，说，我没有听到过。

这时候，他们坐的车已经到了一个火车小站，在这里他们要去买火车票，然后坐火车往南，往东，再往南，再往东，到一个很远的城市去。中国的城市很多，从来没有出过门的王才，连东南西北也搞不清的王才，怎么知道自己要到哪个城市呢。毫无疑问，是自清的账本指引了王才，在自清的账本的扉页上，不仅记有年份，还工工整整地写着他们生活的城市的名称。他写道：自清于某某年记于某某市。

在这里停靠的火车都是慢车，它们来得很慢，在等候火车到来的时候，王才又看账本了，他想看看这个记账的人有没有关于火车的记载，但是翻来翻去也没有看到，最后王才"啪"地打了一下自己的嘴巴，说，你真蠢，人家是城里人，坐火车干什么？乡下人才要坐火车进城。

其实自清最后还是去了一趟甘肃。他和王才一家走的是反道，他先坐火车，再坐汽车，再坐残疾车，再坐驴车，最后在甘肃省

dream, in which a butterfly said to him, "Wang Cai, Wang Cai, get up!" Wang Cai panicked, "Butterflies can't talk. You can't be a butterfly!" The butterfly laughed, and Wang Cai woke up in a fright. For a long while after waking up his heart was still wildly going pitter-patter. Eventually, he couldn't help but ask his son, "Hey, can butterflies talk?"

Wang Xiaocai thought for a bit and replied, "Never heard of it."

Just then, their bus pulled into a little train station. Here, they had to buy train tickets, and then take the train south, then east, then south, then east again, to go to a city far, far away. There were many cities in China, and how would Wang Cai—who had never left his home village, and who couldn't tell east from west—know which city he wanted to go to? Needless to say, it was Ziqing's ledger that gave him guidance. On the cover of Ziqing's ledger he not only put down the year, but also the name of the city they lived in, written in neat handwriting. He wrote, "By Ziqing in the City of..., in the Year of ..."

The trains that stopped at the little train station were the slow trains, and they didn't come frequently at all. While waiting for their train, Wang Cai looked at the ledger again, trying to see if the author had written anything about taking the train. Despite flipping through the volume from cover to cover, he found nothing. At the end, Wang Cai slapped himself on the mouth and said, "You moron! He's city folk. Why would he take the train? Only country folk have to take the train, for getting to the city."

Actually, Ziqing did end up making a trip out to Gansu. Going

的西部找到了小王庄，也找到了小王庄小学，最后也知道了自己的账本确实是到了小王庄小学，是分到了一个叫王小才的学生手里，王小才的家长还对此有意见，还跑到学校来论理，最后还在乡教育办拿了另一本书作补偿。自清这一趟远行虽然曲折却有收获，可是他来晚了一步，王小才的父亲带着他们全家进城去了。他们坐的开往火车站的汽车与自清坐的开往乡下的汽车，擦肩而过，会车的时候，王才正在看自清的账本，而自清呢，正在车上构思当天的账本记录内容。但他在车上的所有构思和最后写下的已经不是一回事了，因为在车上的时候，他还没有到达小王庄。

这一天晚上，自清在小旅馆里，借着昏暗的灯火，写下了以下的内容："初春的西部乡村，开阔，一切是那么的宁静悠远，站在这片土地上，把喧嚣混杂的城市扔开，静静地享受这珍贵的平和。我到小王庄小学的时候，校长不在学校，他正在法庭上，他是被告，学校去年抢修危房的一笔工程款，他拿不出来，一直拖欠着。校长当校长第四个年头，已经第七次成为被告。中午时分，校长回来了，笑眯眯地对我说，对不起，蒋同志，让你等了。他

the opposite direction as Wang Cai's family, he first took the train, then the bus, then the motor scooter, then the donkey cart, and finally in the western reaches of Gansu Province he found Wang Village, and there he found Wang Village Primary School.

And there he found out that his ledger did indeed arrive at the school, and was given to a student named Wang Xiaocai. And that Wang Xiaocai's parents took issue with that and came to the school to protest. And that at the end they received another book from the village Education Bureau as compensation.

Ziqing's own journey, while less than straightforward, was an informative one; nonetheless he had come too late. Wang Xiaocai's father had already brought their whole family to the city. The bus that they took to get to the train station and the bus that Ziqing took to get to the village passed by each other. At that instance, Wang Cai was looking at Ziqing's ledger, and Ziqing was thinking about what to write in his ledger that day. However, whatever he thought about on the bus and what ended up being written were two completely different things, because when he was on the bus, he had not arrived at Wang Village yet.

That evening, under the dim light in the little guesthouse, Ziqing wrote down the following:

"It's early spring in a village in the West, a vast and open place, where everything is so serene and remote. As soon as I set foot on this land, I could liberate my mind from the clamour and confusion of the city, and enjoy this precious tranquility in peace. When I arrived at Wang Village Primary School, the principal wasn't there. He was in court standing trial. The school had incurred an

好像不是从法庭上下来。平静，也许是因为无奈，也许是因为穷困，才平静。我说，校长，听说你们欠了工程款，校长说，本来我们有教育附加费，就一直寅吃卯粮，就这么挪下去，撑下去，现在取消了教育附加费，挪不着了，就撑不下去了。我说，撑不下去怎么办？校长说，其实还是要撑下去的，学校总是要办的，学生总是要上学的，学校不会关门的，蒋同志你说对不对。面对贫困的这种坦然心态，在日新月异的城市里是很难见着的。今天的开支：旅馆住宿费，3元；残疾车往，5元（开价2元）；驴车返，5元（开价1元）。早饭，2角。玉米饼两块，吃下一块，另一块送给残疾车主吃了。晚饭：5角。光面三两。午饭，5角（校长说不要付钱，他请客，还是坚持付了，想多付一点，校长坚决不收），和小学生一起吃，白米饭加青菜，还有青菜汤。王小才平时也在这里吃，今天他走了，不知道今天中午他在哪里吃，吃的什么。"

自清最后在王小才家的门上，看到了那张纸条，字写得歪歪扭扭，自清以为就是那个分到他的账本的小学生写的，却不知道

amount for emergency repairs that he was unable to pay; the school had been in arrears. This is his fourth year as principal and the seventh time standing trial.

Around lunch time, he came back. He said to me grinning, 'I'm sorry, Comrade Jiang, to keep you waiting.' He didn't look like one who had just stood trial. He was unruffled—probably out of helplessness, and probably out of sheer poverty. I said, 'Sir, I heard that you were owing construction costs.' He said, 'In the past, our school received education subsidies, and we held out by spending on deficit. But the subsidies have since been cancelled, and we can't hold out anymore.' I said, 'Then what can you do?' He said, 'Well, we still have to hold out. The school has to keep running, and the students have to go to school. The school cannot close down. Don't you agree, Comrade Jiang?' This kind of calm acceptance in the face of abject poverty is a rare sight in modern cities that are undergoing dramatic changes.

Today's expenses: Guesthouse, 3 *yuan*; motor scooter fare outgoing, 5 *yuan* (original offered price 2 *yuan*); donkey cart returning, 5 *yuan* (original offered price 1 *yuan*). Breakfast, 20 cents. Two corn cakes, ate one and gave one to the owner of the scooter. Dinner, 50 cents. Three *liang* of plain noodles. Lunch, 50 cents. The principal said I need not pay and it's on him, but I insisted on paying anyway. Wanted to pay a bit more but he firmly refused to take it. Ate it along with the students. Plain rice with cabbage, with cabbage soup on the side. Wang Xiaocai would eat here normally too, but today he is gone. I wonder where he had lunch today and what he ate."

这字是小学生的爸爸写的，虽然王小才已经念到五年级，他的爸爸王才才四年级的水平，平时家里的文字工作，都是由王小才承担的，但这一回不同了，王才似乎觉得王小才承担不起这件事情，所以由他出面做了。

自清最终也没有找回自己丢失的账本，但是他的失落的心情却在长途的艰难的旅行中渐渐地排除掉了，当他站到那座低矮的土屋前，看到"一笔勾消"这四个字的时候，他的心情忽然就开朗起来，所有的疙疙瘩瘩，似乎一瞬间就被勾销掉了，他彻底地丢掉了账本，也丢掉了神魂颠倒坐卧不宁的日子。

自清从大西北回来，看到他家隔壁邻居的车库里住进了一户外来的农民工家庭。在自清住的这个小区里，家家都有车库，有些人家并没有买车，也或者车是有的，但那是公车，接送上下班后，车就走了，不停在他家，这样车库就空了出来，有的人家就将车库出租给外来的人住。

这个农民工就是王才。王才做的是收旧货的工作，所以他和

At long last, Ziqing saw that note on the front door of Wang Xiaocai's house. The handwriting was crooked and uneven, so Ziqing assumed that it was the work of the primary school student who received his ledger. He would not have figured out that it was the handiwork of the schoolboy's father. Wang Xiaocai was in fifth grade, but his father, Wang Cai, had only a fourth grade education. Normally, if any writing had to be done at home, it fell to Xiaocai. However, this time, Wang Cai apparently felt that his son was incapable of handling the gravity of the task, and so he took charge of it himself.

Ziqing never found his lost ledger. However, his feeling of loss dissipated over the course of this arduous journey. The moment he stood before the little mud hut and saw the words "let bye gones be bye gones", he suddenly cheered up. All the knots and gnarls in his heart were gone. His ledger was gone forever, but so were his restless, anxious days.

When Ziqing returned home from the Great Northwest, he saw that a migrant farmer family had moved into the garage next doors. Every house in Ziqing's neighbourhood had a garage. Some families never bought their own car. Some of them had access to a company car which was only used for pick-ups and drop-offs, and which wouldn't be parked at home. And so their garage would be free. Some families rented out their garages for migrant worker families to live in.

That migrant family was none other than Wang Cai's. As he worked as a junk collector, he got to know the inhabitants of the neighbourhood very well in a short time.

The days were getting hotter. One day, Ziqing passed by the

小区里的人很快就熟悉起来。天气渐渐地热了，有一天自清经过车库门口，看到王才和他的妻子在太阳底下捆扎收购来的旧货，他们满头大汗，破衣烂衫都湿透了。小区里有一只宠物狗在冲着他们叫喊，小狗的主人要把小狗牵走，还骂了它，王才说，不要骂它，它又不懂的。狗主人说，不懂道理的狗东西。王才说，没事的，它跟我们不熟，熟了就不叫了，狗都是这样的。下晚的时候，自清又经过这里，他看到他们住的车库里，堆满了收来的旧货，密不透风，自清忍不住说，师傅，车库里没有窗，晚上热吧？王才说，不热的。他伸手将一根绳线一拉，一架吊扇就转起来了，呼呼作响。王才说，你猜多少钱买的？自清猜不出来。王才笑了，说，告诉你吧，我捡来的，到底还是城里好，电扇都有得捡。自清想说什么却没有说得出来，王才又说，城里真是好啊，要是我们不到城里来，哪里知道城里有这么好，菜场里有好多青菜叶子可以捡回来吃，都不要出钱买的。王才的老婆平时不大肯说话的，这时候她忽然说，我还捡到一条鱼，是活的，就是小一点，鱼贩子就扔掉了。自清说，可是在乡下你们可以自己种

front of the garage, and saw that Wang Cai and his wife were there under the sun, tying the junk they had bought into bundles. They were covered in sweat, and the rags on their backs were soaked through. One of the neighbourhood dogs was barking furiously at them. The dog's owner came to lead it away, and scolded it.

Wang Cai said, "Don't scold it. It's not like it understands."

The dog owner said, "Stupid son of a *itch!"

Wang Cai said, "It's fine. It's just because it doesn't know us well. Once it gets used to us, it won't bark anymore. Dogs are all like that."

At dusk, Ziqing walked by again. He saw that the garage they lived in was packed to the rafters with their wares, and not a waft of outside breeze got in. Ziqing felt compelled to ask, "Sir, it must be hot inside at night, since you don't have windows in the garage?"

Wang Cai answered, "Not at all." He reached out and tugged on a piece of cord. A ceiling fan started to spin, making swooshing noises. Wang Cai continued, "Guess how much this cost me?"

Ziqing couldn't guess correctly. Wang Cai laughed and said, "I'll tell you. I found this on the streets. City living is definitely better than country living—never thought you can scrounge electric fans just off the streets!" Ziqing wanted to say something, but could utter no word. Wang Cai continued, "It's so great here in the city. If we hadn't come here, we'd never know how nice it is to live in the city. In the vegetable market you can pick up all sorts of greens, and not pay a cent for them."

Wang Cai's wife, though normally reticent, suddenly added, "I've picked up a fish once, and a live one at that! There ain't nothing wrong with it except it's a bit small, and so the fishmonger threw it out."

菜吃。王才说，我们那地方，尽是沙土，也没有水，长不出粮食，蔬菜也长不出来，就算有菜，也没得油炒。自清从他们说话的口音中，感觉出他们是西部的人，但他没有问他们是哪里人。他只是在想，从前老话都说，金窝银窝，不如自家的狗窝，但是现在的人不这么想了，现在背井离乡的人越来越多了。

王才和自清说话的时候，是尽量用普通话说的，虽然不标准，但至少让人家能听懂大概的意思，如果他们说自己的家乡话，自清是听不懂的。后来他们自己就用家乡话交流了。王小才从民工子弟学校放学回来的时候，王才跟王小才说，我叫你到学校查字典你查了没有？王小才说，我查了，学校的大字典有这么大，这么厚，我都拿不动。王才说，蝴蝶兰是什么呢？王小才说，蝴蝶兰就是一种花。王才说，贼日的，一朵花也能卖这么多钱，城里到底还是比乡下好啊。

这些话，自清都没有听懂，但他听出了他们对生活的满意。后来他们还说到了他的账本，他们感谢这本账本改变了他们的生活，让他们从贫穷的一无所有的乡下来到繁华的样样都有的城市。

Ziqing said, "But back in the country you could have grown your own greens."

Wang Cai replied, "Back where we're from, it's just sand and rocks everywhere, and there ain't no water neither. We couldn't grow no grain or vegetables. And even if we had vegetables, we wouldn't have any oil to cook them with anyway."

From their accent Ziqing fathomed that they were from the west, but he didn't ask what their hometown was. All he could think of was, "People used to say, 'Gold dish, silver dish, they cannot compare to your own dog's dish'. But nowadays people don't think like that anymore. There are more and more people leaving their hometowns now."

When Wang Cai talked to Ziqing, he tried to speak in Standard Mandarin as much as possible. Even though he had an accent, at least others could get the gist of his meaning. If they spoke in their local dialect, Ziqing would have no way of understanding anything. Later on, however, they talked among themselves in their own dialect. And when Wang Xiaocai came home from the School for the Children of Migrant Workers, Wang Cai asked him, "Did you go look at the dictionary at school like I told you to?"

Wang Xiaocai replied, "I did! The dictionary at school is *this* big and *this* thick. I couldn't even pick it up."

Wang Cai said, "So what's a phalaenopsis orchid?"

Wang Xiaocai replied, "It's a kind of flower."

Wang Cai said, "Son of a * itch, you can sell a flower for that much money? City living is definitely better than country living!"

Ziqing didn't understand what that was about, but he could sense

自清也一样没有听懂，他也不知道现在王才每天晚上空闲下来，就要看他的账本，而且王才不仅看自清的账本，王才自己也渐渐地养成了记账的习惯，王才记道："收旧书35斤，每斤支出5角，卖到废品收购站，每斤9角，一出一进，净赚4角/斤×35斤，等于14元整。到底城里比乡下好。这些旧书是住在楼上那个戴眼镜的人卖的，听说他家的书多得都放不下了，肯定还会再卖。我要跟他搞好关系，下次把秤打得高一点。"

一个星期天，王小才跟着王才上街，他们经过一家美容店，在美容店的玻璃橱窗里，王才和王小才看到了香薰精油，王小才一看之下，高兴地喊了起来，哎嘿，哎嘿，这个便宜哎，降价了哎，这瓶10毫升的，是407块钱。王才说，你懂什么，牌子不一样，价格也不一样，便宜个屁，这种东西，只会越来越贵，王小才，我告诉你，你乡下人，不懂就不要乱说啊。

2006年

their satisfaction with life. Later on, they also talked about his ledger: they were grateful to the ledger for having changed their lives, allowing them to move from the deprived countryside to the prosperous city, where everything was available. Ziqing didn't understand that either, nor did he know that, every evening, when he had some time to himself, Wang Cai would read his ledger. Not only did Wang Cai read Ziqing's ledger, but he got into the habit of keeping his own records too. This day, he wrote, "Received 35 *jin* of old books, paid 50 cents for each *jin*, sold for 90 cents a *jin* at the recycling centre. Net profit for this transaction was 40 cents×35 *jin*, or 14 *yuan*. City living is definitely better than country living. The old books were sold to me by the man with the glasses living upstairs. They say he's got more books at home than he has space for, so he'll have more to sell for sure. I should develop a good relationship with him. Next time I'll tip the scale a bit more for him."

One Sunday, Wang Xiaocai went out for a walk with his father. They passed by a beauty parlour, in whose display window they finally saw their first Essential Oil. Upon spotting it, Wang Xiaocai shouted out in delight, "Oho! Oho! This one is cheap! The price went down! This 10 ml bottle is just 407 *yuan*."

Wang Cai snapped, "What would you know? It's a different brand, so the price is different. Cheap, my ass. This kind of thing only ever gets more and more expensive. Xiaocai, lemme tell you, you're just country folk, so shut up if you don't know what you're talking about."

2006

鹰扬巷

　　太阳暖暖地照在墙上,照在地上,老太太在院子里晒太阳,她们的脸被太阳晒得有些红润起来,有一个小孩跑过来说,汤好婆,外面有个人找你。

　　找我吗?汤好婆说,谁找我呢?

　　小孩说,我不知道,是一个老老头。

　　有一个老太太笑了,她没牙的嘴嘻开,像孩子一样笑。

　　那个老人已经走进来了,他戴着一顶鸭舌帽,样子有点像小

Ying Yang Alley

Translated by Helen Wang

The sun was shining warmly on the walls and on the ground, and three old ladies were in the yard enjoying the sunshine. As their faces turned a rosy pink, a small child ran in, saying,

"Grandma Tang, you've got a visitor."

"A visitor for me?" said Grandma Tang, "Now who could that be?"

"I don't know," said the child, "it's an old man."

One of the ladies giggled, with a toothless grin, like a child.

The old man had already come inside. He was wearing a peaked cap, like a young man, and he stood in front of the old ladies, not quite sure what to do with his hands and feet, and squinting in the sunlight.

The ladies cast their somewhat blurry eyes at his face. He

青年,他站在老太太面前有一点手足无措的,因为有太阳光,他只好眯着眼睛。

老太太有些昏花的目光都投到他的脸上。他的脸有一点红了,他说,我找黄夫人,她姓汤,她自己是姓汤的。

一个老太太笑了笑。

汤好婆也有一点点难为情。你找我吗,她说,我姓汤。

噢,老人高兴地说,我找到你了,你是黄夫人。

汤好婆没有认出他是谁。你从哪里来?她问道。

我吗?老人说,我从火车站来的。

你刚下火车吗?

是的,他从口袋里摸出一张名片,递给汤好婆,这是我的名片,我姓麦。

噢,汤好婆看了看名片,但是她看不清名片上的字。我去拿眼镜,她说,你到屋里坐一坐。

卖,有姓卖的?一个老太太说。

老人跟着汤好婆进屋去。一个老太太说,天要下雪了。

另一个老太太说,太阳这么好,会下雪吗?

会的,一个老太太说,冬天总是要下雪的。

blushed a little.

"I'm looking for Mr Huang's wife," he said, "she's called Tang. Tang's her family name."

One of the ladies laughed.

Grandma Tang felt a bit awkward too. "You're looking for me?" she said, "My name's Tang."

"Oh," the old man said happily, "then I've found you. You must be Mr Huang's wife."

Grandma Tang didn't recognize him.

"Where are you from?" she asked.

"Me?" said the old man. "I came from the train station."

"You just got off the train?"

"Yes." He pulled a name-card out of his pocket, and handed it to Grandma Tang, "Here's my name-card. My name's Mai."

"Oh." Grandma Tang looked at the name-card, but she couldn't see the characters clearly. "I'll go and fetch my glasses," she said. "Take a seat inside."

"My? Are there people called My?" asked one of the ladies.

The old man followed Grandma Tang inside the house.

"It's going to snow," said one of the ladies.

"Do you think so? When the sun is so lovely?" asked the other lady.

"Yes," said the other, "it always snows in winter."

Grandma Tang put on her glasses. She read the old man's name. "I'm afraid I don't remember who you are." She was quite apologetic. "I'm old now, and my memory's not so good."

"You don't know me," said the old man, "we've never met,

汤好婆戴了眼镜看清了老人的名字。我仍然想不起你是谁，汤好婆有些抱歉，她说，人老了，记性会差的。

你不知道我的，老人说，我们没有见过面，你也不会知道我的名字。

噢，汤好婆说，你刚才说，你刚下火车，你从哪里来？

从南方。

你要到哪里去？

到北方。

北方，是北京吗？汤好婆说。

是北京，我在北京谋了一份差事，我现在就是坐火车去北京做事的，老人说。

北京，汤好婆说，我年轻的时候，跟着先生住过北京的，北京是个大地方，其实冬天也不太冷。

我知道的，老人说，你们住北京我知道的。

汤好婆先是有些奇怪，但后来她想通了，她说，你从前和我们黄先生熟悉的。

不熟悉，老人说，其实我也没有见过黄先生，只是久仰先生的大名，却一直无缘见到。他老早就去了，汤好婆说，有四十多年了。

我知道的。

你说你坐火车到北京去，汤好婆说，那你是中途下车来的。

and you wouldn't know my name."

"Oh," said Grandma Tang, "You said that you'd just got off the train. Where have you come from?"

"From the south."

"Where are you going?"

"To the north."

"Do you mean Beijing?" said Grandma Tang.

"Yes, Beijing, I'm on a work trip to Beijing. I've got some work to do there, so I took the train."

"When I was young, I moved to Beijing with my husband," said Grandma Tang. "Beijing's a big place, and it doesn't get too cold in winter."

"I know," said the old man, "I know that the two of you lived in Beijing."

At first Grandma Tang was a bit bewildered, and then she worked it out. "Ah, you must have known our Mr Huang back then," she said.

"I didn't know him," said the old man, "actually, I never met him. I admired him greatly, but our paths never crossed."

"He's been gone a long time," said Grandma Tang, "over forty years now."

"I know."

"You say you're taking the train to Beijing," said Grandma Tang, "so you broke your journey to come here?"

"Yes."

"You got off the train specially to come and visit me?" asked Grandma Tang, a little suspiciously.

是的。

你专门下了火车来找我？汤好婆有些疑惑地说。

我是事先打听了你的地址，才找得到，老人说，我很早就知道你回家乡了，但是一直不知道你住在哪里的，后来才打听到。

这地方小街很多的，不太好找，汤好婆说，难找的。

倒也不难，老人说，这个鹰扬巷，很多人都晓得的，到底黄先生在这里住过，人家能够记得的。

你吃茶，汤好婆将茶杯往老人面前推一推，吃点茶。

这是碧螺春，老人说，我对茶不大讲究的，也不大懂的，吃不太出好坏。

我倒是讲究的，汤好婆说，我对茶的要求高的，我能看出茶的好坏来。

我知道的，老人说，你年轻的时候就讲究吃茶的。

汤好婆有些不好意思地笑了一下，她说，到现在还是这样的，我要吃好茶的，不好的茶我不要吃的。

院子里的声音响起来，汤好婆出去看了一下，又进来了，她说，来了一个要饭的。

噢，老人说，你这个院子，有一百年了。

差不多一百年了，汤好婆说。

我在书上看到过有人写这个院子的，老人说，那个人会写文

"I had to find out your address first," said the old man. "I'd known for a long time that you'd gone back home, but I never knew where that was. I had to make some enquiries."

"There are lots of little streets here, it's not easy to find," said Grandma Tang, "not easy at all."

"It wasn't so difficult," said the old man, "lots of people knew of Ying Yang Alley, and could remember where Mr Huang lived."

"Have some tea," Grandma Tang pushed a teacup in front of the old man. "Have some tea."

"This looks like *Biluochun*, gunpowder tea," said the old man, "I don't know very much about tea. I don't really understand it. I can't tell what's good and what's not."

"I do know about tea," said Grandma Tang, "I'm very particular about tea, I can tell by looking whether it's good or not."

"I know," said the old man, "you knew a lot about tea when you were young too."

Grandma Tang was a bit embarrassed, and smiled. "It's still the same, I only drink good tea," she said, "if it's not good, I won't drink it."

There was a noise in the yard. Grandma Tang went out to see what it was, then came back inside and said, "It's a beggar."

"Oh," said the old man, "this courtyard house of yours must be a hundred years old."

"More or less a hundred," said Grandma Tang.

"I read about it in a book," said the old man, "it was in a book of essays that was unputdownable."

"So you got off the train specially to come and visit me," said

章,写得有感染力的。

你专门下火车来找我,汤好婆说。

但是书上写的街名不叫鹰扬巷,老人说,所以,我一直搞不懂。

从前叫阴阳巷,汤好婆说。

老人和汤好婆一起笑了笑。老人说,阴阳,拿阴阳做街名,好像不大多的。后来就改名了,汤好婆说,叫鹰扬巷,念起来还是一样的,但是写到书上就不一样了。

小孩跑了进来。汤好婆,小孩说,汤好婆,收旧货的来了,他问你报纸卖不卖。

今天不卖了,汤好婆说,改日吧,今天我有客人。

小孩朝老人看看。你是客人,小孩边说边跑出去。

老人吃了一口茶。汤好婆说,茶有些凉了,我替你倒掉一点再加满,就热了。

不用的,老人说。

温茶不好吃的,吃茶就要吃滚烫的茶,才好吃,汤好婆说,你专门下了火车来找我的。

你从前在沪上的振华女校读书的,那时候我在你们墙那边的务同学校,老人说,一墙之隔的。

务同,汤好婆说,务同是很好的学校,那时候不收女生的。

Grandma Tang.

"But the street is not called Ying Yang Alley in that book. And it took me a while to work it out."

"It used to be called Yin-Yang Alley," said Grandma Tang.

The old man and Grandma Tang both laughed. "Yin-Yang, it's quite an unusual name for an alley." said the old man.

"Then the name was changed and it became Ying Yang Alley (Majestic Eagle Alley)," said Grandma Tang, "It sounds much the same when you say it, but the written characters are completely different."

The small child ran in again. "Grandma Tang, Grandma Tang, the rag-and-bone man is here. He wants to know if you have any newspapers to sell."

"Not today," said Grandma Tang, "tell him to come another time. I've got a visitor today."

The child looked at the old man. "You're a visitor," the child said, then ran out again.

The old man took a sip of tea.

"The tea's gone cold," said Grandma Tang, "let me pour a bit out and fill it up, so it will be hot."

"There's no need," said the old man.

"Lukewarm tea's not nice. Tea should be drunk boiling hot. That's when it tastes best," said Grandma Tang. "You got off the train specially to come and visit me."

"You used to go to Zhenhua Girls' School in Shanghai. I was at Wutong School next door," said the old man, "just the other side of the wall."

所以你不知道我的,老人说,我是很早就知道你,你是女校的校花,我们男生都知道,很多人老是在振华女校门口绕来绕去,是想看一看你的。

汤好婆有一点不好意思。是吗？她说,我不大晓得的。

是的,老人说,我也一直想看到你的,可是总没有机会的,每天从女校出来的女生中,也不知道哪一个是你。

是吗？汤好婆的脸有一点红的,她说,好多年了。

好多年了,老人说,好多好多年了。

后来你在哪里呢？汤好婆说。

后来我走过好多地方,老人说,后来听说你和黄先生结姻缘,我们都知道黄先生是很有才气的,是郎才女貌。

后来先生开讲习所,汤好婆说,我做他的助手。

我知道的,老人说,其实也不仅是郎才女貌的,黄夫人是女才子,才貌双全的。

汤好婆微微地笑了一下,老人也笑了一下。有一阵他们都没有再说话,院子里和巷子里的声音时隐时现地传进来,屋子显得空旷起来。

你吃茶,汤好婆说。

吃的,老人说。

好多年了,汤好婆说。

"Wutong," said the old lady, "Wutong was a very good school, but they didn't take girls in those days."

"That's why you didn't know me," said the old man, "but I knew you. You were the school's beauty queen. All the boys knew you. We would hang around the gates of Zhenhua Girls' School, hoping to see you."

Grandma Tang was a bit embarrassed. "Is that so?" she said, "I wasn't really aware of it."

"That's how it was," said the old man, "I wanted to see you for ages, but I never had the chance. When all the girls came out of school, I didn't know which one was you."

"Is that so?" Grandma Tang was blushing a little. "It was such a long time ago."

"It was a long time ago," said the old man, "a very long time ago."

"Where did you go afterwards?" said Grandma Tang.

"Afterwards I went to many places," said the old man. "I learnt that you and Mr Huang had tied the knot. We all knew Mr Huang was a gifted young man. It was a perfect match: truly, 'wit and beauty.'"

"Afterwards, my husband opened a school," said Grandma Tang, "and I was his assistant."

"I know," said the old man, "actually, it was more than 'wit and beauty.' You yourself were a gifted young woman; you had brains as well as beauty."

Grandma Tang smiled, and the old man smiled. For a while neither of them said anything. Noises from the yard and from the

好多年了,老人说,我的心愿一直在心里的,所以我无论如何要下火车,专门来看一看你,我就这样来的。

你下了火车,要转车的,汤好婆说,转车麻烦不麻烦?

不麻烦的。

要买下一趟的车票,汤好婆说。

是的,他们已经替我买好了,老人说。

他们是谁?

和我一起去北京的两个同事。

他们也跟你一起在这里下车的?

是的。

他们再买好下一趟的车票?

是的。

噢,汤好婆说。

我很高兴,老人说。

我也高兴的,汤好婆说。

汤好婆,汤好婆,有人在外面喊着,人就进来了。

林阿姨,汤好婆说,有什么事?

你有客人,林阿姨说,要不要帮你去买一点菜来?

不用的,老人说。

难得来的,要在这里吃饭的,林阿姨说。

street came and went, and the atmosphere in the room seemed to open.

"Have some tea," said Grandma Tang.

"I'm fine," said the old man.

"Such a long time ago," said Grandma Tang.

"Such a long time ago," said the old man, "I've held this wish in my heart all these years. That's why I'm here. Nothing was going to stop me getting off the train, specially to come and visit you."

"You got off the train. That means you'll have to catch another one," said Grandma Tang. "Is it a lot of trouble to change trains?"

"It's no trouble."

"You'll have to buy a ticket for the onward journey," said Grandma Tang.

"Yes, they've already bought it for me," said the old man.

"They?"

"The two colleagues who are going to Beijing with me."

"They got off with you?"

"Yes."

"They had to buy tickets for the onward journey too?"

"Yes."

"Oh," said Grandma Tang.

"I'm so happy," said the old man.

"I'm happy too," said Grandma Tang.

"Grandma Tang! Grandma Tang!" A voice called from outside, then hurried in.

"What is it, Auntie Lin?" asked Grandma Tang.

"You've got a visitor," said Auntie Lin, "would you like me to

他们在车站等我,老人说,我要告辞了。

老人站起来,汤好婆也站起来。老人说,我要告辞了。

咦咦,林阿姨说。

不是的,老人说,我是要走了。

汤好婆陪着老人走出来,老人回头看看院子。和我想象的是一样的,他说,几乎没有差别。

是吗?

是的,老人说,我一直想象你住的地方就是这样。

是吗?

是的,老人说,我一直想象你就是这样。

一辆三轮车过来。汤好婆,三轮车夫说,这是你的客人?

是的。

要三轮车吗?

要的。

上哪里?

火车站。

哦,三轮车夫说,坐火车,到哪里去呢?

到北京。

哦,很远的。

老人上了三轮车,他回身向汤好婆挥手。我走了,他说。

buy you something for dinner?"

"There's no need," said the old man.

"But you must stay and eat," said Auntie Lin.

"They're waiting for me at the station," said the old man, "I'd better say goodbye."

The old man got up. Grandma Tang got up too. The old man said, "I'd better say goodbye."

"You're leaving? But you must stay!" said Auntie Lin.

"Thank you," said the old man, "but I have to go."

Grandma Tang saw him off at the door. The old man glanced back at the yard, "It's almost exactly as I imagined," he said.

"Is that so?"

"Yes," said the old man, "I always imagined you would live in a place like this."

"Is that so?"

"Yes," said the old man, "I always imagined you like this."

A tricycle came along. "Grandma Tang, is this your visitor?" asked the driver.

"Yes."

"Does he need a trike?"

"Yes."

"Where to?"

"The train station."

"Oh," said the driver, "you're taking the train. Where are you going?"

"To Beijing."

"Oh, that's a long way."

汤好婆点了点头,三轮车就走远了。

汤好婆回来,他们问她,他是谁呢?

一个老朋友,汤好婆说。

他是哪里的?

从前的朋友,汤好婆说。

他叫什么?

他叫,汤好婆想了一想,说,他姓麦。

卖?一个老太太说,有姓卖的?

              1999 年

The old man got into the tricycle, looked back at Grandma Tang and waved. "I'm going now," he said.

Grandma Tang nodded, and the tricycle headed off into the distance.

Grandma Tang went back inside. "Who was he?" everyone asked.

"An old friend."

"Where from?"

"He's a friend from the past," said Grandma Tang.

"What's his name?"

"He's called..." Grandma Tang had to think for a moment, "he's called Mai."

"My?" said one of the old ladies, "are there people called My?"

1999

生于黄昏或清晨

单位里一位离休老同志去世了。这是一件正常的事情。人老了,都会走的。但这一次的情况稍有些不同,单位老干部办公室的两位同志恰好都不在岗,小丁休产假,老金出国看女儿去了,单位里没人管这件事,那是不行的,领导便给其他部门的几个同志分了工,有的上门帮助老同志的家属忙一些后事,有的负责联系殡仪馆布置遗体告别会场,办公室管文字工作的刘言也分到一个任务,让他写老同志的生平介绍。这个任务不重,也不难,内

Born in an Unknown Hour

Translated by Shelly Bryant

An elderly comrade who had retired from the work unit passed away. This was a normal occurrence—when a person is old, he will die. But there was something slightly different about this situation. Two comrades in the veteran cadre's office were not currently on duty. Ding was on maternity leave, and Jin was overseas visiting his daughter, so there was no one in the work unit to attend to the matter. That wouldn't do, so the unit chief divided up the duties between the various departments, with some of the staff going to the home of the old comrade to help with funeral preparations, and others contacting the funeral parlour for the burial service when people could pay their last respects to the deceased. The staff member in charge of paperwork in the work unit, Liu Yan, was

容基本上是现成的,只要到人事处把档案调出来一看,把老同志的经历组织成一篇文字就行了,对吃文字饭的刘言来说,那是小菜一碟。

虽然这位老同志离休已经二十多年,他离开单位的时候,刘言还没进单位呢,但是刘言的思维向来畅通而快速,像一条高质量的高速公路,他只在人事处保险柜门口稍站了一会,翻了几页纸,思路就理出来了,老同志一辈子的经历也就浮现出来了。档案中有多年积累下来的各种表格,它们相加起来,就是老同志的一生了。这些表格,有的是老同志自己填的,也有是组织上或他人代填的,内容大致相同,即使有出入,也不是什么大的原则性的差错,比如有一份表格上调入本单位的时间是某年的六月,另一份表格上则是七月,年份没错,工作性质没错,只是月份差了一个月,也没人给他纠正,因为这毕竟不是什么大不了的事情。

本来这事情也就过去了,刘言的腹稿都打好了,以他的写字速度,有半个小时差不多就能完成差事了,他把老同志的档案交回去的时候,有片刻间他的目光停留在最上面的这张表格上了,

assigned the task of writing the old comrade's obituary. The task was not heavy or difficult, since most of the content was already there—it only required a visit to the HR office to check the details in the file there, then all he had to do was piece the comrade's experiences together in the obituary. For Liu, whose bread and butter was dealing with paperwork, this was nothing more than preparing a quick bite.

Although the comrade had been retired for over twenty years before Liu had started at the work unit, Liu's mind always worked quickly, like a vehicle moving smoothly along a well-laid highway. He only stood in front of the archive cabinets of the HR office for a few minutes, flipped through a few pages, and his thoughts were already organized, the comrade's lifetime of experiences surfacing in his mind. A variety of forms had accumulated in the old man's file over the years and, when put together, they told the whole life story of the deceased comrade. Some of the forms had been prepared by the comrade himself, and others had been filled up on his behalf by his work units or other people. The information and formalities were basically the same. Where there were discrepancies, they did not amount to much. For instance, one form said he had entered the work unit in June in a certain year, while another said it was July of the same year. The nature of the work was the same on the two forms; it was only the date for starting work that was off by a month. No one had bothered to correct it since, at the end of the day, it was not a big deal.

At first this just could have passed unnoticed. Liu had outlined the obituary in his mind and, based on his usual writing speed,

表格上老同志的名字是张箫生，刘言觉得有点眼生，又重新翻看下面的另一张表格，才发现两张表格上的老同志名字不一样，一个是张箫声，一个是张箫生，又赶紧翻了翻其他的表格，最后总共出现了三个不同的版本，除张箫生和张箫声外，还有一个张箫森。刘言问人事处的同志，人事处的同志有经验，不以为怪，说，这难免的，以本人填的为准。刘言领命，找了一份老同志自己亲自填的表格，就以此姓名为准写好了生平介绍。

生平介绍交到老同志家属手里，家属看了一眼就不乐意了，说，你们单位也太马虎了，把我家老头子的名字都写错了，我家老头子，不是这个"声"，是身体的"身"。刘言说，我这是从档案里查来的，而且是你家老同志亲自填写的。家属说，怎么会呢，他怎么会连自己的名字都填错了呢。刘言说，不过他的档案里倒是有几个不同名字，但不知道哪一个是准的。家属说，我的肯定是准的，我是他的家属呀，我们天天和他的名字在一起，这么多年，难道还会错。刘言觉得有点为难，老同志家属说的这个"身"

thought it would take him about half an hour to put it down on paper. When he started to take the old comrade's file back to the archives, he shot a fleeting glance at the form on the top of the pile, with the old comrade's name listed as Zhang Xiaosheng. Liu felt it a little unfamiliar. Looking at another form beneath the top, he noticed that the name was written with a different character at the end—声 instead of 生. The two words were pronounced exactly the same, but represented by different characters. As he flipped through the rest of the forms, he found a total of three variations of the written name, with the third reading Zhang Xiaosen. Liu asked one of the staff members in the HR office about it. The fellow, being quite experienced, felt it was nothing out of the ordinary. It was inevitable that there would be occasional glitches, and he just needed to go by the name filled in by the old comrade himself. Liu shuffled through the file to find a form written in the old comrade's own hand, took that version of the name and completed the obituary.

When the obituary was in the hands of the old comrade's widow, she was clearly displeased, even at first glance. The old man's widow said, "The work unit is so sloppy, writing the old man's name wrong. It's 'shen', not 'sheng'."

Liu said, "I checked personally in his file. He filled in the form himself."

The woman said, "How could that be? Are you saying he didn't know how to write his own name?"

Liu replied, "There were several different versions of the name in his file, so I wasn't sure which was correct."

字,又是一个新版本,档案里都没有,以什么为依据去相信她呢?

他拿回生平介绍,又到人事处把这情况说了一下,人事处同志说,这不行的,要以档案为准,怎么能谁说叫什么就叫什么呢,那玩笑是不是开大了。刘言说,可即使以档案为准,老同志的档案里,也有着三种版本呢。人事处同志说,刚才已经跟你说过这个问题了,你怎么又绕回来了呢?刘言的高速公路有点堵塞了,他挠了挠头皮说,绕回来了?我也不知怎么就绕回来了,难怪大家都说,机关工作的特点,就是直径不走要走圆周,简单的事情要复杂化嘛。人事处的同志笑了笑,说,你要是实在不放心,不如到老同志先前的单位再了解一下,他在那个单位工作了几十年,调到我们单位,不到两年就退了,那边的信息可能更可靠一点。

刘言开了介绍信就往老同志先前的单位去了,找到老干部处,是一位女同志接待他,看了看介绍信,似乎没看懂,又觉得有些不解,说,你要干什么?刘言把事情经过简单说了,女同志"噢"了一声,说,我也是新来的,不太熟悉,我打个电话问问。就打

The woman replied, "But I'm sure. We're family! I have lived with this name every day for many years. Do you think I'm mistaken?"

Liu felt he was in a tight spot. The old comrade's widow was telling him the name was "shen", a completely new version. But it wasn't anywhere in the archive, so how could he just accept her story?

He took the obituary back and consulted the HR office. The staff there said, "This won't work. Everything should go by what is found in the archives, you can't just assign a name arbitrarily. That would be a big joke."

Liu said, "But I can't even confirm it based on the archive, because there are three different versions of his name there."

The staff said, "I told you earlier what to do, so why are you coming around with the same problem?"

Liu's normally high-speed mind seemed to hit a roadblock. He scratched his head and said, "Coming around? I'm not sure how I came around to the same problem. No wonder everyone says working with bureaucracy is so difficult. You wind around and around, making everything so complicated."

The HR staff smiled and said, "If you're really worried, go back to his previous work unit, and that should clear it up. He had worked there for decades before transferring to us. He was here for just a couple of years and then he retired. Maybe the information there is more reliable."

Liu got a letter of introduction and went to the comrade's previous work unit. It was a female comrade who attended to him. This woman looked at the letter and, seemingly at a loss, asked,

起电话来，说，有个单位来了解老张的事情，哪个老张？她看了看刘言带来的介绍信，说，叫张箫声，这个声，到底对不对，到底是哪个 sheng（shen、seng、sen），是声音的声，还是身体的身？还是——她看了看刘言，刘言赶紧在纸上又写出两个，竖起来给她看，她看了，对着电话继续说，还是森林的森，还是生活的生——什么？什么？噢，噢，我知道了，原来是这样。女同志放下电话，脸色有点奇怪，有点不乐，对刘言道，这位同志，你搞什么东西，老张好多年前就去世了，你怎么到今天才写他的生平介绍？刘言吓了一跳，说，怎么可能，张老明明是前天才去世的，我们领导还到医院去送别了他呢。女同志半信半疑地看了看他，最后还是相信了他的话，说，肯定老胡那家伙又胡搞了。他以为女同志又要打电话询问，结果她却没有打，自言自语说，一个个信口开河，胡说八道，谁都不可靠，还是靠自己吧。就自己动手翻箱倒柜找了起来，翻了一会，才发现了自己的问题，停下来说，咦，不对呀，他人都已经调到你们那里了，材料怎么还会在我这

"What do you want?"

Liu laid out the problem as simply as he could. The woman cried, "Oh, I'm new here too, so I'm not very familiar with things yet. Let me make a phone call and ask."

When she had dialed, she said, "There's someone here from some work unit enquiring about Mr. Zhang's situation. Which Mr. Zhang?" She looked at the introductory letter from Liu Yan and said, "He's Zhang Xiaosheng—no, the other 'sheng'. But, actually, that's the problem. We're not sure if it's 'sheng', 'shen', 'seng', or 'sen', nor which character it should be. Maybe—" She looked at Liu Yan, who quickly wrote out the various characters he had encountered so far. The woman looked, then read off the options before saying, "What? What? OK... OK... got it. So, that's what's wrong."

She put the phone down, her expression a mixture of puzzlement and displeasure. She looked at Liu Yan and said, "What do you want to bring up this old comrade for? Mr. Zhang died many years ago. Why are you writing his obituary now?"

Shocked, Liu Yan said, "How is that possible? Mr. Zhang clearly died the day before yesterday. Our department head went personally to the hospital to offer his condolences."

The woman looked at him dubiously, but finally seemed to believe him. She said, "Hu must have made a mistake."

He expected her to make another phone call to enquire but, instead, she began muttering to herself, When everyone is talking nonsense, who can I trust? I have to depend on myself. I'll look for information myself and see what I can turn up. But after a bit of

里？刘言说，我不是来找材料的，我只是来证实一下他的名字到底是哪一个。女同志说，噢，那我找几个人问问吧。丢下刘言一个人在她的办公室，自己就出去了。这个女同志有点大大拉拉，刘言却不想独自待在陌生人的办公室里，万一有什么事情也说不清，就赶紧跟出来，看到女同志进了对面一间大办公室，大声问道，张箫声，张箫声你们知道吗？大家都在埋头工作，被她突然一叫，有点发愣，闷了一会，有一个人先说，张箫声，知道的，是位老同志了，什么事？女同志说，走了，名字搞不清，他现在的单位来了解，他到底叫张箫哪个"sheng（shen、seng、sen）"。

另一个同志说，唉，人都走了，搞那么清楚干什么，又不是要提拔，哪个"sheng（shen、seng、sen）"都升不上去了。女同志说，别搞了，人家守在那里等答案呢。大家就七嘴八舌地说起来，说什么的都有，但好像都没有什么依据，有分析的，有猜测的，有推理的。不一会儿，大伙儿给老同志名字的最后一个字，又添加了好几个新版本，有一个人甚至连肾脏的肾都用上了。女同志头

rummaging and shuffling through the files, she realized that there was a problem. She stopped and said, "*Aiyah*, this won't work. Mr. Zhang was transferred to your department, how would his files still be here?"

Liu said, "I don't come here to find more records. I just come to find out the correct way to write his name."

The woman said, "Oh, then I'll find some people you can ask."

Leaving Liu Yan alone in her office, she went out. That seemed a bit careless. Liu Yan did not like being left alone in a stranger's office. What if something happened? He quickly got up and followed her out. He saw the woman entering an office across the corridor, calling loudly, "Do any of you know Zhang Xiaosheng?"

Everyone in the other office was burying himself in work. At her loud question, they were dazed for a while before someone said, "I knew Zhang Xiaosheng. He's an old comrade. What do you need?"

The woman said, "Yes, he's gone now. We're not sure how to write his name. His new work unit wants to know whether it was 'sheng' 'shen' 'seng' or 'sen', and which character."

Another said, "Hey, if he's already gone, why all the bother for such details? But anyway, it's not 'sheng'"—and he added yet another possibility to their list of characters which means "promotion."—"Can someone dead still hope for a promotion?"

The woman snapped, "Don't be silly. The fellow from his new unit is waiting for an answer now."

There was a commotion as everyone spoke at once. There were all sorts of options raised, but none had any real grounds on which

都大了,说,哎哟哎哟,人家就是搞不准,才来问的,到咱们这儿,给你们这么一说,岂不是更糊涂了?刘言也觉得这些人对老同志也太不敬重了,说话轻飘飘的,好像老同志不是去世了,而是坐在办公室里等着大家调侃呢。

女同志一喳哇,大家就停顿下来,停顿了一会,忽然有个人说,是老张吗,是张萧 sheng(shen、seng、sen)吗,我昨天还在公园里遇见他的呢,怎么前天去世了呢?女同志惊叫一声说,见你的鬼噢!另有一个女同志失声笑了起来,但笑了一半,赶紧捂住嘴。先前那人想了半天,才想清楚了,赶紧说,噢,噢,我收回,我收回,我搞错了,昨天在公园里的不是他,是老李,我对不起。于是大家纷纷说,也没什么对不起的,时间长了就这样,这些老同志退了好多年,平时也见不着他们,见了面也不一定记得,搞错也是难免的。

刘言不想再听下去了,悄悄地退了出来,那女同志眼尖,看见了,在背后追着说,喂,喂,你怎么走啦?可是你自己要走的,

to treat it as trustworthy, being based merely on speculation. Before long, many new potential characters had been offered for the last word in the old comrade's name. Fed up, the woman in charge said, "*Aiyah!* Everyone's just spouting nonsense. He just came in here to ask a simple question, and all you can do is muddy the waters further."

Liu Yan felt the group had been a bit disrespectful to the deceased. The way they spoke so lightly, one wouldn't think an old comrade had just passed away, but that he was sitting right there in the office, the object of their barbs and banter.

At the woman's protest, they stopped chattering. After a moment had passed in silence, one person suddenly said, "Are you talking about Mr. Zhang? Zhang Xiaosheng? I saw him at the park yesterday—how can you say he passed away the day before?"

Surprised, the woman said, "Maybe you saw your own ghost!"

Another woman stifled a laugh, quickly covering her mouth. The person who spoke before thought for quite a long time before he said in haste, "Oh! I take it back! I was mistaken. He wasn't the one I saw yesterday. That was Mr. Li. Sorry."

Everyone told him not to feel bad, and that there was nothing to apologize for. It had been a long time, many years since the fellow retired, in fact. And it wasn't like they met often, so it would be easy to make a mistake. Things like that just happened sometimes.

Not wishing to hear anymore, Liu quietly backed out, but the woman in charge had a sharp eye. She followed him and said, "Hey! Where are you going? We haven't done with it yet. If you have to

回去别汇报说我们单位态度不好啊。刘言礼貌道,说不上,说不上,跟我们也差不多。

刘言重新回到老同志家,看到老同志的遗像挂在墙上,心里有些不落忍,对他家属说,还是以您说的身体的"身"为准吧。老同志家属说,果然吧,肯定还是我准,如果我都不准,还有什么更准的?刘言掏出生平介绍,打算修改老同志的姓名,不料却有一个人出来反对,她是老同志的女儿。女儿跟母亲的想法不一样,女儿说,妈,你搞错了,我爸的"sheng"字是太阳升起来的"升"。她妈立刻生起气来,当场拉开抽屉,拿出户口本来,指着说,在这儿呢。刘言接过去一看,张箫身,果然不差。刘言以为事情终于可以告一段落了,可是那女儿却也掏出一个户口本来,说,这是我家的老户口本。两个户口本的封皮不一样,一个是灰白色的硬纸板封皮,一个是暗红色的塑料封皮,一看就知道是时

leave, at least don't go and report that we have a bad attitude!"

Liu Yan answered as politely as he could, "Don't worry. It's the same in our unit."

Liu made his way back to the old comrade's home, where he saw the fellow's portrait hanging on the wall. Feeling a surge of compassion, he said to the widow, "We'll use 'shen', like you said."

She replied, "Of course you will. After all, I'm right. If I'm mistaken, who could possibly be correct?"

Liu took out the draft of the obituary, intending to make the amendment. Just then, someone came into the room, objecting loudly. It was the old man's daughter. She disagreed. "Ma," she said, "you're mistaken. My father's name was Zheng Xiaosheng."

Enraged, her mother took their *hukou*, the household registration booklet, out of a drawer. Pointing, she said, "Look here."

Liu looked and saw that it said, "Zhang Xiaoshen," without a doubt, just as the woman had said. He felt the dispute could be settled, finally, but the daughter produced another *hukou*, saying, "This is the family's old *hukou*."

The two booklets were not the same. One had a grey cardboard cover, the other red plastic one. At one glance, one could tell that they were legacies from two different eras. But what was strange was that the widow held the newer *hukou*, while the daughter had the old one.

Liu said, "When you made the new *hukou*, you didn't return the old one?"

代的标志和差异。但奇怪的是母亲拿的是新户口本,女儿拿的反而是老户口本。刘言说,你们换新本的时候,老本没有收走吗?那女儿说,我们不是换本,我们是分户,我住老房子,所以收着老本,老本上,我爸明明是张箫升,升红旗的升。老太太仍然在生气,说,反正无论你怎么说,老头子是我的老头子,不会有人比我更知道他。女儿见妈不讲理了,说话也不好听了,说,难道你亲眼看见我爷爷奶奶给我爸取名的吗?老太太说,哼,一口锅里吃了六十多年,就等于是亲眼看见一样。女儿说,就算亲眼看见,都八十多年了,说不定早就搞浑了。老太太气得一转身进了里屋,还重重把门关闭了。

刘言手里执着那份生平介绍,陷入了僵局,不知该怎么办了。那女儿却在旁边笑起来,说,咳,这位同志,别愁眉苦脸的,没什么为难的,你就按我妈说的写罢。刘言说,那你没有意见,你不生气?那女儿说,咳,我生什么气呀,哪来那么多气

The daughter replied, "We didn't make a new one. We split his residence. I live in the old house, so I have the old booklet. In it, my father is clearly named Zhang Xiaosheng."

The old woman was furious. She said, "Anyway, no matter what you say, the old man was my old man. No one can be more certain about this than I am."

The daughter, seeing that her mother was being unreasonable, turned tough herself and said, "Surely you didn't personally witness my grandparents naming him?"

The old woman said, "Well, we ate from the same pot for some sixty years, so I might as well have been there to see it with my own eyes."

The daughter shot back, "Even if you saw it with your own eyes, it has been over eighty years now. Maybe your mind is muddled!"

The old woman turned and went back into the room in a huff, slamming the door behind her.

Liu Yan, at an impasse with the task at hand, was uncertain what to do next. Beside him, the daughter smiled and said, "Well, comrade, don't frown. It's not that difficult. You can just write what my mother said."

Liu Yan replied, "Is it fine with you? You won't be angry?"

The daughter said, "Why so much anger? I just can't stand my mother. She thinks she's always right. I just want to fight with her a little. Anyway, the fight is over. Whether my father was Zhang Xiaoshen or Zhang Xiaosheng, he isn't here now, so what's the point worrying about it?"

Pleased to have come to a truce, Liu was about to modify the

呀,我也就看不惯我妈,样样事情都是她正确,我得跟她扭一扭,现在扭也扭过了,至于我爸到底是"声"还是"身"还是"升",人都不在了,管那还有什么意思呢。刘言如遇大赦,正要改写,忽见那老太太又出来了,手里举着几张证件,说,搞不懂了,搞不懂了。

原来老太太被女儿一气之下,就进里屋找证据去了,结果找出来好些证件,有身份证、工作证、医疗证、离休证,老年证,乘车证等等,可是这些证件上的名字,居然都不统一。老太太气得说,怎么搞的,怎么搞的,这些人,不像话。那女儿却劝她妈说,妈,你怎么怪别人呢,你自己平时就没注意没关心嘛,你要是平时就注意就关心了,错的早就改了嘛。老太太说,改?这么多不同的字,照哪个改?那女儿嘻嘻一笑,说,照你的改罢。老太太这才把气生完了,看着刘言按照她的说法改了老张的全名叫张箫身,接过那生平介绍,事情算是办妥了。

name. Just then, the old woman burst into the room, carrying several papers and crying, "I don't understand!"

The woman, enraged at her daughter, had gone into the bedroom to search for evidence. She had turned up several documents, including the old man's identity card, work permit, health permit, retirement card, senior citizen card, and travel documents, but the names on these documents were not uniform. The woman said furiously, "How could this happen? What's wrong with these people? It's outrageous!"

Her daughter advised, "Ma, how can you blame others? You didn't pay attention or take note yourself. If you had, you could have corrected the errors earlier."

The old woman snapped, "Correct? With so many different names, which one do I change it to?"

The younger woman laughed and said, "Just pick the one you thought it should be."

This seemed to quell the old woman's anger. Watching Liu modify Mr. Zhang's name to Xiaoshen in the obituary, she seemed satisfied that the matter was complete.

Liu went back to the work unit and told everyone about his experience. Hearing it, one colleague said, "Liu Yan, you took the task too seriously. The old fellow's not around anymore. Do you really need to be so meticulous?"

Another said, "Why all the trouble, do you really think it can bring some comfort to Mr. Zhang?"

Another added, "You may end up comforting the wrong Mr. Zhang. That would be embarrassing!"

刘言回到单位,把这遭遇说给大家听,大家听了,说,刘言你这么认真干吗,人都不在了,搞那么准,有必要吗?另一同事说,你追查清楚了想干什么呢,告慰老张吗?又说,你可别告慰错了,弄巧成拙。刘言想辩解几句,但想了半天,却不知道该辩解什么,也不知道该替谁辩解,最后到底也没有说出一句话来。

那天回家,刘言把自己的几件证件找出来,一一核对,不同证件上自己的名字是完全一致的,这才放了点心。但是老婆觉得奇怪,问他干什么,刘言说,我看看我的名字。老婆更奇了,说,这有什么好看的,名字生下来就跟着你了,难道今年会换一个名字?刘言既然心里落实了,也就没再吱声。

不几日就到清明了,刘言带着老婆女儿回家乡上坟,遇到一老乡,稀开嘴朝他笑。他认不出老乡了,但看着那没牙的黑洞洞,觉得十分亲热,但也有点不好意思,便也笑了笑,点点头,想蒙

Liu wanted to say something in his own defense but, after thinking for a long while, he could not come up with a single word, not knowing how to defend and for whom.

When he went home that evening, he took out a few of his own important documents and felt reassured after he found that the names on all these papers were uniform in print. Surprised, his wife asked what he was doing.

"I'm looking at my name," Liu replied.

Even more surprised by his answer, she said, "What's to look at? Your name followed you from the time you were born. Surely you don't think it just changed one day?"

Feeling comforted, Liu did not reply.

A few days later, the Qing Ming Festival rolled around, so Liu Yan took his wife and daughter to his hometown to visit the ancestral graves. On the way, they came across an old villager grinning at them from ear to ear. He did not recognize the fellow, but seeing his toothless grin, Liu felt a rush of warm affection for him. At the same time, he felt a little awkward, and so just smiled, nodded, and tried to shuffle past. Unexpectedly, the villager blocked his path and said warmly, "Hey, Bunny, you're back."

His daughter tittered and parroted, " Hey, Bunny! Hey, Bunny!" The more she thought about it, the harder she laughed, until her stomach ached and she doubled over with it.

Caught off guard, Liu said to the old man, "Uncle, I think you've got the wrong person. I'm not Bunny."

The man said, "Who says you're not Bunny? You are, and you

混过去。不料老乡却亲热地挡住他,说,小兔子,你回来啦?女儿在旁边"哧"的一声笑了出来,说,哎嘿嘿,小兔子,啊哈哈,小兔子。越想越好笑,竟笑疼了肚子,弯着腰在那里"哎哟哎哟"地喊。刘言愣了一会说,大叔,你认错人了,我不是小兔子。老乡说,你怎么不是小兔子,你就是小兔子,你打小就是小兔子。刘言说,我排行第四,所以小名就叫个小四子。那老乡说,我不是喊你小名,你是属兔的,所以喊你小兔子。刘言"啊哈"了一声,说,果然你记错了,我不属兔,我属小龙。老乡见他说得这么肯定,也疑惑起来,盯着他的脸又看了一会,说,你是老刘家的老四吗?刘言说,是呀。老乡一拍巴掌道,那不就对了,就是你,小兔子,你小时候都喊你小兔子。刘言说,我怎么不记得了。老乡奇怪说,你们从乡下人变成城里人,难道连属相都要跟着变吗?刘言说,我可没有变,我生下来就属小龙的。老乡也不跟他争了,喊住路上另外两个老乡,问道,老刘家的老四,属什么的?

have been since you were little."

Liu said, "I was the fourth child in my family, so my nickname was always Fourth Boy."

The old man said, "It's not your nickname. You were born in the year of the rabbit, so we always called you Bunny."

"Aha!" cried Liu Yan. "Then you are mistaken. I wasn't born in the year of the rabbit, but of the snake."

Seeing him speak so convincingly, the old man hesitated. After staring at Liu's face for a moment, he said, "You're the fourth child in the Liu family?"

"That's right."

The old man clapped his hands. "Then, I'm right, it's you! Bunny. When you were small, that's what we called you."

Liu said, "Then why don't I remember it?"

The old man looked surprised, and said, "You people become city dwellers, and you have to change your zodiac sign too?"

Liu said, "I don't change anything. I was indeed born in the year of the snake."

The old man did not seem to bother enough to argue with Liu. Calling two other elderly villagers over, he asked, "The fourth kid in the Liu family—what year was he born?"

The two villagers glanced at Liu Yan. One said, "Fourth kid in the Liu family... he was born in the year of the dog. We called him Puppy."

The other said, "No! It was the year of the monkey."

Liu sighed. "So you called him Little Monkey?"

His wife and daughter were convulsed with laughter. "Stop it,"

那两老乡也朝刘言瞧了几眼，一个说，老刘家老四，属狗的，小时候叫个小狗子。另一个说，不对不对，老四属猴。刘言赶紧说，小时候叫个小猴子吧。他老婆和女儿都笑得前仰后合，说，不行了，不行了，肚子要断掉了。老乡不知道她们俩笑的什么，感叹说，城里人日子好过，开心啊。

刘言也不再跟他们计较了，上了坟就赶紧到大哥家去。他兄弟四个，只有大哥一家还在农村，俩兄弟到饭桌上，先洒了点酒在地上祭了父母，然后就喝起来。大哥寡言，喝了酒也不说话，刘言代二哥三哥打招呼说，本来他们也是要回来的，因为忙，没走得成。大哥说，忙呀。刘言又说，不过他们都挺好的，让大哥放心。大哥跟着说，放心。刘言说一句，大哥就跟着应一句，刘言不说话，大哥也就不作声，就好像刘言是大哥，而大哥是老四似的。后来大嫂过来给刘言斟酒，说，老四啊，明年是你大哥的整生日，做九不做十，今年就要做了，你跟老二老三说一下。大

they said, "My stomach hurts from laughing so much."

Not knowing what they were laughing at, one of the old villagers said, "City life must be good. Look how happy they are."

Not wanting to fuss over this with the old villagers, Liu left, making his way first to the ancestral grave, then hurrying to his oldest brother's house. Of the four brothers, only the oldest remained living in the countryside. The two of them went to the dinner table, where they went through the ritual of sprinkling wine on the floor as an offering to their deceased parents before drinking a cup themselves. His oldest brother was reserved, not saying much as he drank. Liu Yan spoke up on behalf of his other two brothers, saying, "They meant to come back, but got held up and can't make it."

His brother said, "Held up."

Liu Yan added, "But they're fine. You don't need to worry about them."

His oldest brother repeated, "No need to worry."

When Liu Yan said something, his brother responded. When he said nothing, his brother remained silent. It was as if Liu Yan was the oldest and his brother the youngest. After a while, his sister-in-law came over and poured him some wine, saying, "Fourth Boy, next year is a big birthday for your brother. But by convention, we are going to have the celebration this year. Let your other two brothers know."

His brother said, "*Aiyah,*" meaning that his wife was being a busybody. But whatever his brother said, Liu Yan did not hear it. The words *big birthday* somehow touched his heart. And he said to

哥说,咳呀。意思是嫌大嫂多事,但大哥话没说出口来,刘言也没听进耳去,因为刘言心里被"整生日"这说法触动了一下,说,大哥,你都六十啦。本来他已经把路上那老乡的事情丢开了,但喝了喝酒,又听到说大哥六十了,就觉得那岁月的影子还在心里搁着,一会就隐隐地浮上来,忍不住说,大哥,你属什么的?大嫂笑道,老四你做官做糊涂啦,你跟你大哥差十二岁,同一个属相。刘言说,属小龙?大嫂说,咦,哪里是小龙,属大龙的。刘言说,奇了,我一直是属小龙的呀。大嫂说,噢,也可能你小时候给搞差了吧。见刘言有点懵,又劝说,老四,没事的,小时候搞差的人多着呢,我姐的年龄给搞差了五岁呢,也不照样过日子。口气轻描淡写。还是大哥知道点儿刘言的心思,说,城里人讲究个年龄,不像乡下人这样马马虎虎。大嫂有点儿不高兴,说,那就算我没说,老四你该几岁还几岁,该属什么还属什么。大家就没话了。

his brother, "So you're sixty!"

He had forgotten all about the conversation with the elderly villagers on the road, but now, after the wine, and after realizing that his oldest brother was sixty, he felt that age was like a shadow, vague but constantly looming up in one's mind. He blurted out, "Which year were you born?"

His sister-in-law laughed and said, "Fourth Boy, you've been an official for so long that you get muddled up. You and your brother are twelve years apart—one cycle on the lunar calendar. You're of the same sign."

"So the snake?" he said.

"What snake?" his sister-in-law replied. "It's dragon."

"That's odd. I always think I am a snake."

His sister-in-law replied, "Maybe they made a mistake when you were little." Seeing Liu Yan's consternation, she added, dismissing it in a light tone, "Never mind. A lot of people make these mistakes when they are small. My oldest sister had her age wrong by five years, and her life went on fine."

As if reading Liu Yan's mind, his brother said, "City folk are very particular about dates and ages, not like we are here in rural parts. We're a little lax about such things."

His sister-in-law was not quite happy to hear that. She said, "Whatever age Fourth Boy says he is, that's what he is, and whatever year he says he was born, that's when he was born. That does it!" Everyone was silent after that.

Leaving his oldest brother's house, Liu Yan went with his wife

离了大哥家，刘言三口人到乡上的旅馆住下。那娘儿俩嫌刘言打呼噜，便合睡一间，让刘言单独睡一间。刘言夜里听到乡下的狗叫，想起小时候的许多事情，结果就梦见了母亲，刘言赶紧问道，娘，老四是属小龙的吧。母亲笑眯眯的，眼睛雪亮，说，生老四的时候，天气好热，天都快黑了，还没生下来，后来就点灯了，也巧了，一点灯，就生了。刘言说，娘，你记错了吧，我是冬天生的，早晨七八点钟，太阳升起来的时候。母亲摇了摇头，转身就走了。刘言急得大喊，娘，你不能走，你走了，我再也不知道我是什么时候生的了。可是母亲还是头也不回地走了。刘言大哭起来，把自己哭醒了，好半天才回过神来，心里悠悠的，摸不着底。看看窗外，天已亮了，乡镇的街上已经人来人往了。刘言起来到隔壁房间门口听了听，那娘儿俩还睡着呢。刘言给老婆发了一个短信，自己就出来了。

到得街上，打听到乡派出所，刘言进去一看，已经有很多人

and daughter to the village hotel, checking his wife and daughter into one room. He stayed alone in another room since he snored. In the middle of the night, he heard a dog barking, calling to mind many things from his childhood. In the end, he dreamt of his mother. He asked her urgently, "Ma, your fourth son was born in the year of the snake, right?"

His mother smiled, eyes lighting up, and said, "When my fourth was born, it was very hot. And he wasn't born when it had gotten dark. But as soon as we lit the lamp, he was born. What a coincidence!"

He said, "Ma, you're mistaken. I was born in the winter, at about seven or eight in the morning, when the sun had come up."

His mother shook her head and turned to go. He cried anxiously, "Ma! You can't go! If you go now, I'll never know when I was born."

But his mother did not even glance back.

Liu Yan cried out so loudly he woke himself up. It took him quite a while to pull himself out of the trance. He felt empty and disoriented. He looked out the window. It was light out, and there were many people moving about on the streets. Liu Yan got up, went to the door of the adjoining room, and put his ear to it. His wife and daughter were still asleep. He sent a text message to his wife, then went out by himself.

Once on the street, he asked his way to the town's police station. Getting there, he found it was already crowded with people. They surrounded a desk in a noisy crowd. He pushed his way forward, poking his head through the throng, causing the

来办事了，围着一张办公桌，吵吵嚷嚷的，他插上去探了一脑袋，那守在办公桌边的警察朝他看看，说，排队。又看他一眼说，你是外面来的？刘言赶紧说，是，是。警察说，那也得排队。刘言空欢喜了一下，发现大家都朝他看，有点尴尬，往后退了退，心里着急，这么多人，也不知道要等多长时间才轮到他，在后边站了站，听出来警察正在断事情呢，听了几句，觉得这警察虽然歪瓜裂枣、其貌不扬，说话倒是很在理，很有水平，也很利索，刘言干脆安下心等了起来。

两个老乡争吵，是为了一头猪，说是一家的猪跑到了另一家的猪圈去了，怎么也不肯回去，后来硬拖回来了，总觉得不是他家那头，咬定邻居偷梁换柱，又上门去闹，结果打起来，一个打破了头，一个撕破了衣裳。警察听了，问道：猪呢？那两人同时说，带来了，在院子里等着呢。警察就离了办公桌往外拱，大家自觉地让出一条道，除了那俩当事人，无关的人也一起出来围在

officer behind the desk to look his way and say, "Queue up!"

Eyeing him again, the officer said, "You aren't from around here?"

Liu Yan quickly replied, "No."

The officer said, "You still have to wait in line."

Liu Yan's heart sank. He noticed that everyone was looking at him. Feeling a little awkward, he went to the back of the pack. Anxious, he thought, there are so many people. Who knows how long I'll have to wait for my turn. He stood at the back, listening to the officer address each issue. After listening for a while, he felt the officer knew what was what. Although he was quite an ugly-looking fellow, he spoke sensibly, and seemed level-headed and mentally agile. Liu Yan settled down and waited.

Two fellows from the village were quarreling over a pig. One said his pig had run to the other's sty and refused to return. When the owner finally managed to drag the animal back home, he kept having the distinct feeling it was not his pig, but one the neighbor had secretly swapped for his own. When he went to the neighbor's house to settle it, a fight broke out, resulting in one man having his head injured and the other having his clothes ripped.

The officer listened, then said, "Where are the pigs?"

The pair answered in unison, "We've brought them along. They're in the yard."

The officer stood up from his desk, elbowing his way to the door. The crowd made a path for him and everyone—though none, aside from the two farmers, had any stake in the argument—followed the officer into the yard, where two pigs were tied to a tree. The officer inspected the creatures, smiled, and said, "Oh,

院子里，那两猪果然被牵在树上。警察朝那两猪瞄了一眼，笑了起来，说，嚯，真像呐，难怪分不出来了。那逃跑的猪的主人指着其中一头猪说，喏，这是我家的。说过之后，却又怀疑起来，挠了挠脑袋，说，咦，是不是呢？警察说，你自己都分不清，怎么说人家偷换了呢。那老乡上前抓住猪的一条腿，扯了起来，神气地说，看吧，我做了记号的。一看，果然猪腿上扎了一根红绳子，因为沾满了猪粪，黑不溜秋，不仔细看是看不出来的。警察说，这猪是你的？那老乡说，本来是我的，逃到他家去了，他又还给我了，但我看来看去，觉得不是它。警察问另一老乡，你说呢。那一老乡委屈说，他说他做了记号的，记号明明在他猪身上，他却又不承认。这一老乡说，谁晓得呢，猪在你家圈里待了两天，不定你把记号换过来了。警察说，你有证据吗？老乡说，我有证据就不来找你了。警察说，找我我也是要找证据的，证据就是这猪腿上的这根绳子，既然这根绳子在你这猪腿上，这就是你的猪，

they really do look alike! No wonder you two can't tell them apart."

The owner of the escaped pig pointed to one of the beasts and said, "That one's mine." But right away, he became dubious, scratching his head and said, "Or... is it that one?"

The officer said, "Even you can't tell them apart. How can you say someone furtively swapped the two?"

The fellow caught the pig, pulled up its hind leg, and said, "Look, I marked mine."

They looked and saw there was a red thread on its leg, which they had overlooked before because it was covered with dark manure. The officer said, "Is this your pig?"

The man said, "At first, it was, but then it ran away to his pen, then when he returned it, I looked and looked, and it just doesn't seem to be mine."

The officer asked the other villager, "What do you have to say about it?"

The accused man replied, "He says he marked it, and the mark is clearly on the pig's body, but he won't acknowledge it."

The other fellow said, "Who knows? The pig was in your pen for two days. Maybe you placed the mark on the other pig."

The officer said, "Can you prove it?"

The man said, "If I could prove it, I wouldn't have to come to you."

The officer replied, "But when you come to me, I need to see evidence too, and the evidence here is the mark on the pig's leg. And since this pig has the mark on its leg, that's your pig. Isn't it fine with you?"

你服不服？老乡倔着脑袋，说，我不服。警察说，那你的意思是什么呢，你觉得那猪是你的？老乡被问住了，走到那猪跟前，蹲下来，仔仔细细地看来看去。警察说，看够了没有，它是不是你的猪？老乡说，我吃不准，反正，反正，我心里不踏实。警察说，你是觉得你那猪变小了，变瘦了？老乡说，小多了，瘦多了。警察说，你是想要胖一点的那猪？老乡说，那当然，我猪本来就比他猪胖。警察说，那你觉得它们俩哪个胖一点？老乡又朝两头猪看了半天，也看不出来哪个更胖一点，说，我眼睛看花了。警察指了其中一头说，喏，这头胖一点。那老乡不依，说，我怎么觉得那头胖。警察说，弄杆秤来。刘言起先以为警察在挖苦他们，哪里想到真有人弄了秤来，是个带轮子的秤，轰隆轰隆地推过来，把猪绑了抬上去称，在猪的撕心裂肺杀猪般地叫喊声中，两猪分量称出来了，它俩商量好了似的，居然一般重。警察笑道，随你挑了。那老乡还是不依，说，分量虽是一样重，但肉头不一样，

The stubborn fellow scratched his head and said, "No, it is not."

The officer said, "Then what do you want? Do you think that pig is yours?"

Stumped by the question, the man squatted and looked the pig over once and again.

The officer said, "Have you seen enough? Do you think it's yours?"

The fellow said, "I can't be sure. Anyway, I'm just not comfortable with it."

The officer asked, "Do you think it's smaller? Thinner?"

The man said, "A lot smaller and thinner."

The officer said, "Do you want a fatter pig?"

The man replied, "Of course. My pig was always fatter than his."

The officer said, "So, which of these two pigs do you think is fatter?"

The man looked at the two animals for a long time, but couldn't tell which was fatter. He said, "My eyes are now blurry..."

The officer pointed at one of the pigs and said, "There, that one's fatter."

Not yet ready to give in, the man said, "Why do I have the feeling that the other one's fatter?"

The officer said, "Bring me the scales."

At first Liu Yan thought the officer was toying with them. He never imagined that someone would actually push a weighing machine out, one rumbling along on wheels. The two creatures were

我家的猪吃得好，他家的猪吃的什么屁。给猪吃屁的那老乡见两头猪一般重，就想通了，不恼了，说，换就换吧。就把腿上带绳子那猪牵到自己手里。给猪做记号这老乡换了一头猪之后，牵着猪走了几步，又觉不靠谱，说，这是我的猪吗？警察骂道，你就是个猪。老乡说，你警察怎么骂人呢。警察说，你连自己是什么你都搞不清，还来搞猪的身份。这老乡不作声了，朝着被别人牵走的那头猪看了又看，有点依依不舍，说，我们还是换回来吧。那老乡好说话些，说，换回就换回。两人重又交换了猪。警察又笑道，白忙了吧。

两个人和两头猪走了以后，下面轮到的是一桩不养老的事情。一个老娘，两个儿子，都不肯养老，老大老二各自有新房子，老母亲住在旧屋里，七老八十了，没有生活来源。警察说，老大出二百，老二出一百。结果两个儿子均不承认自己是老大。问那老母亲，哪个是老大，老母亲老眼昏花，支支吾吾竟然连哪

tied and put on the machine, squealing for all they were worth. The pair of animals was weighed, and as if they had been working out a conspiracy, they weighed exactly the same. The officer laughed and said, "Choose whichever you want."

The fellow was still doubtful. He said, "The weight might be the same, but the meat's not. My pig ate well. His ate rubbish."

Seeing there was no difference in the two animals' weight, the other man—more liberal-minded and seemingly able to laugh off the remarks that his pig was fed on rubbish—said, "There's no need to argue. If you want to swap, let's swap." And with that, he took the rope of the pig with the marked leg and pulled it to him.

The man who had marked his pig took the lead of the other animal. When he had walked a few steps, still dubious, he said, "Is this my pig?"

The officer cursed and said, "*You're* a pig."

The old man said, "How can a cop curse people?"

The officer said, "You don't even know yourself, and you want to come here to dispute over a pig's identity."

The man kept quiet. He looked at the pig being led away by the other man, and felt a little reluctant to part with it. He said, "Let's swap back."

The other man, a little more easy-going now, replied, "If you want to swap back, that's fine."

The pair traded pigs. The officer laughed again and said, "What a waste of time."

When the two men and the two pigs had walked away, the next case involved failure to care for an elderly parent. An old woman had

个是大儿子都说不清。警察恼了,说,两个儿子,不分大小,一人二百。两个儿子不服,说,这事情不该你警察管,该法官管。警察说,那你们找法官去。两儿子说,找法官也没用。警察说,知道没用就好,走吧走吧,一人二百。两儿子又互相责怪起来,言语难听,不过没动手,最后还是领了警察的命令走了。那老母亲蹒跚地跟在后面,撵不上两个儿子,喊着,等等我,等等我。

轮到刘言的时候,警察已经很辛苦了,但仍然认真地听了刘言的话,说,你想要证明一下自己的年龄?又说,你身份证丢了吧?刘言说,身份证没丢。警察怀疑地看看他,说,身份证没丢?拿来我看看。刘言拿出身份证交给警察,警察一看,笑了起来,你要查出生年月日,这上面不就是你的出生年月日。刘言说,可是这次我回乡,老乡说我是属兔子的,又说是属大龙的。警察说,老乡的话你也听得?刚才你都见了吧,猪也分不清,老大老二也分不清,他们还想搞清你属什么?刘言说,不是他们想

been denied financial help from her two sons. Both sons had new houses, and their mother stayed in the old familial home. She was old and frail, and had no source of income. The officer said, "The elder son should give you two hundred *yuan*, and the younger one a hundred."

Hearing this, neither son was willing to admit he was older. When the woman was consulted, she faltered, saying that her eyesight was poor and she could not be sure which was the older son.

Angry, the officer said, "You two sons, we won't differentiate between older and younger. You'll each give your mother two hundred."

Neither son was happy with this. They said, "This matter shouldn't be settled by the police. It should be settled by a judge."

The officer said, "Then take it to the court."

The two sons said, "It's no use going to court either."

The officer replied, "You know it's no use?—That's good. Go away now, and each of you give your mother two hundred."

The two brothers started bickering, blaming each other in the crudest terms they could find. But they did not go so far as to fight with each other and, in the end, did as the officer had said, and then left the station. Their elderly mother stumbled along behind them, crying, "Wait for me! Wait for me!"

When it was finally Liu Yan's turn, the officer was obviously very tired, but he still listened carefully to everything Liu Yan had to say. When he had finished, the officer said, "You want to confirm your age?" Then he added, "So you lost your ID

搞清,是我自己想搞清。警察说,笑话了,你自己的年龄你自己都不知道,那你自己是谁你知不知道呢?刘言同志,你可是有身份证的人,你可是有身份的人噢。刘言说,可有时候身份证上的信息并不可靠。警察说,身份证都不可靠,什么可靠呢?刘言说,所以我想来了解一下,就是我小时候家里头一次给我上户口时到底是怎么写的,到底是哪一年哪一月哪一日。警察听了,沉默了一会,眼神渐渐地警觉起来了,说,你查自己的年龄干什么,想把年龄改小是吧?少来这一套,你这样的人我见多了,要提干升官了,把你娘屙你出来的时辰都敢改掉,不过你别想在我这儿得逞。刘言说,我不是要改小,也不是要改大,只是要弄清楚自己到底属什么,查清楚了,说不定是要改大呢。警察惊讶说,改大?那你岂不傻了,改大了有什么好处?现在当官进步,年龄可是个宝,万万大不得,别说大一年两年,不巧起来,大一天两天都不行。刘言说,我不是要改,我只是想弄清楚了。警察

card, huh?"

Liu said, "No."

The officer stared at him suspiciously. "You didn't lose your ID? Let me have a look at it."

Liu took out his ID card and handed it to the officer. With one glance, the officer smiled and said, "Look, isn't this your date of birth? Here!"

Liu said, "But when I came back to the village this time, one old fellow said I was born in the year of the rabbit, and another said the year of the dragon."

The officer said, "You mean you believe the chatter in your old hometown? You have seen for yourself just now, they can't tell their pigs, or even their sons, apart. You think they can verify what year you were born?"

Liu replied, "It's not them who wants to verify. It's me."

The officer said, "You must be joking. You don't know your own date of birth? Do you even know who you are? Comrade Liu Yan, you are a man with an identity card, and you are a man with some status."

Liu said, "But sometimes the details on an identity card are unreliable."

The officer said, "Unreliable? If you can't rely on your identity card, what can you rely on?"

Liu said, "That's why I want to get a clearer picture. In my childhood when my parents first registered my *hukou*, what was the date of birth under which I was registered? What year, month, and date?"

听了,又想了一会,理解了刘言的心情,同情地说,倒也是的,一个人连自己的出生年月日都搞不准,那算什么呢。刘言赶紧道,是呀,警察同志,就麻烦你替我查一查吧。警察说,你知道我这派出所管多少人多少事,要是什么烂事都来找我,我不叫派出所,我叫垃圾站得了。警察虽然啰里啰唆,废话不少,但还是起了身朝里边走,嘴里嘀咕说,我去查,我去查,几十年前的存根,在哪里呢。

刘言感觉就不对,果然那警察刚一进去就出来了,脸色很尴尬,说,对不起,那些存根不在这里,我大概翻错了地方。刘言想,我几乎就料到你会这么说。话没出口,感觉有人在拉扯他的衣服,回头一看,女儿不知什么时候已经站到了他的身后,老婆也跟来了,站在一边,抿着个嘴笑。刘言被女儿拉着揪着,分了心,眼睛也花了。再看警察时,就觉得警察的脸很不真切,模模糊糊的,刘言顿时就泄了气,他是指望不上这个认真而又模糊的

Hearing this, the officer was silent for a moment. Then he became vigilant and said, "What do you want to check your age for? Are you trying to make yourself younger? It's an old trick. I've seen plenty of people like you, trying to change their age, so they can get a promotion. Don't think you'll get anywhere with me."

Liu said, "I don't want to make myself younger, or older either. I just want to find out once and for all which year I was born. When I do find out, who knows, maybe I'll see I'm older."

The officer was surprised. "Older? Then you really are an idiot. What benefit is there in being older? To get a promotion nowadays, being young is a precious privilege. No way would anyone want to be older. In the worst cases, even being a day or two older makes a difference, not to mention a year or two."

Liu said, "I don't want to change anything. I just want to verify."

Hearing this, the officer thought for a moment, then, seemingly understanding Liu's feelings, said sympathetically, "That's true. If one doesn't even know his own date of birth, what kind of life is that?"

Liu replied, "That's right, comrade. Can I trouble you to check for me?"

The officer said, "Do you have any idea how many people and how many issues cross my desk here? Any little thing happens, and people come looking for me. I don't call this a police station; I call it a junk yard."

Though the officer was rattling on with endless complaints, at least he got up and made his way to the inner room, grumbling as he went, "I'll check. I'll check decades of records. Now, where are they...?"

警察了,他也不想证明自己到底是大龙小龙还是小兔子了,跟着女儿就往外走。那警察却不甘心,在背后喊道,哎,哎,你怎么走了?你等一等,我帮你查。刘言说,算了算了,我不查了。警察说,不查怎么行,一个人连自己的出生年月都搞不清,那算什么?刘言说,我搞得清,身份证上就是我的出生年月。警察说,身份证也有出错的时候。他见刘言执意要走,有些遗憾,最后还顽强地说,那你留一个联系电话吧,等我空一些,一定帮你查,查到了我会立刻打电话告诉你。眼睛就直直地盯着刘言手里的手机,刘言只得留下了手机号码。

一家人往外走的时候,有一个老乡正在往里挤,边挤边大声叫喊,钱新根,钱新根,你不要老卵钱新根。那警察说,我老卵怎么啦。刘言才知道这警察叫钱新根。那老乡说,钱新根,你再老卵,我就把你捅出来。警察说,你捅呀,你有种现在就捅。那老乡见钱新根无畏,反而缩退了,口气软下来,大喊大叫变成了

Liu felt something was not quite right. No sooner had the officer gone into the room than he came back out, an embarrassed expression on his face, and said, "Sorry, those records aren't here. I must have looked in the wrong place."

Liu thought, I know you were going to say that. But he did not say it. Feeling someone tug on his shirt, he turned and saw that his daughter had been standing behind him since who-knew-when. His wife was also there, standing in a corner snickering. As his daughter pulled on his shirt, Liu got distracted, and his vision blurred, so that when he looked back at the officer, he felt the man's face was vague and fuzzy. He suddenly felt deflated. He could not count on this serious, yet fuzzy officer. Having no more desire to know whether he was born in the year of the dragon, snake, or rabbit, he turned and followed his daughter out.

But the officer was not so willing to let him go. He shouted at Liu Yan from behind, "Hey! Where are you going? Wait, I'll help you search."

Liu said, "Never mind."

The officer said, "How can you not verify it? If someone doesn't know his own date of birth, what kind of life is that?"

Liu said, "I'm clear. What's on my ID is my birthdate."

The officer replied, "But sometimes there are mistakes on the ID." Seeing that Liu Yan was determined to leave, he seemed to feel some regret. Finally, he insisted, "Leave me your contact details. When I'm free, I'll definitely help you check. Then, I'll call and let you know."

The officer stared so intently at the cell phone in Liu's hand

小声嘀咕，说，你以为我不敢？你以为我不敢？警察说，我正等着你呢。刘言三人走出了派出所的院子，后面的话，也就听不清了。

开车回去的路上，老婆和女儿对乡下人的这些可笑之事，又重新笑得个人仰马翻的。刘言心里不乐，想起单位里刚去世的老同志张箫 sheng（shen、seng、sen）的事情，说，你们也别这么嘲笑人家，有些事情，并不是城里人和乡下人的区别。老婆和女儿不知道他的遭遇，所以不理解他的心思，不同意他的说法，说，城里没见过这等事，下乡来才见到。

快到家的时候，刘言接到学校老师的电话，喊家长到学校去谈话。刘言问女儿在学校犯什么错了，女儿说，我犯什么错，我才不犯错，喊你们去是表扬我呢。刘言跟老婆商量谁去，老婆说，那老师年纪不大，倒像更年期了，说话呛人，我不去。

就只好刘言去了，老师告诉刘言，他女儿把学校填表的事情当

that he felt he had no choice but to leave his number.

As the family walked out, a villager pushed his way in, shouting as he squeezed past, "Qian Xingen, you bastard!"

The officer said, "Who are you calling a bastard?"

It was only then that Liu knew the officer was called Qian Xingen. The villager said, "You bastard! You fraud, I'm going to rip off your mask."

The officer replied, "Come on. If you have real guts, do it now."

Seeing that the officer wasn't bothered by his bluster, the other man softened, and speaking almost in a whisper, he said, "Do you think I don't dare?"

The officer said, "I'm waiting."

Liu and his family hurried out of the police station, so they could not hear clearly what was said after that.

All along their drive back to the city, his wife and daughter laughed about the old villagers, laughing so hard they could hardly keep from falling off their seats. Liu was not pleased. Thinking of what he had encountered at work with Mr. Zhang Xiaosheng/shen/seng/sen, he said, "You shouldn't laugh at others. Some things are not just a matter of urban-rural differences."

Not knowing what had happened to him, his wife and daughter couldn't understand, so of course they did not agree with his conclusions. His wife said, "I've never seen such things in the city. I had to go to the countryside to encounter it."

When they got back home, Liu received a phone call from a teacher at his daughter's school, asking the parents to go to the

儿戏，一式两份表格，父亲的职务级别居然不同，一份填的是科长，一份填的是处长。老师说，刘先生，你有提拔得这么快吗？在填第一张表格和第二张表格的时间里，你就由科长当上处长了？刘言目前既不是科长，也不是处长，是个副处长，熬那处长的位置也有时间了，没见个风吹草动，正郁闷呢，女儿倒替他把官升了。

刘言回家责问女儿捣什么蛋，女儿说，噢，我没捣蛋，一不留神随随便便就写错了罢。刘言批评说，你也太没心没肺了，表格怎么能随便瞎填呢。女儿不服，说，这有什么，填什么你不都是我爸？又说，你还说我呢，你自己又怎么样，从来不出差错吗，小兔子同志？刘言一生气，说，你怎么不把自己的生日填错呢。老婆在一边替女儿抱不平了，说，刘言你吃枪子了，女儿的生日怎么会错？她又不是你，她的出生证就在抽屉里，你要不要再看一看？刘言火气大，呛道，那也不一定，医院也有搞错的时候。老婆见刘言平白无故发脾气不讲理，性子也毛躁了，言语也呛人

school for a meeting. When Liu asked his daughter what she had done wrong at school, she replied, "I didn't do anything wrong. It can be for some commendation."

Liu asked his wife which of them should go. She said, "The teacher isn't very old, but it seems like she's going through menopause. She is always so aggressive. I'm not going."

So Liu Yan had to go. When he met the teacher, she told him that his daughter treated certain formalities like a trifling matter. She had been asked to fill up a form in duplicate and, when she wrote in her father's post at work, she wrote in two different answers. On one, she said he was Section Chief, and on the other, Department Head. The teacher said, "Mr. Liu, were you promoted so quickly? Were you promoted in that brief instance between the time the first form was filled up and the second?"

In fact, Liu Yan was currently neither Section Chief nor Department Head. He was Deputy Department Head, and had been for quite some time without a sniff of promotion in sight. It was depressing, while his daughter just made it happen—on paper.

When he went back home, he asked his daughter what she was up to. The girl replied, "Oh, I wasn't up to any sort of mischief. Just a slip of the pen."

Liu said, "You're reckless. How can you just blindly fill up the forms like that?"

Unhappy with this criticism, his daughter said, "What's the big deal? Whatever your post, you're still my father, right?" Then she added, "Why are you so upset with me? It's not like you never made a mistake, Comrade Bunny."

了，说，那医院还会犯更大的错呢，护士还会抱错孩子呢，你还可以怀疑她不是你亲生的，你要不要去做个亲子鉴定啊？刘言投了降，说，算了算了。

过了些日子，刘言的一个朋友过生日，办个生日派对，刘言去了，就问那朋友，你这生日，这年这月这日，最早是谁告诉你的？朋友愣了半天，说，咦，你这算什么问题，生日当然是从父母那里知道的啦，难道你不是？刘言说，我父母都不在了。朋友又愣了愣，捉摸不透刘言要干什么，说，怎么，父母不在了，生日就不是生日啦？刘言说，趁你父母健在，赶紧回去搞搞清楚，父母说的话，未必就是真相啊。朋友说，生你养你的人，怎会不知道真相啊？刘言说，最真实的东西也许正是最不真实的东西。朋友见他神五神六，不理他了，忙着去招呼其他人。一位来参加派对的客人听了他们的对话，又看了看刘言，说，刘言，你好像话里有话嘛。刘

Enraged, Liu shot back, "Why didn't you fill in your own date of birth wrongly!"

His wife took up for their daughter and cried, "Liu Yan, what's wrong with you? Why would our daughter's birth date be wrong? She's not you. Her birth certificate is in the drawer. You want to see it?"

Liu Yan's anger rose, and he snapped in retort, "Don't be so sure! Even hospitals make mistakes."

Seeing Liu lose his temper without reason and fly into such a blind rage, his wife also became bitter, "Maybe the hospital made an even bigger mistake and confused her with another family's baby. Do you want a paternity test to make sure she's yours?"

Liu relented, "Forget it."

Several days later, a friend of Liu Yan celebrated his birthday. When Liu went to the party, he asked his friend, "Your birthday—the day, month, and year—who first told you what day it was?"

His friend thought for a while, then said, "Eh? What sort of question is that? Of course it's our parents who tell us our birthdate. You mean that isn't the case for you?"

Liu said, "My parents are deceased."

His friend hesitated, as if not sure what Liu wanted. He said, "So what? Your parents are gone. Does that mean your birthday isn't your birthday?"

Liu said, "Since your parents are still alive, you'd better check it out with them. And who says what your parents tell you is necessarily true?"

言说,你呢,你的生日你是怎么知道的?你父母告诉你的吗?这客人说,我家户口本上写着呢。刘言说,你那户口本是哪里来的呢?这客人翻了翻白眼,撇开脸去,不再和刘言搭话了。

大家喝酒庆生,刘言喝了点酒,指着过生日的朋友说,今天真是你的生日吗?朋友见刘言一而再再而三地对他的生日提出异议,不满道,刘言,你什么意思?刘言又说,你能肯定你真是今天生出来的吗?你能肯定你这几十年日子是你自己的日子吗?你真的以为你就是你自己吗?你有没有想过,你辛辛苦苦努力的,可能根本就不是你的人生呢。大家都被刘言的话怔住了,怔了半天,有一个人先回过神来了,一拍桌子大笑起来,指那过生日的朋友说,啊哈哈哈,原来你是个私生子啊?朋友气得不行,手指着刘言,有话却说不出来,憋得嘴唇发紫发青。大家赶紧圆场,说,喝多了喝多了,刘言喝多了。也有人说,奇了奇了,从前他再喝三五个这么多,也不会醉。还有人说,废了废了,刘言废了。

His friend replied, "They gave birth to you and raised you. Why wouldn't they know the truth?"

"Maybe the truest things are least true," Liu replied.

His friend, not knowing what Liu was driving at with this babble, ignored him and turned to greet other guests. Having overheard the conversation, another friend attending the party looked at Liu and said, "Liu Yan, it seems there's something behind your words."

Liu replied, "What about you? Do you know your birthdate? Is it your parents who told you?"

The man said, "It's written on my *hukou*."

Liu retorted, "Where did your *hukou* come from?"

The fellow rolled his eyes and turned to go away, saying nothing more to Liu.

Everyone had a lot to drink. Liu, having had his share, pointed at the birthday boy and said, "Is today really your birthday?"

Hearing Liu challenge his birthdate again, his friend was not pleased. He said, "Liu Yan, what are you getting at?"

Liu replied, "Can you be sure you were born on this date? Can you confirm with absolute certainty the year, month, and day when you were born? Are you sure you are yourself? Has it ever crossed your mind that you work so hard, and maybe it's not even your life?"

Everyone stopped upon hearing Liu's words, stunned into a long silence. The first to recover pounded the table and laughed. Pointing at the birthday boy, he said, "Aha! So, you're a bastard?"

Livid, the fellow celebrating his birthday pointed at Liu,

其实刘言并没有喝多,他只是听到大家左一口生日快乐右一口生日快乐,句句不离生日,搞得跟真的一样,心里犯冲,就觉得"生日"那两字很陌生,很虚无,他不能肯定到底是谁在过生日,也不能肯定这生日到底是谁的,便借着点酒意发挥了一下,让自己逃了出来,逃离了那个不真切的,模糊的,虚幻的"生日"。

刘言走出来的时候,手机响了,是一个陌生的号码,那个人说,刘先生你好,我就是那个警察呀。见刘言不回答,那警察又说,刘先生你忘记我了?我就是乡下那个叫钱新根的警察,其实我又不是那个叫钱新根的警察。刘言说,你帮我查到出生年月日了吗?警察说,我打电话给你,就是要跟你说一声对不起,我现在不当警察了,不过不是因为我干得不好,是因为我是个冒名顶替的。刘言说,原来警察也是假的。那警察说,也不能算是假的噢,钱新根是我的堂兄,他部队转业回来,上级安排他当民警,开始他答应了,后来又不想干了,要出去混,可是放弃警察又太

looking like he wanted to say something, but could not, his lips turning purple in his rage. Several people hastened to smooth things over, saying, "He's drunk! Liu Yan had drunk too much."

Others retorted, "Can't be. In the past, I've seen him have four or five times more without getting drunk."

Still others said, "He's wasted!"

In fact, Liu was not drunk. He just kept hearing "Happy Birthday" right and left, over and over, as if it were something real. It made him feel upset, estranged from the very words "Happy Birthday," that empty phrase. He was not even sure whose birthday it was, nor who was supposed to be celebrating it. He drank just enough to be tipsy—a subterfuge to escape the vague, phantasmagorical "birthday."

When he made his way out, his cell phone started ringing. It was an unfamiliar number. The person on the other end said, "Hello, Mr. Liu, I'm the police officer." Receiving no reply from Liu, the officer went on, "Do you remember me? I'm the officer from your hometown, called Qian Xingen. Though, actually, I'm not Qian Xingen..."

Liu said, "Did you find out my birthdate?"

The officer replied, "I am calling to ... well, just apologize. I'm not a police officer anymore. But it's not because I wasn't good at it. It's because I was an impostor."

Liu said, "So, even the cop was fake?"

The officer said, "Well, not exactly a fake. Qian Xingen is my cousin. When he was discharged from the military, his superior arranged for him to become a policeman. At first he agreed to it,

可惜,就让我去顶替了,我是他的堂弟,长得很像的。刘言说,你被发现了?那警察说,我不是被发现的,我堂兄在外面混不下去,又回来要当警察了,就把我赶走了,我下岗了。刘言说,荒唐。那警察说,不荒唐的,只可惜我没有来得及替你查到出生年月,其实我已经快要接近真相了,我已经知道那些存根在哪里了。刘言说,那些存根就很可靠吗,也许当初就有人写错了呢。那警察说,所以呀,所以说很对不起你,我正在争取重新当警察,以后如果能够重新当上,我一定替你寻找证明,我一定查出你的真正的不出一点差错的出生年月日。刘言说,你不叫钱新根,你叫个什么呢。那警察说,我叫钱新海,跟我堂兄的名字就只差一个字。刘言听了,眼前就浮现出那警察的面貌来,心里有些苍凉,说,谢谢你,钱新海。就挂断了手机。

2010 年

then decided he wanted to explore some other opportunities, but it seemed a pity to lose his officer's post, so I went in and posed as him. My cousin and I look a lot alike."

Liu asked, "So you were discovered?"

The officer replied, "No, I wasn't caught, but my cousin could no longer drag out a decent living outside and wanted to come back and be a cop. He chased me out of the job, so I guess you could say I am laid off."

Liu said, "That's absurd."

The officer replied, "Not really. It's just a pity I didn't have time to look up your birthdate before it happened. Actually, I had almost got to the bottom of it. I know where the records are kept."

Liu asked, "But are those records reliable? Maybe someone made a slip from the beginning?"

The officer replied, "That's why I'm apologizing to you! I'm applying to be a cop and, if I succeed, I'll definitely look for more evidence on your behalf. I'll find irrefutable evidence to prove your date of birth."

Liu said, "So you're not Qian Xingen. What's your name then?"

The officer said, "I'm Qian Xinhai. Just one character different from my cousin's name."

Hearing this, Liu could see the officer's face clearly in front of him. Feeling a little desolate, Liu said, "Thank you, Qian Xinhai." And then he hung up the phone.

2010

我们都在服务区

天快亮时,桂平才朦朦胧胧要睡去了,结果手机设的闹钟却响了,喳喳喳地叫个不停,桂平翻身坐起来,和往常一样,先取消噪耳的铃声,再打开手机,又和往常一样,片刻之后,手机里的信息就接二连三地响了起来,桂平感觉至少有五六条,结果数了一下,还不止,有七条,都是昨晚他关机后发来的,还有一条竟是凌晨五点发的,也没什么了不起的大事,那个人天生醒得早,一个人起来,全家人还睡着,窗外、路上也没有什么人气人声,

We're All in the Service Area

Translated by Shelly Bryant

Just before dawn, Gui Ping was drifting into the haze of sleep when the alarm on his cell phone started clanging nonstop. He rolled over, sat up and, as usual, first canceled the ringing sound, then turned on the phone. A moment later, also as usual, his phone sounded with one incoming message after another. Gui Ping thought there were at least five or six, but after counting, he realized he had underestimated. There were seven, all sent after he had turned off the phone the previous night—one was actually sent around five that morning. It wasn't even anything urgent or important. The sender was someone who always woke up early. When he woke up, the whole family was still sleeping and there were no signs of life on the streets outside the window either. He had probably just sent that

大概觉得寂寞了，就给他发个信，消解一下早起的孤独。这些来自半夜和凌晨的短信，只有一封是急等答复的，其他都没有什么太重要的事情，桂平也来不及一一回复了，赶紧就到会场，将手机放到震动上。开了一上午的会，会议结束时，才发现事情也像短信和未接来电一样，越开越多，密密麻麻。中午又是陪客，下午接着还有会。总算午饭抓得紧一点，饭后有二十分钟时间，赶紧躲进办公室，身体往沙发上一横，想闭一闭眼睛，放松一下，结果在这短短的时间里，手机上又来了两条短信和三次电话，桂平接了最后一个电话，心里厌烦透了，一看只剩五分钟了，"的"地一下关了手机，强迫自己闭上眼睛，可那眼皮却怎么也合不拢，突突突地跳跃着。就听到办公室的小李敲他的门了，桂主任，桂主任，你手机怎么不通？你在里边吗？桂平垂头丧气地坐起来，说，我在，我知道，要开会了。

他抓起桌上的手机，忽然气就不打一处来，又朝桌上扔回去，劲使大了一点，手机"嗖"地滑过桌面，"啪"地摔到地上，桂平

message as a way of getting rid of the loneliness of an early bird. Of these messages sent from midnight to dawn, only one required an immediate reply. None of the others were very important, and Gui Ping did not have time to answer each one. He rushed to the venue, put the phone into vibrate mode, and began the meeting.

When the meeting ended, he found that matters, like the unanswered messages and phone calls, were stealthily piling up. Midday he met a client, and there was another meeting in the afternoon. At least he was able to finish his lunch in good time, and still had twenty minutes left after his meal. He quickly escaped into his office and lay flat on the sofa, closing his eyes to relax. But even in this brief time, his phone sounded with two more messages and three calls. Gui Ping answered the last one, feeling irritated. As soon as he saw that there were only five minutes left, click, he turned off the phone, forcing himself to close his eyes. But he felt they started to twitch involuntarily and simply could not close them as if his eyelids were stuck together.

He heard his office clerk Xiao Li knock on the door. "Director Gui, what happened to your phone? Are you in there?"

Gui Ping sat up and said dejectedly, "I'm here. I know, it's time for the meeting."

He grabbed the phone from the table and then, suddenly deciding otherwise, tossed it back on the table—perhaps a little too forcefully, for the phone swished across the table and fell to the ground with a thud. Startled, Gui Ping rushed to pick it up. Then, remembering he had turned it off, he hurried to switch it on, checked, and only relaxed when he found it undamaged. Grabbing

一急,赶紧去捡起来,这才想起手机刚才被他关了,急忙又打开,检查一下,确定没有被摔坏,才放了心。抓着手机就要往外走,就在这片刻间,手机响了,一接,是一老熟人打来的,孩子入学要托他找教育局领导,这是为难的事情,推托吧,对方会不高兴,不推托吧,又给自己找麻烦,正不知怎么回答,小李又敲门喊,桂主任,桂主任!桂平心里毛躁得要命,对那老熟人没好气说,我要开会,回头再说吧。老熟人在电话里急巴巴说,你开多长时间会?我什么时候再打你手机?桂平明明听见了,却假作没听见,挂断了电话,还不解气,重又下狠心关了机,将手机朝桌上一扔,空着手就开门出来,往会议室去。

小李跟在他后面,奇怪道,咦,桂主任,你的手机呢,我刚才打你手机,怎么关机了?不是被偷了吧?桂平气道,偷了才好。小李说,充电吧?桂平说,充个屁电。小李吐了一下舌头,没敢再多嘴,但是总忍不住要看桂平的手,因为那只手,永远是捏着手机的,现在忽然手里空空的了,连小李也不习惯了。

the phone, he started to walk out of his office, but just then the phone rang. When he answered, it was an old acquaintance whose child was going to enter school, and he was hoping Gui Ping could put him in touch with some officials from the Education Bureau. Feeling the situation awkward, he knew that if he tried to get out of it, his friend would not be happy, but if he did not get out of it, he would be inviting trouble for himself. As he was thinking of what to say, Xiao Li again knocked on the door, calling "Director Gui! Director Gui!"

Mind alight like the flames of hell, Gui Ping told the acquaintance on the phone: "I can't talk now. I've got a meeting. Let's talk about it later."

The acquaintance said urgently, "Will it be a long meeting? What time shall I call back?"

Though Gui Ping heard it clearly enough, he pretended he had not, hanging up the phone. Still feeling frustrated, he resolutely turned off the machine once again. He tossed it on the table, flung the door open with his hands empty, and went out to the conference room.

Xiao Li followed him in confusion. "Um, Director Gui... Where is your phone? I tried to call you just now. Why was it off? It wasn't stolen, was it?"

Gui Ping snapped, "I wish."

Xiao Li said, "Is it charging?"

"Charging my ass."

Xiao Li stuck his tongue out, not wanting to speak out of turn. Still, he couldn't help but look at Gui Ping's hand, because that

曾经有一次会议，保密级别比较高，不允许与会者带手机，桂平将手机留在办公室，只觉得那半天，心里好轻松，了无牵挂，自打开了这个会以后，桂平心烦的时候，也曾关过手机，就当自己又在开保密会议吧。结果立刻反馈来诸多的不满和批评，上级下级都有意见，上级说，桂平，你又出国啦？你老在坐飞机吗？怎么老是关机啊？下级说，桂主任，你老是关机，请示不到你，你还要不要我们做事啦？总之很快桂平就败下阵来，他玩不过手机，还是老老实实恢复原样吧。

跟在桂平背后的小李进了会议室还在唠唠叨叨，说，桂主任，手机不是充电，是你忘了拿？我替你去拿来吧。桂平哭笑不得说，小李，坐下来开会吧。小李这才住了嘴。

下午的会，和上午的会不一样，桂平不是主角，可以躲在下面开开小差，往常这时候，他定准是在回复短信或压低声音告诉来电者，我正在开会，再或者，如果是重要的非接不可的电话，就要蹑手蹑脚鬼鬼祟祟地溜出会场，到外面走廊上去说话。

hand was always carrying the phone. Seeing it suddenly empty now made Xiao Li feel strange.

There was one meeting for which the confidentiality level was high, so cell phones were not permitted. Gui Ping had left his in his office for the half-day meeting, and he felt very relaxed and worry-free. After that meeting, whenever Gui Ping felt frustrated, he would turn his cell phone off, pretending he was attending a confidential session. The dissatisfaction this had caused and the criticism it had invited were immediately evident in both his superiors and subordinates. One of his superiors said, "Gui Ping, have you been traveling abroad again? Are you always on the plane, and that's why you have to turn off your phone?"

His subordinates said, "Director Gui, your phone is always off. If we can't reach you, do you still want us to approach you with these matters?"

Gui Ping knew he was defeated. He couldn't win the game against the phone, and he had to return to how things were.

Xiao Li, still nagging as he trailed behind Gui Ping, said, "Director Gui, your phone's not charging. Did you forget it? Would you like me to get it for you?"

Not knowing whether he should feel amused or annoyed, Gui Ping said, "Xiao Li, sit down and we'll start the meeting."

Xiao Li finally fell silent.

In the afternoon meeting, unlike the one that morning, Gui Ping was not in the lead position, so he could duck out of the limelight and, as he usually did in such situations, take the opportunity to reply to text messages, or softly tell a new caller,

但是今天他把手机扔了，两手空空一身轻松地坐到会场上，心里好痛快，好舒坦，忍不住仰天长舒一口气，好像把手机烦人的恶气都吐出来了，真有一种要飞起来的自由奔放的感受。

乏味的会议开始后不久，桂平就看到坐在前后左右的同事，有的将手机藏在桌肚子里，但又不停地取出来看看，也有的干脆搁在桌面上，但即使是搁在眼前的，也会时不时地拿起来瞄一眼，因为震动的感觉毕竟不如铃声那样让人警醒，怕疏忽了来电来信。但凡有信了，那人脸色就会为之一动，或者喜色，或者着急，或者平静，但无不立刻活动拇指，沉浸在与手机相交融的感受中。

一开始，桂平还是怀着同情的心情看着他们，看他们被手机掌控，逃脱不了，但是渐渐的，桂平有点坐不住了，先是手痒，接着心里也痒起来了，再渐渐的，轻松变成了空洞，潇洒变成了焦虑，甚至有点神魂不定、坐立不安起来，他的心思，被留在办公室的手机抓去了。

"I'm in a meeting", or even, if the call was important, answer it and slid out of the conference room into the corridor to talk.

But today he had tossed his phone aside and now sat, empty-handed and relaxed, in the conference room. He felt so happy and at ease that he could not help but release a deep sigh, as if he had expelled the rancor harbored in his heart against the phone. The feeling of freedom was like flying.

Shortly after the start of the mind-numbing meeting, Gui Ping looked at the colleagues seated around him. Some hid their phones under the conference table and yet couldn't help retrieving them and constantly looking at the screens. Others left them sitting on top of the table, but often picked them up to glance at them because, after all, the vibrating alert was not as noticeable as a ringing sound, so one might inadvertently neglect a call. When a message did come, the person's face might change, showing joy, anxiety, or calm, but none could resist exercising the thumb immediately, quickly immersing themselves in the world of the screen.

At first, Gui Ping watched them with some sympathy, seeing them controlled by their phones, unable to escape. But gradually he became antsy, the fidgeting of his hands turning into a mental unrest. Then, the calm he had felt before turned into a sort of emptiness, uninhibitedness into anxiety, until he grew emotionally volatile. Restless, he felt as if his mind were captured by his mobile phone locked in the office.

The woman sitting beside him noticed that he was uncomfortable—as if thorns were sprouting out of his body—and said, "Director Gui, are you on your monthly flow?"

坐在他旁边的一个女同事,都感觉出他身上长了刺似的难受,说,桂主任,你今天来例假了?桂平说,不是例假,我更了。大家一笑,但仍然笑不掉桂平的不安。他先想了一想今天是什么日子,会不会有什么重要的电话或信息找他,会不会有什么重要的事情要他去做,有没有什么重要的工作忘记了,除了这些,还会不会有一些特殊的额外的事情会找到他,这么一路想下去,事情越想越多,越想越紧迫,椅子上长了钉似的,桂平终于坐不住了,溜出会场,上了一趟洗手间,出来后,站在洗手间门口还犹豫了一下,终究没有直接回会场,却回了办公室。

办公室一切如常,桂平却有一种恍若隔世的奇怪感觉,看到了桌上的手机,他才回到了现世,忍不住打开手机。片刻之后,短信来了,哗哗哗的,一条,两条,三条,还没来得及看,电话就进来了,是老婆打的,口气急切地说,你怎么啦,人又不在办公室,手机又关机,你想躲起来啊?桂平无法解释,只得说,充电。老婆说,你不是有两块电池吗?桂平说,前一块忘记充了。

He replied, "No, I stopped flowing—I've already gone through menopause."

Everyone laughed, but it was not enough to settle Gui Ping's unease. He thought first about what day it was, then whether there might be some important phone call or message for him, or something important he needed to do, or some urgent work he had forgotten. And on top of all this, whether some extra responsibilities might be landed with him. Once he started thinking this way, more things came to mind and he grew more anxious. His seat seemed to have sprouted a bed of nails. Finally unable to sit any longer, Gui Ping left the conference room and went to the washroom. After he finished, he stood at the door to the men's room, hesitating. In the end, he did not go back to the conference room, but to his office.

In his office, nothing was out of the ordinary, but Gui Ping had a strange feeling, as if he had been cut off from the outside world for ages. Seeing his phone on the desk, he snapped back to reality. He quickly turned it on, and a moment later a text came in. Beep beep beep. One message, two, three. Before he could even read them, a call came in. It was his wife, her tone urgent.

"Are you alright? You weren't in the office, and your phone was off. Are you hiding from someone?"

Unable to explain, Gui Ping simply said, "It was charging."

His wife replied, "Don't you have a spare battery?"

He answered, "I forgot to charge the other one."

His wife wondered. "The sun must have risen in the west today. Isn't your nickname 'Always On-call Gui,' and now you

老婆"咦"了一声，说，太阳从西边出来了，你是出了名的"桂不关"，竟然会忘记充电？桂平自嘲地歪了歪嘴，老婆就开始说要他办的事情，桂平为了不听老婆啰嗦个没完，只得先应承了，反正虱多不痒债多不愁，桂平永远是拖了一身的人情债，还了一个又来一个，永远也还不清。

带着手机回到会场，桂平开始看信、回信。旁边的女同事说，充好电了？桂平说，你怎么知道我充电？女同事说，你是机不离手，手不离机的，刚才进来开会没拿手机，不是充电是什么？难道是忘了？谁会忘带手机你也不会忘呀。桂平说，不是忘了，我有意不带的，烦。女同事又笑了一下，说，烦，还是又拿来了，到底还是不能不用手机。桂平说，你真的以为我不敢关手机？女同事说，关手机又不是杀人，有什么敢不敢的，只怕你关了又要开噢。两人说话声音不知不觉大起来，发现主席台上有领导朝他们看了，才赶紧停止了说话。桂平安心看短信、回短信，一下子

forgot to charge your phone?"

Gui Ping twisted his mouth in a self-deprecating smile. His wife started talking about the things she wanted him to do. In order not to prolong his wife's endless chatter, he decided to immediately agree to all her requests. Anyway, whether it's one louse or many lice, it still itches, and whether it's one debt or many debts, one still has to pay up. Gui Ping always seemed to owe other people favors. As soon as he paid one off, the next started to pop up. He was never clear of debt.

Taking his phone back to the conference room, Gui Ping started to read his messages and send replies. The woman next to him said, "Finished charging?"

He asked, "What makes you think it was charging?"

She replied, "Your phone never leaves your hand, and your hand never leaves your phone. Just now when you came to the meeting without your phone, wasn't it charging? Surely you didn't forget. Everyone else might forget to bring their phones, but you never would."

Gui Ping said, "I didn't forget. I purposely left it behind. Irritating."

She laughed again and said, "Even though you were irritated, you still ended up bringing it. You really can't get by without your phone."

Gui Ping said, "Do you really think I wouldn't dare to turn off my phone?"

She said, "Turning off your phone is no crime. There's nothing to 'dare' or 'not dare.' I just think that if you turned it off, you'd go mad."

找回了精神寄托，心也不慌慌的了，屁股上也不长钉了。

该复的信还没复完，就有电话进来了，桂平看了看来电号码，不熟悉，反正手机是震动的，会场上听不到，桂平将手机搁在厚厚的会议材料上，减小震动幅度，便任由它震去，一直等到震动停止，桂平才松一口气。但紧接着第二次震动又来了，来得更长更有耐心，看起来是他非接不可，桂平一直坚持到第三次，不得不接了，身子往下挫一挫，手捂着手机，压低声音说，我在开会。那边的声音却大得吓人，啊哈哈哈，桂平，我就知道你会接我电话的，其实我都想好了，你要是第三次再不接，我就找别人了，正这么想呢，你就接了，啊哈哈哈。不仅把桂平的耳朵震着了，连旁边的女同事都能听见，说，哎哟喂，女高音啊。虽然桂平说了在开会，可那女高音却不依不饶，旁若无会地开始说她要说的说来话长的话，桂平只得抓着手机再次出了会场，到走廊上才稍稍放开声音说，我在开会，不能老是跑出来，领导在台上盯着呢。

Neither of them realized that they were speaking rather loudly until they saw one of the leaders looking at them from the rostrum. They quickly stopped talking. Gui Ping calmly read his messages, replied, and all at once rediscovered his anchor. He was no longer anxious, and did not feel the nails poking his posterior anymore.

Before he had finished answering all the messages that needed replies, a call came in. Gui Ping looked at the number of the incoming call, but did not recognize it. Anyway, his phone was on vibrant mode, and the ringing wouldn't be heard in the conference room. He put his phone down on the thick file of materials he needed for the meeting, buffering the vibrations from his phone. The vibrations went on, and he simply ignored. He finally felt relieved after the vibrations stopped. Then it started vibrating again, buzzing for a longer time, and more insistently. Feeling a little trapped, he finally gave in on the caller's third attempt. He had to pick up the call. He slipped down further in his seat, putting a hand over his phone, and in a muffled voice said, "I'm in a meeting."

The voice on the other end was startlingly loud. "Oh, ha ha! Gui Ping, I knew you would answer. I had already decided that if you didn't answer on the third try, I would look for someone else. But as soon as I thought that, you answered. Ha ha!"

It was a shock not only to Gui Ping's ears, but even the colleague sitting beside him could hear the voice. She said, "Aiyah, a soprano."

Even though Gui Ping said he was in a meeting, the woman did not seem to care—she went on in the same high-pitched voice, launching into the long story she had called to tell him. Gui Ping

女高音说，怎么老是跑出来呢？我打了你三次，你只接了一次，你最多只跑出来一次啊。桂平想，人都是只想自己的，每个人的电话我都得接一次，我还活不活了。但他只是想想，没有说，因为女高音的脾气他了解，她的一发不可收的作风他向来是甘拜下风的，赶紧说，你说吧你说吧。女高音终于开始说事，说了又说，说了又说，桂平忍不住打断说，我知道了，我现在在开会，走不掉，会一结束我就去帮你办。女高音这才甘心，准备挂电话了，最后又补一句，你办好了马上打我手机啊。桂平应声，这才算应付过去。心里却是后悔不迭，要是硬着心肠不接那第三次电话，这事情她不就找别人了么，明明前两次都已经挺过去了，怎么偏偏第三次就挺不过去呢？这女高音是他比较烦的人，所以也没有储存她的号码，可偏偏又让她抓住了，既然抓住了，她所托的事情，也就不好意思不办。桂平又悔自己怎么就不能坚持到底，抓着手机欲再回到会场，正遇上小李也出来溜号，见桂主任一脸懊

could only walk out of the conference room, clutching his phone in his palm. Only when he was in the corridor could he speak a bit louder. "I'm in a meeting. I can't always go out like that. The boss is glaring at me."

The soprano said, "What do you mean 'always go out'? I called you three times, but you only answered once. At most you only go out once."

Gui Ping thought, "People are so self-absorbed. If I answered just one call from everyone, could I survive it?" But he only kept the thought to himself. He knew the soprano's temper, how she could go on a rampage and how it would end up with his defeat, so he hurriedly said, "Right. Go ahead."

The soprano finally turned to the matter she had called about. She talked and talked. Gui Ping could not help but interrupt. "I see. I'm in a meeting now. I can't leave. As soon as I can get away, I'll help you settle it."

Finally the soprano was satisfied, but she was just about to hang up when she added, "When you settle it, call my cell phone right away, OK?"

Gui Ping gave in, and got it done with, at long last. He regretted that he had not resisted. If he had not given in and answered the third call, she would have looked for someone else to take care of this. Obviously he had done fine on the first two times, so why did he give in on the third? This high-pitched woman was the type he felt quite bothersome, so he had not stored her number in his phone. And now that he had allowed her to get in touch with him, he was caught. It would be too awkward to refuse to help her with this

恼,关心道,桂主任,怎么啦?桂平将手机一举,说,烦死个人。小李以为他要扔手机,吓得赶紧伸出双手去捧,结果捧了个空。桂平说,关机吧,不行,开机吧,也不行,难死个人。小李察言观色地说,桂主任,其实也并非只有两条路,还有第三种可能性的。桂平白了他一眼,说,要么开,要么关,哪来的第三种可能性?小李诡秘一笑,说,那是人家逃债的人想出来的高招。桂平说,那是什么?小李说,不在服务区。桂平"切"了一声,说,怎么会不在服务区,我们又不是深山老林,又不是大沙漠,怎么会不在服务区?小李说,桂主任,你要不要试试,手机开着的时候把那卡芯直接取下来,再放上电板重新开机,那就是不在服务区。桂平照小李说的一试,果然说:"对不起,您拨的电话不在服务区,请稍后再拨。"桂平大喜,从此可以自由出入"服务区"了。

如此这般的第二天,桂平就被领导逮到当面臭骂一顿,说,

matter. Regretting that he had not held out until the end, he grasped his phone and went back into the conference room. He ran into Xiao Li, who was sneaking out. Noticing his boss's chagrin, Xiao Li asked in concern, "Director Gui, is everything OK?"

Gui Ping waved his phone toward Xiao Li and said, "Irritating."

Xiao Li, thinking he was going to throw the phone, quickly reached out with his hands, only to grasp at thin air. Gui Ping said, "Turning off the phone is no good. Turning on the phone is no better. It sucks."

Xiao Li observed Gui Ping's expression as he said cautiously, "Director Gui, actually those are not the only options. There is a third possibility."

Gui Ping squinted at him and said, "On, off—what's your third option?"

Xiao Li smiled secretively, and explained that it was an option devised by people who wished to escape their loan sharks.

"What is it?" asked Gui Ping.

"Go out of the service area."

"Pooh!" Gui Ping said, "How can that be—outside the service area? We aren't in a wilderness or a desert. How can we be without service?"

Xiao Li said, "Do you want to try? When your phone is on, take out the card, put back the battery, restart the phone, and then you will be outside the service area."

Gui Ping tried what Xiao Li had suggested. When he dialed his number from his office phone, he heard, "We're sorry, the number you called is not in the service area. Please try again later."

我这里忙得要出人命,你躲哪里去了?在哪个山区偷闲?桂平慌忙说,我没去山区,我一直都在单位。领导说,人在单位手机怎么会不在服务区?桂平说,我在服务区,我在服务区。领导恼道,在你个鬼,你个什么烂手机,打进去都是不在服务区,既然你老不在服务区,你干脆就别服务了吧。桂平受了惊吓,赶紧恢复原状,不敢再离开服务区了。

小李当然也没逃了桂平的一顿臭骂,但小李挨了骂也仍然不折不挠地为桂平分忧解难,又建议说,桂主任,你干脆别怕麻烦,把所有有关手机都储存下来,来电时一看就知道是谁,可接可不接,主动权就在你手里了。

桂平接受了小李的建议,专门挑了一个会议时间,坐在会场上,把必须接的、可接可不接的、完全可以不接的,实在不想接的电话——都储存进手机,储得差不多了,会议也散了,走出会场时,手机响了,一看,是一个可以不接的电话,干脆将手机往

Gui Ping was thrilled. He was now free to move in and out of the service area.

Only one day after Gui Ping had resorted to this trick, the boss caught him and gave him a scolding. "I'm working myself to death. Where have you been hiding? In which mountain resort were you seeking your pleasure?"

Gui Ping hurriedly responded, "I didn't go into any mountains. I was in the office compound the whole time."

"If you were in the compound, why was your phone outside the service area?"

Gui Ping said, "But I was in the service area. I was."

The boss was furious. "Bullshit! What kind of rotten phone are you using that tells me it isn't in the service area? If you are always outside the service area, you might as well stay out of service."

Frightened, Gui Ping rectified the situation with his phone. He did not dare to leave the service area again.

Of course, Xiao Li did not escape Gui Ping's scolding, nevertheless he was a sort of eager beaver, indefatigable in seeking solutions for his boss. He then suggested, "Director Gui, just forget about the trouble and store all numbers in your phone and don't leave anyone out. When you get a call, you will know whose it is and whether or not you will answer it. The decision lies in your own hands then."

Gui Ping took this advice and purposefully applied it during the next meeting. As he sat in the conference room, he sorted through all the numbers—those he had to answer, those he could ignore, those he could afford to ignore and those he wanted to ignore, and stored them all in his

口袋里一兜，任它叫唤去。

桂平找到了一个切实可行的好办法，他已经把和他有关系的大多数人物都分成几个等次储存了，爱接不接，爱理不理，主动权终于掌握在他自己手里了，如果来电不是储存的姓名，而是陌生的号码，那肯定与他没有什么直接关联的人，那就不去搭理它了。

如此这般过了一段日子，果然减少了许多麻烦，托他办事的人，大多和那女高音差不多，知道他好说话，大事小事都找他，现在既然找不上他，他们就另辟蹊径找别人的麻烦去了。即使以后见到了有所怪罪，最多嘴上说一句对不起，没听到手机响，或者正在开会不方便接，也就混过去了，真的省了不少心。

省心的日子并不长，有一天开会时，刚要入会场，有人拍他的肩，回头一看，吓了一跳，竟是组织部的常务副部长，笑眯眯地说，桂主任，忙啊。桂平起先心里一热，但随即心里就犯嘀咕，部长跟他的关系，并没有熟悉亲切到会打日常哈哈的地步，桂平

phone. As he was just about done with the task, the meeting ended. When he went out of the conference room, the phone rang. He glanced, saw it was a call he could ignore, and simply slipped the phone into his pocket, letting it continue to ring there.

Gui Ping found this a very workable solution. He had already stored the numbers of most of the people related to him into different categories, so if he wanted to answer, he would answer, and if he wanted to ignore a call, he would ignore it. He had finally taken over control of his phone. If the caller's number was not stored in his phone, if it was an unfamiliar number, then it was definitely not someone directly associated with him and he could ignore the call.

It went on like this for a few days, and it really reduced the number of hassles he had to deal with. Of those who usually looked for him to do them a favor, most were like the woman with the high-pitched voice. Knowing he was approachable, they came to him with all sorts of issues, big or small. Now that they couldn't reach him, they had to find other people to trouble. Even though it was a little awkward meeting them the next time, all he really had to do was to say sorry, he hadn't heard the phone, or perhaps that he had been in a meeting and it wasn't convenient to answer the call. Then it would blow over, saving him a lot of effort.

But the effort-saving days did not last long. One day he was going to attend a meeting, and just as he was going into the conference room, someone tapped him on the shoulder. Startled, he looked back and saw that it was the Administrative Deputy Minister of the Organization Department of the CPC. With a smile on his face, he said, "Director Gui, you've been busy, huh?"

赶紧反过来试探说,还好,还好,瞎忙,部长才忙呢。部长又笑,说,不管你是瞎忙还是白忙,反正知道你很忙,要不然,怎么连我的电话都不接呢?桂平吓了一大跳,心里怦怦的,都语无伦次了,说,部、部长,你打过我电话?部长道,打你办公室你不在,打你手机你不接,我就知道找不到你了。桂平更慌了,就露出了真话,说,部长,我不知道你给我打电话。部长仍然笑道,说明你的手机里没有储存我的电话,我不是你的重要关系哦。他知道桂平紧张,又拍拍他的肩,让他轻松些,说,你别慌,不是要提拔你哦,要提拔你,我不会直接给你打电话哦。桂平尴尬一笑。部长又说,所以你不要担心错过了什么,我本来只是想请你关照一个人而已,他在你改革委工作,想请你多关心一下,开个玩笑,办公室主任,你们都喜欢称大内总管嘛,是不是,年轻人刚进一个单位,有大内总管罩一罩,可不一样哦。桂平赶紧问,是谁?在哪个部门?部长说,现在也不用你关照了,他已经不在你们单

Gui Ping's heart skipped a bit at first, and then he started to wonder in his mind. His relationship with the deputy minister was not close to the point of bantering with each other. He quickly tried to turn the table on the deputy minister, and tested the waters, "Not too bad. I'm busy, but not nearly as busy as you."

The deputy minister smiled and said, "Whether you're busy or just messing around, whatever the case, all I know is you're busy. Why else would you not answer my phone calls?"

This gave Gui Ping a huge fright, making his heart pound. He stuttered a few times, then said, "Mr.—Mr. Minister, you called me?"

"When I called your office, you weren't there. When I called your cell phone, you didn't answer. Then I know you are a difficult man to reach."

Gui Ping, really panicking now, resorted to the truth. "Mr. Minister, I didn't know it was you calling."

The deputy minister smiled. "You mean you didn't store my number in your phone? I must not be very important to you then." Knowing Gui Ping was nervous, the deputy minister slapped him on the shoulder, making him relax a little. "Don't worry, anyway it is not about your promotion. If it were, I am not supposed to call you in person."

Embarrassed, Gui Ping laughed. The deputy minister continued, "So don't worry, you didn't miss anything. I just wanted to ask you to take care of someone. He was assigned to your Reform Commission. I just wanted to ask you to keep an eye on him, make him feel at home. Just a joke. Don't you office directors all like to be

位了,前两天调走了,放心,跟你没关系,现在的年轻人,跳槽是正常的事,不跳槽才怪呢,由他们去吧。说着话,部长就和桂平一起走进会场,很亲热的样子,会场上许多人看着,后来有人还跟桂平说,没想到你和部长那么近乎。

桂平却懊恼极了,送上门来的机会,被自己给关在了门外,可他怎么想得到部长会直接给自己打电话呢。现在看起来,他所严格执行的陌生号码一概不接的大政是错误的,大错特错了。知错就改,桂平把领导干部名册找出来,把有关领导的电话,只要是名册上有的,全部都输进手机,好在现在的手机内存很大,存再多号码它也不会爆炸。

现在桂平总算可以安心了,既能够避免许多无谓的麻烦,又不会错过任何不应该错过的机会,只不过,过了很长很长的时间,也没有等到一个领导打他的手机。桂平并不着急,也没觉得功夫白费了,他是有备无患,凡事预则立。

called by fancy titles like the palace chamberlain? Well, this young fellow had just entered your unit, and if he had the palace chamberlain's attention, it would have made a great difference, wouldn't it?"

Anxious, Gui Ping asked, "Who is it? Which department is he with?"

The deputy minister said, "I don't need you to look after him now. He's not in your unit anymore. He was transferred a couple of days ago. Don't worry, it's nothing to do with you. Nowadays, it's normal for young guys to job-hop. If he didn't, that'd be rare. So leave them alone."

As they were talking, the deputy minister walked into the conference room with Gui Ping, his manner almost affectionate. Many people in the conference room noticed it and one commented later, "I didn't know you were so close to the deputy minister."

Gui Ping was very upset. The opportunity had been right on his doorstep, and he had slammed the door in its face. But how could he have known the deputy minister would call his line directly? Looking at it now, taking such a strict approach to governing the strange numbers on his phone had been a mistake. A big mistake. Huge. Admitting a mistake meant it was time for change. Gui Ping found the directory of the leading cadres, all the leaders—anyone who was on the directory—and entered the numbers into his phone. Fortunately his current phone's memory was large. Storing that many numbers would not make it explode.

Now Gui Ping could finally relax. He could avoid unnecessary troubles, but also would not miss out on an opportunity when it

过了些日子,桂平大学同学聚会,在同一座城市的同班同学,许多年来,来了的,走了的,走了又来的,来了又走的,到现在,搜搜刮刮正好一桌人,这一天兴致好,全到了。坐下来的第一件事,大家都把手机从包里或者从口袋里掏出,搁在桌上,搁在眼睛看得见的地方,夹在一堆餐具酒杯中。桂平倒是没拿出来,但他的手机就放在裤子后袋里,而且是设置了铃声加震动,如果聚会热闹,说话声音大,听不到铃声,屁股可以感受到震动,几乎是万无一失的。也有一两个比较含蓄的女生并没有把手机拿出来搁在桌上,但是她们的包包都靠身体很近,包包的拉链都敞开着,可以让手机的声音不受阻挡地传递出来,这才可以安心地喝酒叙旧。

这一天大家谈得很兴奋,而且话题集中,把在校期间许多同学的公开的或秘密的恋情都谈出来了,有的爱情,在当时是一种痛苦,甚至痛得死去活来,时隔多年再谈,却已经变成一种享受,

came his way. But after a long, long time, not a single high official called his phone. Still, he was not worried, and did not feel the effort was wasted. He was prepared. Forewarned is forearmed.

A few days later, Gui Ping's classmates from university held a gathering for all those who still lived in the same city. Over the years, some had left, some had come back, some had come back and left again. Now, what was left could just fill up one table. On that day, everyone seemed to be in good mood, and all came.

As soon as they sat down, they all took their cell phones out from a bag or pocket, setting them on the table where they were sure to always be in sight amid the dishes and wine glasses there. Gui Ping did not take his out, leaving it in his back pocket, set on vibrate as well as ring mode. If the gathering was lively and everyone was speaking loudly, and he missed the ringing, he would still feel the vibration on his rear. It was almost foolproof. There were also a couple of the more reserved female classmates who did not take their phones out and place them on the table, but they held their bags close and unzipped, not obstructing the sound of the phones' ringing. In this way they could drink and reminisce without a worry.

The conversation was very lively and engaging, with many of the classmates' old romances—whether open or secret—being the topic of discussion. There were some romances that seemed really heartbreaking at the time, so painful those involved felt like dying. Discussing these romances after so many years had passed, had become a sort of enjoyment. Whether they had been directly involved in the tale or merely spectators, they all enjoyed the light touch of sadness and happiness brought on by time.

无论是当事人，或是旁观者，都在享受时间带来的淡淡的忧伤和幸福。

谈完了当年还没谈够，又开始说现在，现在的张三有外遇吧，现在的李四艳福不浅啊，谁是谁的小三啦，谁是谁的什么什么，怎么怎么。接着就有一个同学指着另一个同学，说那天我看到你了，你挽着一个女的在逛街，不是你老婆，所以我没敢喊你。大家哄起来，要叫他坦白，偏偏这个同学是个老实巴交不怎么会说话的人，急赤白赖赌咒发誓，但谁也不信，他急了，东看看，西看看，好像要找什么证据来证明，结果就见他把手机一掏，往桌上一拍，说，把你们手机都拿出来。大家的手机本来就搁在桌面上，有人就把手机往前推一推，也有人把手机往后挪一挪，但都不知他要干什么。这同学说，如果有事情，手机里肯定有秘密，你们敢不敢，大家互相交换手机看内容，如果有事情的，肯定不敢——我就敢！话一出口，立刻就有一两个人脸色煞白，急急忙忙要抓回手机，另一个人说，手机是个人的隐私，怎么可以交换着看，你有窥视欲啊？当然也有人不慌张，很坦然，

When they had finished talking about old times, they started to discuss the present. Now this one was having an affair, that one had a way with women, who was whose mistress, who was doing what with whom, and so on. Then one classmate pointed at another and said, "I saw you the other day shopping with some woman. It wasn't your wife, so I didn't dare call you."

Everyone coaxed him, urging him to tell all. He happened to be an honest but untactful guy, and he kept swearing and denying anxiously, but no one believed him. Exasperatedly, he looked here and there, as if looking for something to prove his innocence. Then they saw him take out his phone and fling it on the table, "Take out your phones," he said.

Most people's phones were already on the table. Several pushed theirs forward, while others pulled theirs back, but no one knew what he wanted to do. Then he said, "If there is anything going on, the phone will be full of secrets. Who dares? Let's all exchange phones and see each other's contents. If there are secrets, you won't dare. But I dare!"

As soon as he finished saying this, a couple of the friends turned pale and quickly reached for their phones. One said, "A phone is private. How can we just swap and look at each other's phones? What are you, a voyeur?"

And of course there were others who did not panic, but were quite open. Some were even excited by the idea, saying, "Look. Go ahead. Let's lay everything bare here on the table."

Gui Ping didn't care either way, but he did feel that this naive classmate was going a little overboard. He said, "Who would be

甚至有人对这个点子很兴奋，很激动，说，看就看，看就看，大家摊开来看。桂平也是无所谓，但他觉得这同学老实得有点过分，说，哪个傻叉会保留这样的信？带回去给老婆老公看？那同学偏又顶真，说，如果真有感情，信是舍不得马上删掉的。大家又笑他，说他有体验，感受真切等等。这同学一张嘴实在说不过大家，恼了，涨红了脸硬把自己的手机塞到一个同学手里，你看，你看。

结果，同学中分成了两拨，一拨不愿意或不敢把自己的秘密让别人知道，不肯参加这个游戏，赶紧把手机紧紧抓在手心里，就怕别人来抢；另一拨是桂平他们几个，自觉不怕的，或者是硬着头皮撑面子的，都把手机放在桌上，由那同学闭上眼睛先弄混乱了，大家再闭上眼睛各摸一部。桂平摸到了一个女同学的手机，正想打开来看，眼睛朝那女同学一瞄，发现那女同学脸色很尴尬，桂平心一动，说，算了算了，女生的我不看。把手机还给了那女同学，女同学收回手机，嘴巴却又凶起来，说，你看好了，你不看白不看。桂平也没和她计较，但他自己运气就没那么好了，他

silly enough to keep that kind of message? You think anyone would want to bring it home for a spouse to read?"

The classmate obstinately rebutted, saying, "If you really feel that way about someone, you can't bear to delete the messages."

Everyone laughed, saying he obviously had some experience in this area, since he knew how it really felt. It went on for a while until the classmate could not withstand their assault and so, red-faced and angry, he shoved his phone into another classmate's hand and said, "Come on. Take a look."

And so the group was divided into two camps, those willing to share the secrets of their phones and those who refused to participate in the game, keeping their phones firmly clutched in their hands, afraid someone might snatch them. Another group, including Gui Ping, were either not afraid at all, or pretending they didn't care to save their face. They all put their phones on the table, and the one who had suggested the game mixed them up with his eyes closed. Then everyone closed his or her eyes and picked one. Gui Ping got hold of a female classmate's phone. Just as he started to inspect it, he sneaked a look at her, noticing how embarrassed she looked. Something inside him stirred, and he said, "Forget it. I don't want to look at a woman's phone."

He handed the phone back to her and she put it away. However, she would not rest her sharp tongue. She said, "Why don't you look? It's your own loss if you don't."

He didn't bother about her, but his own luck was not so good. His phone had been taken by one of the nosiest guys in the group. The first thing the fellow did was to look through the messages.

的手机被一个最好事的男生拿到了，先翻看他的短信，失望了，说，哈，早有准备啊。桂平说，那当然，不然怎么肯拿出来让你看。那男生不甘心，又翻看他的储存电话，想看看有没有可疑人物。

真是不看不知道，一看吓一跳，那男生脸都涨红了，脱口说，哇，桂平，你厉害，连大老板的手机你都有？接着就将桂平手机里的储存名单给大家一一念了起来。这可全是有头有脸有来头的大人物啊。惊得一帮同学一个个朝着桂平瞪眼，说，嗬，好狡猾，这么厉害的背景，从来不告诉我们。也有的人，说，这是低调，你们懂吗，低调，现在流行这个。桂平想解释也解释不清，只好一笑了之。

却不知他这一笑，是笑不了之的。第二天，就有一个同学找到他办公室去了，提了厚重的礼物，请桂平帮忙联系分管文化的副市长，他正在筹办一个全市最大也最规范的超霸电玩城，文化局那头已经攻下关来，但没有分管市长的签字，就办不成，他已经几经周折几次找过那副市长，都碰了钉子被弹回来了，现在就

Disappointed, he said, "Hm. You're well prepared."

Gui Ping said, "Of course. If not, why would I take it out and let you look?"

But the fellow would not give up so easily. He inspected the phone book to see if he could find any suspicious characters there.

A look of shock came over him. The fellow's face reddened and he blurted out, "Gui Ping, you're so influential. You even have the higher-ups' cell numbers." He went through the names stored in Gui Ping's phone, reading them out one by one. "These are all the big wigs and VIPs."

The stunned group of classmates all turned to stare at Gui Ping, saying things like, "Wow, you are sly. Such an impressive background, and you never told us."

One also said, "It's called keeping a low profile, you know? A low profile is the thing these days."

Gui Ping, unable to offer a good explanation, could only laugh it off.

He had not imagined how long the echoes of this laughter would follow him. The next day, a former classmate sought him out at his office, a weighty gift in hand, asking Gui Ping to help contact the Deputy Mayor in charge of the cultural industry. The classmate was planning the city's biggest, highest standard video game arcade. The Department of Culture had given the green light, but the documents were not signed by the Deputy Mayor, and they could not proceed without his signature. He had tried to get in touch with the Deputy Mayor several times, but always came back empty-handed. Now it all depended on Gui Ping's power.

看桂平的力度了。

桂平知道自己的手机引鬼上门了，只得老老实实说，我其实并不认得该副市长。同学说，不可能，你手机里都有他的电话，怎么会不认识？桂平只得老实交代，从头道来。那同学听后，"哈"了一声，说，桂平，你当了官以后，越来越会编啊，你怎么不把国家领导人的电话也输进去？桂平开玩笑说，我知道的话一定输进去。那同学却恼了，说，桂平，凭良心说，这许多年，你在政府工作，我在社会上混，可我从来没找过你麻烦是不是，这是第一次，第一次求你你就这么对付我，你说得过去吗？桂平知道怎么说这同学也不会相信他了，但他也无论如何不可能去替他找那副市长的，只得冷下脸来，说，反正你怎么理解、怎么想都无所谓，这事情我不能做。同学一气之下，走了，礼物却没有带走，桂平想喊他回来拿，但又觉得那样做太过分，就没有喊。

那堆礼物一直搁在那里，桂平看到它们，心里就不爽，搬到墙角放着，眼睛还是忍不住拐了弯要去看，再把办公室的柜子清

Gui Ping, knowing that this sort of apparition came through the door opened by his phone, had to say frankly, "Actually, I don't know the deputy mayor."

His classmate said, "Impossible. You have his number in your phone. How can you not know him?"

Gui Ping confessed the truth of what had happened, beginning to end. Hearing it, his classmate said, "Ha! Gui Ping, since you became an official, you've become more twisted. I'm surprised you don't have state leaders' numbers stored in your phone."

Gui Ping joked, "If I knew their numbers, I would have stored them too."

His classmate was angry. He said, "Tell me in good conscience, all these years you've been working for the government and I've been struggling in the private sector, have I ever come to you with any kind of trouble? Just this once. One time I come to you and you refuse me. Is that fair?"

Gui Ping knew that no matter what he said, his classmate would not believe him, but there was also no way he could approach the Deputy Mayor. He could only put on a cold expression and say, "Anyway, you can think what you like, it doesn't matter. There's nothing I can do to help in this matter."

Angry, his classmate left, but did not take the gift with him. Gui Ping felt like shouting for him to come back, but he thought that would be going too far, so he did not call after his friend.

The pile of gifts was left sitting there. Whenever Gui Ping saw them, he felt awful. He moved them into a corner of the room, but his eyes kept roaming there involuntarily. He cleared a space in the

理一下，放进去，关上柜门，总算眼不见为净。本来他们同学间都很和睦融洽，现在美好的感觉都被手机里的一个错误的储存电话破坏了，右想左想，也觉得自己将认得不认得的领导都输入手机确实不妥，拿起手机想将这些电话删除了，但右看左看，又不知道哪些是该删的哪些是不该删的，全部删了肯定也是不妥，最后还是下不了手。

原来以为得罪了同学，就横下一条心了，得罪就得罪了，以后有机会再给弥补吧。哪知那同学虽然被得罪了，却不甘心，过了两天，又来了，换了一招，往桂平办公室的沙发上一坐，说，你不答应我，我就不走了。桂平说，我要办公的，你坐在这里不方便。同学说，我方便的。桂平说，我不方便呀。同学说，有什么不方便，你就当是自己在沙发上搁了一件东西就行，你办你的公，你又不是保密局安全局，你的工作我听到了也不会传播出去的，即使传播出去别人也不感兴趣的。就这样死死地钉在桂平的办公室里。

即便如此，桂平还是不能打这个电话，因为他实在跟这位副

cupboard, put them inside, and closed the cupboard door, feeling better once they were rid of the sight. All along he had enjoyed a harmonious rapport with his classmates, but now that perfect feeling was ruined by the mistake he had made in storing these numbers in his phone. He went back and forth in his mind, trying to decide if it was really wise to input the numbers of all those officials, both those he knew and those he didn't. He picked up his phone, ready to delete the unnecessary numbers, but could not decide which to keep and which to discard. It didn't feel right to delete them all, so in the end he did nothing.

At first he worried that he had offended his classmate, but then he hardened his heart. If he's offended, he's offended. I'll make up for it when I get the chance.

But he did not realize that the offense would not be so easily resolved. After a couple of days, the classmate came again. Changing his tactic, he came into the office and sat on the sofa. He said, "I'm not leaving until you promise to help me."

Gui Ping said, "I have work to do. It's not convenient for you to just sit there."

His classmate said, "It's convenient for me."

"But not for me," Gui Ping replied.

"What's not convenient? Just pretend that you've set something on the couch, it should be fine. Do your work. It's not like you're in the secret service. If I overhear you working, I'm not going to announce it to anyone. And even if I do, no one is interested." And with that he attached himself to Gui Ping's office with a death grip.

Even so, Gui Ping could not make this phone call because he really

市长没有任何交往，没有任何接触，这副市长并不分管他们这一块工作，即使开什么大会，副市长坐主席台，桂平也只能在台下朝台上远远地看一眼，主席台上有许多领导，这副市长只是其中一位，除此之外，就是在本地电视新闻里看他几眼，他和副市长，就这么一个台上台下屏里屏外的关系，怎么可能去找他帮忙办事呢，何况还不是他自己的事，何况还是办超霸电玩城这样的敏感事情。

同学就这样坐在他的沙发上，有人进来汇报工作，谈事情，他便侧过脸去，表示自己并不关心桂平的工作，就算桂平能够不当回事，别人也会觉得奇怪，觉得拘束，该直说的话就不好直说了，该简单处理的事情就变复杂了，半天班上下来，桂平心力交瘁，吃不消了，跟同学说，你先坐着，我上个厕所。同学说，你溜不掉的。

桂平只是想溜出去镇定一下，想一想对策，但又不能站在走廊上想，就去了一趟厕所，待了半天，没理出个头绪来，也不能老在厕所待着，只得再硬起头皮回办公室。哪曾想到，等他回到

had no contact with this deputy mayor at all, no connections—his line of work was not under the supervision of this mayor. And even if they had been together in any meeting, the deputy mayor would be sitting at the rostrum, and Gui Ping could only catch a glimpse of him from a distance. There were always many officials at the rostrum, and this deputy mayor would have just been one in the crowd. Besides that, he might have glimpsed the deputy mayor on the local news on TV. They only shared an on-rostrum-off-rostrum/onscreen-offscreen sort of relationship. How would it look for him to approach this deputy mayor with some business not his own—and especially such sensitive business as planning a giant video game arcade?

So his classmate sat on the sofa. When people came in to report or discuss work matters, he just looked away, showing he was not interested in Gui Ping's work. Even if Gui Ping felt it was nothing, others would find it strange and feel stifled, so that they could not say directly what they had come to say. What should have been simple matters thus became complicated. After a half-day of it, Gui Ping was both physically and mentally exhausted. It was too much. He said to his classmate, "You stay here. I'm going to the washroom."

The classmate said, "You can't escape."

Gui Ping just wanted to slip outside, regain his composure, and think of countermeasures, but he could not just stand there in the corridor while he thought, so he went to the washroom. After spending quite some time there, he still had no clue what to do, and he couldn't simply stay in the toilet, so he made his way back to his office again. But who would have imagined that the classmate would gleefully greet him at the door. Gui Ping said, "What are you

办公室，那同学已经喜笑颜开地站在门口迎候他了。桂平说，你笑什么？同学说，行了，我拿你的手机打过市长了，市长叫我等通知。桂平急得跳了起来，你，你，你怎么——同学说，我没怎么呀，挺顺利。桂平说，你跟市长怎么说的？同学说，我当然不说我是我，我当然说我是你啦。桂平竟然没听懂，说，什么意思，什么我是你？同学说，我说，市长啊，我是改革委的桂平啊。桂平急道，市长不认得我呀，市长怎么说？同学笑道，市长怎么不认得你，市长太认得你了，市长热情地说，啊，啊，是桂平啊。后来我就说，我有个亲戚，有重要工作想当面向您汇报。桂平说，你怎么瞎说，你是我的亲戚吗？同学说，同学和亲戚，也差不多嘛，干吗这么计较。我当你的亲戚，给你丢脸了吗？桂平被噎得不轻，顿住了。那同学眉飞色舞又说，市长说了，他让秘书安排一下时间，尽快给我，啊不，不是给我，是给你答复。话音未落，桂平的手机响了，竟然真是那副市长的秘书打来的，说，改革委办公室桂主任吧，市长明天下午四点有时间，但最多只能谈半小时，五点市长有接待任务。桂平愣住了，但也知道没有回头路了，

smiling about?"

His classmate said, "Everything is fine. I used your phone to call the deputy mayor, and he said to wait for his call."

Gui Ping started. "You—you—what have you done?"

"I didn't do anything wrong. It all went just fine!"

"What did you say to the deputy mayor?"

"Of course I didn't say it was me. I said it was you."

For a moment, Gui Ping didn't understand. "What do you mean it was me?"

I said, "Deputy Mayor, this is Gui Ping from the Reform Commission."

Anxiety flooded over Gui Ping. "He doesn't even know me. What did he say?"

"Oh, Come on! He knows you very well! He said very warmly, 'Oh yeah, Gui Ping!' Then I said, 'I have a relative who needs to see you about an important document.'"

Gui Ping said, "How come you talk such nonsense? You, my relative?"

"Classmate, relative—it's all the same. Why the fuss? If I were your relative, would that be a loss of face?"

Gui Ping felt he was being choked, and couldn't speak for a moment. Enraptured, his classmate continued, "The deputy mayor said he would get his secretary to arrange a time, and inform me as soon as he could. Oh! Not me, but you."

Hardly had he finished when Gui Ping's phone rang again, and it really was the deputy mayor's secretary, asking, "Is that Director Gui with the Reform Commission? The deputy mayor has time

总不能告诉人家，刚才的电话不是他打的，是别人偷他的手机打的。同学怕他坏事，拼命朝他挤眉弄眼，桂平狠狠地瞪他，却拿整个事情无奈，赶紧答应了市长秘书，明天下午四点到市长办公室，谈半小时。

挂了电话，那同学大喜过望，桂平却百思不得其解，说，怎么可能，怎么可能？同学也不生气了，说，反正事情就是这样，你明天得陪我去，你放心，我不会空手的。桂平气得说，没见过你这样的。同学却高兴而去了。

同学走后，桂平把小李叫来，说，小李，我认得某副市长吗？小李被问得一头雾水，说，桂主任，什么意思？桂平说，我不记得我和他打过什么交道呀，他才当副市长不久呀。小李说是，年初人大开会时才上的，不过两三个月。桂平说，何况他又不分管我们这一块，最多有时候他坐在主席台上，我坐在台下，这是八竿子也打不着的呀。小李说，那倒是的，我也在台下看见领导坐在台上，但是哪个领导会知道台下的我呢。小李见桂平愁眉不展，

tomorrow afternoon at four, but at most he only has half an hour. At five he has a reception."

Gui Ping was astounded, but he knew there was no way out. He could never say that the person who had just called was not him, that someone had used his phone without his knowledge. Fearing Gui Ping might give the game away, his classmate winked at him desperately. Gui Ping glared at him, but he was really helpless in the whole affair, so he promised the deputy mayor's secretary that he would be at the office the next day at four for a half-hour meeting.

When he hung up, his classmate was overjoyed. Gui Ping, on the other hand, was puzzled, and kept saying, "How could that be? How could that be?"

His classmate wasn't angry anymore. He said, "Anyway, as things stand, you'll have to come with me tomorrow. Don't worry. I won't come empty-handed."

Angry, Gui Ping said, "I've never encountered a person like you."

The classmate, on the other hand, left happily.

When his classmate had gone, Gui Ping called Xiao Li in and asked, "Xiao Li, do I know this Deputy Mayor?"

Confused, Xiao Li replied, "Director Gui, what do you mean?"

Gui Ping said, "I don't remember having any dealings with him, but he hasn't been the deputy mayor for very long, has he?"

Xiao Li said, "Since the beginning of the year during the session of National People's Congress, so not more than two or three months."

Gui Ping said, "Well, he's never been in charge of our division. At most, he's been on the rostrum once or twice when I was seated below. He's way beyond my reach I believe."

又积极主动为主任分忧解难,说,桂主任,会不会从前他没当市长的时候,你们接触过,时间长了,你忘记了,但是市长记性好,没忘记。桂平说,他没当市长前,是在哪里工作的?小李说,我想想。想了一会,想起来了,说,是在水产局,他是专家,又是民主党派,正好政府换届时需要这样一个人,就选中了他,后来听说他还跟人开玩笑说,我做梦也没有想到我会当副市长哎。桂平说,水产局?那我更不可能认得了,我从来没有跟水产局打过交道。小李又想了想,说,要不然,就是另一种可能,市长不是记性好,而是记性不好,是个糊涂人,把你和别的什么人搞混了,以为你是那个人?桂平说,不可能糊涂到这样吧?小李说,也可能市长事情太多,他以为找他的人,打他手机的人,肯定是熟悉的,你想想,不熟悉不认得的人,怎么会贸然去打领导的手机呢?

无论小李怎么分析,也不能让桂平解开心头之谜,等小李走了,桂平把手机拿起来看看,看到刚才市长秘书的来电号码,这是一个座机号码,估计是市长秘书的办公室电话,就忽然想到,自己

Xiao Li said, "That's true. I've also seen those leaders high on the rostrum from way below where I was sitting. Which leader would notice me sitting there below the rostrum?"

Xiao Li, noticing Gui Ping's frown, wanted to take the initiative to play the role of problem-solver. He said, "Director Gui, maybe sometime before he was the deputy mayor, you two came into contact. Maybe it was a long time ago, so you forgot, but the deputy mayor has an exceptional memory, so he didn't forget."

Gui Ping said, "Before he was the deputy mayor, where was he working?"

Xiao Li said, "Let me think." After a moment, it came to him. "He was in the Fisheries Bureau. He was an expert, and also a member of one of the democratic parties. When the government changed, they saw a need for this kind of people, so they selected him. Later I heard that he joked about it, 'I never dreamed I would become a deputy mayor.'"

Gui Ping said, "The Fisheries Bureau? Then all the more I don't know him. I've never had any dealings with the Fisheries Bureau."

Xiao Li thought for a moment, and then said, "Or else, there is another possibility. Perhaps the deputy mayor's memory isn't exceptionally good, but exceptionally bad. Maybe he's confused and has you mixed up with someone else. Maybe he thinks you're that person."

Gui Ping said, "Surely he couldn't be that confused."

Xiao Li replied, "Or maybe the deputy mayor is really busy and he assumed that anyone who approached him or anyone who called his cell phone must at least be an acquaintance. Think about it, a stranger surely wouldn't just call a deputy mayor's cell phone."

连这位副市长的这位秘书姓什么也没搞清楚，只知道他是刚刚跟上市长不久的，桂平赶紧四处打听，最后才搞清了这位秘书姓什么，于是又拿起手机，手指一动，就把那秘书的电话拨了回去。那边接得也快，说，哪位？桂平说，我是改革委办公室的桂平，刚才，刚才——那秘书记性好，马上说，是桂主任啊，明天下午市长接见已经安排了，四点，还有什么问题吗？桂平支吾了一下，一时不知道该怎么说，停顿片刻后，才说，我想问一问，你今天晚上有没有时间——？那秘书立刻有习惯性的过度反应，说，桂主任，不用客气。桂平想解释一下，但那秘书认定桂平是要给他请客送礼，又拒绝说，桂主任，你真的不必费心，我知道你跟市长关系不一般，市长吩咐的事，我们一定会用心办的。桂平赶紧试探说，你怎么知道我跟市长关系不一般。那秘书一笑，说，市长平时从来不接手机的，他的手机都是交给我处理的，一般都是我先接了，再请示市长接不接电话，但是今天你打来的电话，却是市长亲自接的，这还不能说明问题？桂平被问得哑口无言，只

But no matter how Xiao Li analyzed it, nothing worked to clear it up for Gui Ping. After Xiao Li left, Gui Ping took out his phone and looked at it. Looking at the number of the deputy mayor's secretary who had just called, he thought, "This is a landline, probably the secretary's office phone." Then it suddenly struck him that he did not even know the surname of this deputy mayor's secretary. He only knew that the secretary had not been in this post very long. Gui Ping frantically asked around and learned the secretary's surname, then his fingers flew over the phone and he called the secretary again.

The call was answered promptly. The voice on the other end said, "May I ask who's calling?"

Gui Ping said, "This is Gui Ping, from the Reform Commission. Just now—just now—"

The secretary had a good memory. He immediately said, "Director Gui, your meeting with the mayor has already been arranged for tomorrow afternoon at four. Is there anything else?"

Gui Ping faltered for a moment, not quite sure what to say. He paused, then said, "I wanted to ask, are you free tonight—?"

Out of habit, the secretary immediately reacted strongly. "Director Gui, there's no need."

Gui Ping wanted to explain, but the secretary seemed to think Gui Ping wanted to treat him to dinners and present him with gifts, so he refused, saying, "Director Gui, you don't need to bother. I know you are one of the deputy mayor's close associates, and whatever the deputy mayor asks us to do, we'll give it our best effort."

Gui Ping, testing the waters, asked, "What makes you think

得作罢。

桂平下班回家,心里仍然慌慌的,虚虚的,老婆感觉出来了,问有什么事,桂平也说不出到底是个什么事,只能长叹几声,老婆心里就起疑,正在这时候,桂平的手机响了,桂平一看,正是那同学打来的,人都被他气疯了,哪里还肯接,就任它响去,它也就不折不挠地响个不停。老婆说,怎么不接手机,是不是我在旁边不方便接?桂平没好气说,我就不接。老婆疑心大发,伸手一抓,冲着那一头怪声道,谁呀,盯这么紧干吗呀。一听是个男声,就没了兴致,把手机往桂平手里一塞,无趣地走开了。桂平捏着手机,虽然心里一千一万个不情愿,但听得手机那头喂喂喂的叫喊,也只得重重地"嗯"了一声,说,喊个魂。正想再冲他两句,那同学却抢先道,桂平啊,明天不用麻烦你了。桂平心里一惊,一喜,还没来得及说话,那同学却又说了,明天不麻烦,不等于永远不麻烦噢。就告诉桂平,刚接到文化局的通知,上级文件刚刚到达,电玩城电玩店一律暂停,市长也没权了,审批权

I'm one of the deputy mayor's close associates?"

The secretary laughed and said, "The mayor usually doesn't answer his cell phone. He gave it to me to manage. Most of the calls are screened by me before I ask the mayor for his decision. But when you called today, he answered himself. Doesn't that say it all?"

Speechless, Gui Ping could only give up.

When his work day ended and Gui Ping went home, his mind was a mess. His wife noticed and asked, "What happened?"

Gui Ping could not even say what all had happened, but could only sigh heavily several times. Just as his wife was growing suspicious, his phone rang. Gui Ping looked and saw that it was his classmate calling. He was already driven mad by this classmate, so why would he answer his call? He let the phone ring. The ringing continued insistently. His wife said, "Why don't you answer? Are you afraid to take the call with me sitting here?"

Gui Ping snapped, "I just don't want to answer."

Overwhelmed by her suspicions, his wife reached out, grabbed his phone, and yelled. "Who is that? Why are you so clingy?"

When she heard a male's voice on the other end, she lost interest. She shoved the phone into Gui Ping's hand and walked away bored. Gui Ping held the phone. Even though he was overwhelmed with reluctance, he could hear the "Hello? Hello? Hello?"on the other end of the line.

"Yeah?" he said sharply. "What are you hollering at?"

He was about to throw in a few more harsh words, but his classmate started, "Gui Ping, I don't need to bother you tomorrow after all."

被省里收去了。桂平愣了半天，竟笑了起来，说，笑话笑话，这算什么事，人家市长那边已经安排了时间，难道要我通知市长，我们不去见市长了？那同学笑道，那你另外找个事情去一下吧。桂平气道，你以后别再来找我。那同学仍然笑，说，那可不行，以后还要靠你的。桂平说，你不是说审批权被省里收去了么，我又不认得省领导。同学说，得了吧，你能认得这么多的市领导，肯定就是一个四通八达的人，省领导必定也能联系上几个的。不过现在还不到时候，情况还不明确，我马上会了解清楚的，如果省里可以松动，到时候要麻烦你帮我一起跑省厅省政府呢。桂平差点喷出一口血来，说，我要换手机了。同学笑道，你以为穿上马甲别人就认不出你了。

第二天桂平硬找了个借口去了市长办公室，见到正襟危坐的市长，心里一慌，好像那市长早已经看穿了他的五脏六腑，忽然就觉得自己找的那借口实在说不出口来，正不知怎么才能蒙混过关，市长却笑了起来，说，你是桂平吧，改革委的办公室主任，

Gui Ping felt surprised, then joy, but before he could say anything, his classmate continued, "I won't trouble you tomorrow, but it doesn't mean I won't bother you forever." Then he added, "I just got word from the Cultural Affairs Department that a file from high-level administration has arrived, saying that the planning of all video game arcades or shops has been suspended. The project is to be overseen at the provincial level now and it is no longer within the mayor's capacity."

Gui Ping hesitated for a long time, and then started laughing. "You're joking, right? What is going on? The guy at the deputy mayor's office has already made the appointment, and now you want me to inform the mayor that we don't need to see him?"

The classmate laughed, "Then you just go see him about another matter."

Gui Ping said furiously, "Don't come asking me for help again."

The classmate was still laughing. "No way," he said. "I'll still have to rely on you later."

Gui Ping said, "You just said all your approvals will come from the provincial level. I don't know anyone at the provincial level."

His classmate said, "Come on. If you know so many city leaders, your contacts must be very far-reaching. I'm sure you can get in contact with a few provincial leaders. But, it's not time yet. Things are not very clear. I'll know something soon, though, and if I need help with the provincial leaders, I'll have to get you to run to the provincial office with me when the time comes."

Gui Ping, so angry he could spit blood, said, "I'm changing my cell phone number."

桂主任，其实我根本就不认得你噢。桂平大惊失色，说，市长，那你怎么？市长说，嘿，说来话长——市长看了看表，说，反正我们被规定有半小时谈话时间，我就给你说说怎么回事吧——你们都知道的，我们的手机，一直是秘书代替用的，一直在他手里，我自己从来都看不到，听不到，什么也不知道，个个电话由他接，样样事情由他安排布置，听他摆布，我一点主动权也没有，一点自由也没有，因为机关一直就是这样的，前任是这样，前任的前任也是这样，我也不好改变。停顿一下又说，你也知道，我原来是干业务的，忽然到了这个岗位，真的不怎么适应，开始一直忍耐着，一直到昨天下午，我忽然觉得自己忍不下去了，就下了一个决心，试着收回自己用手机的权力，结果，我刚让秘书把手机交给我，第一个电话就进来了，就是你的。当时秘书正站在我面前，看着我，我就让他给安排时间，我要让他知道，没有他我也一样会布置工作，事情就是这样。桂平愣了半天，以为市长在说笑话，但看上去又不像，支吾了一会，实在不知道说什么才好，

His classmate laughed, "Do you think people won't recognize you anymore just because you put on a disguise?"

The next day, Gui Ping had to think hard to find an excuse to go to the deputy mayor's office. When he saw the stately deputy mayor, he started to panic, as if the fellow could see right through him. Suddenly he was unable to articulate the excuse he had made up for this meeting. Just as he was wondering how he could extricate himself from the mess, the deputy mayor smiled and said, "You're Gui Ping, from the Reform Commission? Actually, I don't remember meeting you before."

Gui Ping, terrified, said, "Then why did you agree to see me?"

"Ah, that's a long story," the deputy mayor said, looking at his watch. "Anyway, since we've got half an hour to talk, I'll tell you about it. I'm sure you all know that my cell phone is always managed by my secretary, so he always has my phone in hand. I never look at or listen to it. I know nothing at all about it. All the calls are answered by him, and he arranges all my appointments. I am at his mercy, and led by the nose. I have no freedom, because it's always been like that in bureaucracy. It is much the same with the former deputy mayor as with the one before him. I am in no position to change it." He paused for a moment, then went on, "And you also know, I had my own specialty before and was suddenly put in this post. I have not really adapted to it yet, and have just been bearing with it here at first. Right up until yesterday afternoon, when I finally couldn't stand it anymore, I was determined to take back my right to use my own cell phone, so I just asked my secretary to return it to me. Just as he handed me the

好在那市长并不要听他说话，只是叹息一声，朝他摆了摆手说，不说了，不说了，今后没有这样的事情了，你也打不着我的手机了——我又把手机还给秘书了，我认输了，我玩不过它，就昨天一个下午，从你的第一个电话开始，我一共接了二十三个电话，都是求市长办事的，我的妈，我认输了。停顿了一下，末了又补一句说，唉，我也才知道，当个秘书也不容易啊，更别说你办公室主任了。桂平说，是呀，是呀，烦人呢。市长又朝他看了看，说，对了，我还没问你呢，桂主任，我并不认得你，你怎么会直接打我的手机呢？桂平也便老老实实地把事情的来龙去脉说了出来，市长听了，哈哈地笑了几声，桂平也听不出市长的笑是高兴还是不高兴。

桂平经历了这次虚惊，立刻就换了手机号码，只告知了少数亲戚朋友和工作上有来往的人，其他人一概不说，结果给自己给大家都带来很多麻烦，引来了很多埋怨。但无论出现什么情况，桂平都咬牙坚持住，他要把老手机和手机带来的烦恼彻底丢开，

phone, the first call came in—it was you. My secretary was standing there watching me. I wanted him to know that I was perfectly capable of managing my work without him, so I instructed him to arrange a time for our meeting. See, that's what happened."

Gui Ping froze for quite a while, thinking the deputy mayor was joking. But then from the look on the man's face, that did not seem to be the case. He faltered, uncertain what to say. The good news was that the deputy mayor did not want to hear anyway. He sighed and waved Gui Ping off. "Never mind. From now on, this sort of thing won't happen. You won't be able to reach me on my cell phone. I returned it to my secretary. I threw in the towel, since I can't win anyway. Yesterday, I spent the whole afternoon from the time you called onward answering twenty-three phone calls. All were asking for help from the mayor. Damn, I give up." He paused, and then added one final thought, "Alas, now I know it's not easy being a secretary, let alone an office director."

Gui Ping said, "That's true. It's aggravating."

The deputy mayor looked at him, and then said, "Right. I still haven't asked, Director Gui, since I've never met you, how did you come to call my cell phone?"

Gui Ping also laid the matter out before him honestly. The deputy mayor listened, and then laughed for a moment. Gui Ping could not tell whether or not there was any amusement in the laughter.

After experiencing this false alarm, Gui Ping immediately changed his number. He only informed a handful of friends, family, and close work associates, not saying anything about it to the rest. As a result, he created for himself, and others, a lot of hassles and

他要和从前的日子彻底告别，他要活回自己，他要自己掌握自己，再不要被手机所掌控。

现在手机终于安安静静地躺在办公桌上，但桂平心里却一点也不安静，百爪挠心，浑身不自在，手机不干扰他，他却去干扰手机了，过一会儿，就拿起来看看，怕错过了什么，但是什么也没有，桂平怀疑是不是手机的铃声出了问题，就调到震动，手机又死活不震动，他拿手机拨自己办公室的座机，通的，又拿办公室的座机打手机，也通的，再等，还是没有动静，就发一条短信给老婆，说，你好吗？信正常发出去了，很快老婆回信说，什么意思？也正常收到了。老婆的信似乎有点火药味。果然，回信刚到片刻，老婆的电话就追来了，说，你干什么？桂平说，奇怪了，今天大半天，居然没有一个电话和一封短信。老婆说，你才奇怪呢，老是抱怨电话多，事情多，今天难得让你歇歇，你又火烧屁股。老婆搁了电话，桂平明明知道自己的手机没问题，仍然坐不住，给一个同事打个电话说，你今天上午打过我手机吗？同事说，

invited a lot of criticism. But no matter what happened, Gui Ping just gritted his teeth and bore with it, determined to put his old cell phone troubles behind him. He wanted to say farewell to the bygone days, to live for himself, to take himself firmly in hand and not be controlled by the phone.

But now that his phone lay quietly on his desk, Gui Ping still had no peace of mind, feeling as uncomfortable as if hundreds of tiny worries were clawing at his heart. The phone did not disturb him, but he went and disturbed the phone. After a while, he picked it up and looked at it, wondering if he had missed something. But there was nothing. Gui Ping began to suspect that the problem was with the ring tone. So he switched it to vibrate mode. The phone would not vibrate. He picked it up and dialed the office number. The call went through. Then he picked up the office phone and dialed his mobile number. It went through too. He waited, but still nothing came from the phone. He messaged his wife. "You OK?" The message went out normally, and his wife quickly replied, "What do you mean?" He received that without any problem either.

His wife's reply seemed to contain some smell of gunpowder. Sure enough, no sooner had he received her message than she called, "What are you up to?"

Gui Ping replied, "It's strange, no one has called or texted all day."

"You're the strange one. When you get lots of calls, you always complain. Today when you have a rare moment of rest, it's like you have ants in your pants."

After his wife hung up, Gui Ping was certain that there was no problem with his phone, but he still couldn't sit still. He called a

没有呀。又给另一朋友打个电话问，你今天上午发过短信给我吗？那人说，没有呀。

桂平守着这个死一般沉寂的新号码，不由得怀念起老号码来了，他用自己的新号码去拨老号码，听到"对不起，您拨打的电话已停机"，桂平心里一急，把小李喊了过来，责问说，你把我手机停机了？小李说，咦，桂主任，是你叫我帮你换号的呀。桂平说，我说要换号，也没有说那个号码就不要了呀，那个号码跟了我多少年了，都有感情了，你说扔就扔了？小李说，桂主任，你别急，没有扔，我帮你办的是停机留号，每月支付五元钱，这个号码还是你的，你随时可以恢复的。桂平愣了片刻，说，你怎么会想到帮我办停机留号？小李说，桂主任，我还是有预见的嘛，我就怕你想恢复嘛。桂平还想问，你凭什么觉得我想恢复。但话到嘴边，却没有问出来，连小李一个毛头小子，都把自己给看透了，真正气不过，发狠道，我还偏不要它了，你马上给我丢掉它！小李应声说，好好好，好好好，桂主任，我就替你省了这五块钱吧。

colleague and said, "Did you call my cell phone this morning?"

"No." the colleague replied.

He called another friend and asked, "Did you text me this morning?"

"No." his friend replied.

Gui Ping kept watch over this new number, which was as quiet as death, and he could not help missing his old number. Using his new number, he dialed the old line. He heard the message, "We're sorry, the number you are dialing has been disconnected." He started to panic.

He called Xiao Li to come in and took it out on him, "You disconnected my old line?"

Xiao Li replied, "Eh, Director Gui, didn't you ask me to change your number?"

Gui Ping said, "I told you to change my number, but I didn't say I don't want the old one anymore. I've had that number for many years. There's sentimental value. Now you've just tossed it away?"

Xiao Li said, "Director Gui, don't worry. It hasn't been tossed aside. I suspended the number, but still held it for you. It just costs five *yuan* a month, and the number is still yours. You can restore it whenever you want."

Gui Ping was distracted for a moment, and then said, "What made you decide to hold the number?"

Xiao Li said, "Director Gui, I had a sixth sense. I just thought you might want it back."

Gui Ping wanted to ask, What made you think I'd want it restored? But before the words reached his lips, he decided not to

到这天下午,情况忽然发生了很大的变化,打到他手机上的电话多起来,发来的短信也多起来,其中有许多人,桂平明明没有告诉他们换手机的事情,他们也都打来了。桂平说,咦,奇怪了,你怎么知道我的电话。对方说,哟,你以为你是谁,知道你的电话有什么了不起的。也有人说,咦,你才奇怪呢,我凭什么不能知道你的电话?也有心眼小的,生气说,唏,怎么,后悔了,不想跟我联系了?

桂平又恢复了从前的生活,手机从早到晚忙个不停,那才是桂平的正常生活,桂平早已经适应了这样的生活,他照例不停地抱怨手机烦人,但也照例人不离机,机不离人。他只是有点奇怪,这许多人是怎么会知道他的新手机号码的。

一直到许多天以后,他才知道,原来那一天小李悄悄地替他换回了老卡。

2010 年

ask. Even such a lightweight as Xiao Li could see him through and this was simply too much for him, so he hardened himself and said, "I don't want it. Go now and get rid of the number for good."

Xiao Li said, "OK. Sure. Director Gui. I'll save that five *yuan* for you."

By that afternoon though, the situation had changed dramatically. The calls coming into his phone had increased greatly, as had the incoming messages. There were many from people whom Gui Ping was sure he had not informed of his new mobile phone. Still, they kept calling. Gui Ping said, "Ah, this is strange. How did you know my number?"

The caller said, "Who do you think you are? Is it a big deal to know your number?"

There were also some who retorted, "You're the one acting strange. Why can't I know your number?"

Then there were some who were overly sensitive, "Boo! So what? Do you regret it? You don't want to be in contact with me anymore?"

And so Gui Ping resumed his old life, the cell phone busy from morning until night. This was normal life for Gui Ping. He had adapted to it early on. He resumed complaining about how irritating the cell phone was, but he also resumed being attached to it. He only found it strange how so many people came to know his new number.

It was many days later that he finally learned the reason. After his talk with Xiao Li, the latter had secretly replaced his new phone memory card with the old.

2010

梦幻快递

有一天我送快递到一个人家，收件人是个年轻的女孩，就是最热衷网购的那种，从屋里出来，接了快件就向我要笔签收，我提醒她说，先开箱看一下货吧。

这可不是因为我有责任心，这是公司的规定，公司规定一定要让收件人开箱后再签收，否则后果一律由我们送货人自负，我才不想负这么多的后果，所以我坚持要她先开箱后签收。她似乎有些不耐烦，对我送来的货物看起来也不怎么在乎，马马虎虎说，

The Hallucinated Courier

Translated by Edward Allen

One day I made a courier delivery to someone's home. The receiver was a young girl—just the type fiercely loyal about shopping online. She came out of her room, took her delivery and asked me for a pen to sign her receipt. So as to remind her, I said: "Open up first and check the goods."

This was on no account due to my own sense of responsibility. It's a company regulation. The company stipulates that we must first have the recipient open it up before signing for receipt. Otherwise, any later consequences will invariably befall us couriers. Since there was no wish on my part to put up with so many consequences, I was firm in having her open her parcel first before she signed. The young girl seemed a bit impatient, as if she didn't

哎呀，不开了吧，我忙着呢。我说不行，不开箱不能签收的，除非——她赶紧问我，除非什么？我说，除非你在单子上写明。她又问要写什么，我说，写收件人自愿不开箱验货，与递送员无关，一切后果自负等等，再签上你的名字。她又嫌烦，说，哎哟，烦死人，要写那么多字，算啦算啦，就打开来看看吧。可是箱子包裹得很严实，她又皱眉，又想马虎过去。还好，我随身带着小刀子，将包扎箱子的胶带划开来。我这小刀子是专门对付那些嫌麻烦的收件人的。他们会以没有工具打开箱包为由，就强行直接签收，马虎了事。这种做法我是不能允许的。

当然你们也都知道的，其实收件人并不都是这样的人，有些人的习惯正好相反，他们对付快递来的货物的顶真程度让你简直忍无可忍。比如一个妇女喜欢从网上购买衣服，每次拿到衣服，她都上上下下前前后后里里外外反复检查，甚至连线缝都扒开来看个仔细，我在旁边看得心里暗笑，她是不是以为这衣服是我本

really care that much for the goods I was delivering. She hummed and hawed and said—

"*Aiyo*, let's just not open it. I'm busy."

"That won't work." I said, "It can't be signed for if it's not been opened, unless..."

"Unless what?" She asked, hurriedly.

"Unless you make it clear in writing on the receipt."

She asked what she should write, and I said, "You write that the receiver of this parcel does voluntarily leave the parcel unopened and uninspected, that this has no connection whatsoever with the person making the delivery, that you are responsible for all consequences, and so on... Then you sign your name."

This got her worked up again. "Aiyo!" She said, once more: "What a bore! You want me to write that much? Oh, whatever! Whatever! I'll just open it up and have a look."

But the parcel was wrapped up very tight, and she frowned and thought once more about humming and hawing through. Fortunately, I carry around a small knife, which cuts through the cellotape gripped around the package. This knife of mine is used especially to deal with those people who take delivery of a package but who are afraid of any bother. Those people will take the lack of any tool to open their package as their excuse to forcibly sign the receipt, to hum and haw away and stumble through the matter. I will not permit such practices.

Of course, as you all know, not all recipients are like this girl. The habits of some people turn out to be the complete opposite. It puts you at your wit's end to see the levels they go to check the

人缝制出来的,就算看出线缝有问题,她拿我有什么办法呢。另有一个妇女也是经常买衣服的,有一次打开箱子验货时闻到一股橡胶味,她坚持说这是假冒伪劣产品,当场就要退货,又说穿这种衣服会得癌的,说得吓人倒怪。但无论是货真价实还是假冒伪劣,都与我无关,她这是在为难我,我耐心跟她解释了条例,验货时只有当货物损坏或原先确认过的尺寸颜色不符才能拒收,没有一条规定说,衣服有异味也能当场拒收的。最后磨了半天,她还算讲理,收下了那件可能很恐怖的衣服,决定打客服电话要求退货,后来怎么样我就不知道了,也不关我事。还有一个收件人也很奇怪,一定要问我叫什么名字,我说公司没有规定要报名字,可以不告诉她,但见她执意要问,我就告诉她了,我还心存侥幸地以为她要给我介绍对象呢。不料下次去的时候,她又问我的名字,我说上次告诉你了。她说记性不好,忘了。我又告诉一遍。

如此三番几次的,我心里有疑问,我跟她解释说,其实,送快递

authenticity of goods you hand over. There was, for example, a woman who liked to buy clothes from the internet. Every time she got her hands on the clothes, she would inspect them over and over, looking up and down, front and back, inside and out, even poking around the seams to have a good look. I watched from the side, chuckling to myself—maybe she thought that I was the one who'd sown the item together? Although, even if she found a problem with the seams, what could she have me do about it? There was another woman, who would buy clothes with some regularity. On one occasion, she got a whiff of rubber after she'd opened her package for product inspection. She insisted that this was some fake, low-grade product, and demanded on the spot that it be sent back. She then said that wearing such clothes could give you cancer. It scared the hell out of me. Still, whether goods are real and the price is right, or whether they're just shabby fakes, neither has anything to do with me. All she was doing was making my life difficult, and I patiently went through with her the regulation whereby, when goods are inspected, only damaged products or those not matching the agreed-upon size and colors can be returned, explaining that there was no rule stating that odd-smelling clothes could be rejected on-the-spot. Finally, after grinding away for what seemed like half a day, she began to talk sense. She accepted the possibly terrifying clothes, resolving though to make a call later to our customer-service line and demand the product be returned. I don't know what came of this afterwards, and, anyway, it doesn't concern me. Then there was this really odd recipient, who simply had to ask me for my name. I said that the company didn't stipulate that we give our

跟名字没有关系的。她说，怎么没有关系，我连送水工都要问他们名字的。我想她可能是防患于未然吧，生怕哪天出了事找不到人。但其实她不知道快递公司都有规定的，哪一片区域归哪一个快递员，都是清清楚楚的，她只要说出她的地址，公司就能知道是谁送的，除非那是个不规矩的公司，如果是不规矩的公司，你知道快递员的名字有人才通知，你就算知道老板的名字，也同样不能解决问题的。

真是林子大了什么鸟都有。什么鸟你都得小心应付，谁让你是快递员呢。现在快递中的差错很多，无论谁是谁非，最后鸟屎总是要拉在我们头上的，我们只能如履薄冰地保护着自己的脑袋不受鸟的欺负。

不说鸟了，还是回到眼前的这个人身上吧，她终于打开纸箱，拎出那个货物，我才没心思管她是什么货物，就算大变活人也不关我事，可是她还偏偏把那货物扬到我的眼前。喏，看见了吧。

names out and that I could just not tell her. However, when I saw that she persisted, I just told her, kidding myself that she might be thinking of hooking me up with a marriage partner. I wasn't expecting that the next time I went she would ask me for my name again:

"I told you last time." I said.

"My memory's bad," she replied, "I've forgotten."

So I told her again.

This happened over and over, each time I visited. In the end I became quite suspicious about it all. I explained to her that a courier's name was hardly that important.

"How could it not be important?" She asked, "I even ask the names of the men who carry up the water." I supposed she was defending herself against any unforeseen problems, fearing that when someday something should go wrong, she could not find the wrongdoer. In actual fact she was ignorant of a rule in all delivery companies—one courier for one district. It's all very clear, and she'd just have to state her address and the company would know who had delivered her goods. This doesn't hold for those companies that don't play by the rules—they won't notify the seller unless you know the courier's name. But in such a case, what's the difference even if you know the name of the boss—it's useless just the same.

Truly, when the forest grows large, you get all kinds of birds. You've got to be careful in your dealings with each different bird— who forced you to be a courier anyway? Mistakes are frequent in making deliveries nowadays, but no matter who's wrong or right, the bird always shits on our head. Our only choice is to act like

我貌似瞄了一眼，是一条打底裤，还洋红色呢，我心里就很瞧不起她，别以为我不知道，网购一条打底裤，贵不过几十元，最便宜的十块钱就卖了。她倒没为她的低廉的打底裤难为情，扬过打底裤后，又说，行了吧，算验过了吧，可以签收了吧。

当然可以了，我又不是有意要刁难她，只要她按规矩办就行。我请她在单子上签了名，我撕走上面一张，就可以走了，她也回屋里去了，两下刚刚转身，忽然我听到她那里发出一声尖叫，我以为又出错了，赶紧回头看，她却已经笑得直不起腰了，弓着身子在那里哎哟哟，哎哟哟。我不知道她哎哟个什么劲，既然她不是找我麻烦的，我赶紧撤。她见我要撤，才勉强直起了腰，冲我说，哎哟，我买过一条一模一样的哎，哎哟，我怎么忘得干干净净，一点也记不得了，看到它，我才想起来，前几天才买过的呀。这与我无关，我还是得撤。她又说，我不会得老年痴呆了吧，我才二十五岁呀。这仍然与我无关，我再撤。

we're treading on thin ice so as to protect our head from the bullying birds.

But no more of birds—we should return to the person before our eyes. At length, she opened her parcel and took out the goods. I was not in the mood to care that much for what she had—even a magician's Invisibility Box would have nothing to do with me, but she just *had* to take the item and dangle it in front of my face.

"Hey! You see that!?"

I made a pretense of eyeing up the goods: a pair of leggings... magenta, even. In my mind I started to hold her in very low regard: don't think that I don't know full well that those leggings go for nothing more pricey than a few dozen *yuan* online! The cheapest go for just ten! She didn't feel any embarrassment on account of these cheap and cheerful leggings: "Okay, well, I've checked, so I can sign the receipt, now?" she said, her flourishing complete.

Of course you can sign. It's not as if I'm intentionally trying to catch her out here. Everything's fine as long as she goes by the regulations, so I politely asked her to sign her name on the receipt. I tore off the top-sheet, and I was good to go. She had already returned to her room, but as I was turning away I heard her give out a piercing scream from inside. Thinking some mistake had been made, I jerked back my head and had a look in her direction, only to see her doubled up with laughter, arching her back as she howled—

"AI—YO—YO! AI—YO—YO!"

Now, I had no idea what she was 'aiyo'-ing about with such vim, but since she was not trying to make any trouble for me, I hastened my escape. Seeing me make off, she forced herself to

我这才撤走了。

我开始干这一行的时候,还有些新鲜感,但时间一长,什么感也没有了,什么都一个样,收件人呢,恐怕有七八成都是刚才那样的小八婆,手里有一点钱,钱又不多,尽在网上淘些不值钱的甚至没多大用的东西,我真是替她们想不通,她们那手,真的很痒,一天不拿鼠标点一下,又点一下,再点一下,貌似这一天的日子就不下去。当然,就是因为她们天天点一下,又点一下,再点一下,快递公司就那样如雨后春笋般地冒出来了,而且越冒越多,越冒越强,我都听说了,现在有一千多家快递公司。我同事说,一千多?谁统计的,那些连册都不注的黑公司他统计得了吗?我同事比我有想法,按照统计的数字是一千多,按照他的想法,那就不知道是多少家了,难怪竞争这么激烈。

当然,这无数无数的收件人,她们收到的东西,也不一定都是她们自己买的,也有别人赠送或代购的,比如男朋友啦,比如

straighten her back—

"AI—YO!" She blurted at me. "I've already bought a pair that's exactly the same! Ai—yo! How could I have just totally forgotten about it? I couldn't remember at all. But seeing this pair, I was reminded that I had bought one just a few days ago."

But this had nothing to do with me, so I should still run away. Off she went again:

"I can't be going gaga! I'm only twenty-five!"

Even so, this still had nothing to do with me, and I recommenced my escape.

At long last I was able to run off.

There was some novelty value when I started out in this trade, but this feeling has now all gone with the passing of time. Everything's in the same mould. It's like the recipients: I'd say seventy to eighty percent of them are just like that little bitch just now. They get some cash in their hands—not a lot, mind you—and they splurge it all online on some worthless or basically useless stuff. I really cannot make sense of these women, with their itchy hands, as if no day can pass by without placing them on a computer-mouse and clicking here, clicking there, and clicking again over there. Naturally, it's because of this daily clicking, additional clicking and further clicking that the delivery companies have sprouted like bamboo shoots after the spring rain, greater and greater in numbers and power. I've even heard that there are over a thousand delivery companies now. A colleague of mine commented—

"Over one thousand? Whose total is that? Does it cover those shady companies which can't even be found on the records?"

父母啦，比如别的什么人啦，但那个概率是很小的。

说起来，我不应该抱怨她们，更不应该瞧不起她们，有了她们，才有快递公司的生意，才有我们的饭碗。其实她们中间也有好多不错的女孩，如果她们的手不那么痒，其实真是很好的，如果我能够找其中的任何一个做老婆，也都心满意足了。

有一次我到一家送快递，那姑娘开了门，还客气地紧着请我进去，我知趣，才不会进去，但她太热情了，甚至还过来拉我，说，进来呀，进来呀，没事的。那我也只能站在她家门口，就这么一站，我顺便朝她屋里一望，我的个妈呀，堆了半屋子的快递，多半都还没有开包呢，封得死死的。我不知道这是哪家快递公司递送的，怎么能不开箱给货就给她了呢。不过这也不关我事，我只要做好我的工作就行了，还管别家快递公司干什么，各家有各家的规矩。我只是想，这样的老婆我不娶也罢，她这哪里是购物，分明是在做游戏，我一个送快递的，哪有那么多钱给她过家家啊。

This colleague has a more fertile mind than I. There are over a thousand according to the statistics, but according to his way of thinking there's no way of knowing just how many companies there are. No wonder the competition is so intense.

Naturally, again, amongst the countless recipients, it's not certain that these women receive things that they bought with their own money. There are instances of other people sending things as gifts or buying the item for them: "Oh! My boyfriend!", "Mummy and Daddy!" or my someone-else. But this is a very small percentage.

As a matter of fact, I shouldn't moan about these women, much less look down on them, since with these girls comes the business of delivery companies and our rice bowl for the day. In actual fact, there are quite a number of decent girls amongst them. They'd be pretty excellent if their hands didn't get so itchy. I'd be a happy man if I could find any one of them to be my wife.

There was one time I made a delivery to a home. The girl opened the door and, courteously, pressed me to come inside. I knew my place, so I wouldn't go in. Yet she became extremely enthusiastic, even moving over and pulling me inside:

"Come in! Come in! There's no problem!" She said.

Even so I would only stand in the entrance to her home. In this way I could take a casual glance inside. Wow! She'd piled up half her room with courier deliveries, most of them unopened, bundled up dead-tight! I couldn't tell which company had delivered these—how could they make a delivery without having the parcels opened up first? Still, that had nothing to do with me, and I'm alright as long

我这算是自卑呢，还是自卑呢？我这算是一厢情愿呢，还是一厢情愿呢？

这是关于收件人的林林总总，关于寄件人呢，我是看不见他们的，但我也知道，反正五花八门，什么样的都有，因为我看不见他们，我也懒得说。

我还是更关心一下我自己吧。有时候我到了某一个小区的时候，会有一种做梦的感觉。为什么是做梦呢，因为对这些小区太熟悉了，因为这些小区太相像了，我每天进入不同的小区，但它们好像又都是同一个小区，无法区别，不仅梦里会梦到它们，就是醒着的时候，也会把它们当成是梦境。

其实，即使你不进入这些小区，即使你闭上眼睛，想一想，难道不是这样吗，这许许多多新建起来的小区难道不是差不多的模样吗，火柴盒似的竖在那里，一幢贴一幢，只是有的贴得紧密一点，有的贴得宽松一点，这就是小区与小区之间仅有的差别了，

as I get my work done. What's the use in occupying oneself with what other delivery companies are up to? Each company has its rules and regulations... I did think, however, that it would be best not to marry this kind of woman. She was plainly making purchasing a part of her little game. How could a courier such as I have the money to play mummies and daddies with her?

Would you call this a sense of inferiority, or was it truly a sense of inferiority? Would you call this a one-sided wishful thinking, or was it truly a one-sided wishful thinking?

That is a kaleidoscopic picture of those who receive deliveries. As for the senders of these items, I don't see them, but I do know that they come in all shapes and sizes. I just can't be bothered to say more with them out of sight.

It'd be best if I take a little more concern for myself. Sometimes, arriving at a residential district, I will have the feeling that I am dreaming. Why am I dreaming? Because I am so overly familiar with these districts, and they are all so alike that although I go into different districts every day, they appear all the same and indistinguishable from each other. I not only see them in my dreams, but actually take them as a dreamland during my waking life.

In fact, you don't have to go into these districts yourself—you just close your eyes and think about it, can it be any other way? How could those numerous newly built-up districts not come in more or less the same style? Buildings standing like matchboxes in their place, one block glued to the next, with some stuck together a bit more tightly, and some with a bit more space in between—and that

前者呢，就叫个普通小区，后者则可以称作高档小区，至于那些楼的形状和颜色虽略有差异，但这不是问题的关键，只是表面现象而已。我们都是成年人，不会被表面现象蒙蔽了双眼哦。

然后你再找到某一幢，到几零几，是高层的话，就坐电梯，不是高层，就爬楼梯，然后，你敲门，或者按门铃。然后，有一个人在里边问，谁呀。你说，快递。然后，门就开了，你往里边一瞧，别说大楼和大楼相似，这屋里的装饰，也差不多少。

如果你每天都行进在这差不多的空间和时间里，你也许真的会搞不清什么时候是梦，什么时候是梦醒了。

好了好了，别做梦了，现在我已经从打底裤那儿出来，又来到另一个差不多的小区，找到一幢差不多的楼，上了几乎一模一样的楼梯，然后，按响门铃，里边问，谁呀。我答，快递。门立马就开了，都没从门镜里朝外看一看再开门，不知道是他们的警惕性太差，还是对递送来的货物太看重，太着急。

is the sole difference between one district and another. The former we call a common district, and the latter we refer to as a posh district. As for the slight discrepancies in shape and colour that exist between these buildings, this is far from being the key to the point: they are mere superficialities. We're all grown-ups, so such superficialities as these are not going to blinker us.

Then you scout out a certain building, head to a certain room, taking the elevator for the high-rises, or climbing the stairs for the lower ones. You knock on the door or ring the bell, and someone asks—

"Who is it?"

"Delivery!" You say.

Then the door opens, you take a peek inside. Never mind the similarities between one building and another; there's never much difference even in the interior decoration.

If you were to go through every single day in a space and a time much like this, perhaps you, also, would find it hard to make sense between the time when you were dreaming and the time when you were awakened from your dreams.

Alright, alright. No more of dreams. Right then I had already made my way out of the "leggings situation" and came to another, basically similar, district, where I found a basically similar building and climbed up a basically identical staircase. Then I pressed on the doorbell. Someone inside asked—

"Who is it?"

"Delivery!" I replied. The door swung open at once, without the person behind even thinking to look out through the peep-hole

前些时有个新闻说，某女独住，被快递员杀了。这个新闻出来后，我和我的同行以及我们的老板都有些沮丧，有很不好的感觉，以为快递业要下滑了，以为快递件会大大减少了，结果呢，根本就没少，还越来越多了，所以我们老板又神气起来了，到那一年的11月11日凌晨，那个电子购物，不叫购物，叫秒杀。那可是杀得个昏天黑地。

有时候我也很无聊，就幻想着哪一天能够碰到一个不太相同的收件人，但是没有，真的没有。现在站在我眼前的这个，还是那样子，她打开箱子，眼睛往下一扫，算是看过了，说了声，我晕，就签收了。我不知道她"晕"什么，反正我也没注意快递的是什么东西。关于我们递送的货物，每一联单子，无论是最后执在我手里的一联，还是贴在箱子上留给收件人的那一联，上面都有写明，但是我才没那么多时间和那么好的心情将每天要送的东西一一看过来，我只管送，不管知情，更不管收件人对于收到的

before opening up. I couldn't be sure if their sense of caution was rather poor or, on the other hand, whether they were overly anxious and laid great importance on the goods I was delivering.

Sometime recently there was a story in the news about a woman who lived by herself and was killed by a courier. When the story came out, my colleagues, boss and I fell into some despondency and felt generally uneasy. We believed that our trade would soon come off the rails, or that the number of items we deliver was sure to be cut massively. The result was that they never declined, but continued to grow and grow, so that our boss became energized once more, and the online shopping at the crack of dawn on 11th November① turned out to be a fierce battle of seckilling—the stock was literally wiped out in seconds. That was really an awesome spectacle.

Sometimes I'll be feeling really bored, and then I'll fantasize about meeting some recipient for my deliveries who's not like everybody else. But there are none. Really. None at all. This one now standing before my eyes was the same old style: opening the parcel, lowering her eyes and giving a quick scan which counted as having checked the item. She then peeped out—

"Pooh!"—and signed.

I didn't know what she meant by that "pooh", but at any rate I didn't care what it was that I was delivering. The strips from the receipt to any item that we deliver, both the strip left in my hand at

---

① In recent years, the 11th of November (11/11), China's "single's shopping day," has seen huge discounts on online shopping websites, resulting in billions of dollars of purchases.

货物的表情,所以她对于货物晕不晕,不关我事,她既然签了,我就完成任务走了,至少比前面那个不肯验收的打底裤干脆些。

没想到的是,她的这个晕,后来晕到我头上来了。那货送后的第三天,也就是中间隔了两天,我接到一个妇女的电话,问快递怎么没到?这事情不稀罕,多了去,我也不着急,先问她怎么个情况,她说我前天上午给她打过电话,说马上送到,结果等了两天也没到。

这也是个人物呀,等了两天才给我打电话,真不着急啊。我回想了想我前天的工作,没有遗漏呀,前天的任务我都完成了呀,不过我也仍然没有着急,我又问她,你前天接到的电话,确定是我打给你的吗?她说当然呀,我手机上还保留着你的电话呢,要不我怎么会打电话给你呢,幸亏我留着,否则还不知道找谁呢。

其实她的话是不对的,或者说不完全对,快递收不到,不一定全是快递员的问题,也可能是其他的某个环节出了问题。不过我也

the end and the strip stuck on the parcel to be left with the recipient, will have a description of the contents written on them. Still, I don't have the time or the desire to take a look at the things I'm passing on every day. I care only about the delivery, not the story behind it, certainly not the expression of the recipient when taking the goods. It has nothing to do with me whether this woman feels a sense of "pooh-pooh" regarding her parcel. She's signed, so my job is done, and I can go. At least you could say I make a fairer break for it than the case of the leggings in which that lady proved so unwilling to inspect.

I could not have imagined at this time that her pooh-pooh was to befall me three days after completing this delivery. I received a phone call from a lady. "How come my delivery hasn't arrived yet?" she asked. Such events were by no means rare—they came around frequently—and I didn't feel anxious myself. First I asked her what the situation was. She explained that I gave her a call on the morning two days previously, saying I'd be right over, but I had not actually come around after two days of her waiting.

Here was a character! She had waited two days before giving me a call. She was by no means in a rush. I thought back to my work two days earlier—nothing had been left out... I had completed all of my responsibilities on that day. Still I didn't yet feel anxious, so asked if she was certain it was I who had called when she picked up the phone two days ago.

"Of course," She said, "I've still got your number on my phone. If not, how could I call you? Luckily I kept it, actually. Otherwise I wouldn't know who to turn to."

还是理解她的,像她这样的妇女,又不知道快递公司是个什么样子,又看不见公司的操作程序,她不可能想象我们仓库、我们的分拣中心是个什么样子,她能看见的,就是快递员了,她不问我问谁呢,何况我的手机号码已经落在她手里了嘛。我十分耐心地再跟她确认一遍,你是说,前天我跟你联系过,说马上送快递给你?她说,是呀。我很有经验哦,又再跟她核对说,那你报一报你的地址和收件人姓名。她报来,我赶紧拿笔记下,承诺她尽快答复。这种事情,我当然得尽快,像她这样的,看起来性子不算太急,还比较好说话,有些性急的人,根本不问青红皂白,不论谁错谁对,一下子就给你捅到公司里,让你吃不了兜着走,即便是日后查清楚了到底是谁的责任,可你在老板的心目中,已经不是十全十美的了,已经是有了污点的了,亏吧。

前天的运送单早收在公司了,我赶紧挤时间回公司调前天的单子,调出单子我就仔仔细细一一检查,根本就没有疏漏呀,张

Actually the point she made here was wrong, or not one-hundred-percent correct. If you don't receive some delivery, the problem might not lie entirely with the courier: It is always possible that something has gone wrong at some other point along the chain. Still, I could well understand her, since these women don't know the structure of the delivery companies, nor could they see how our outfit is run. She couldn't imagine what our warehouse or our distribution centre is like. All she could see is the delivery guy, and if she wasn't to ask me, then who could she ask? At any rate, hadn't my phone number already fallen into her hands? With great patience, I verified the problem with her once more—

"You're saying that I contacted you the day before yesterday and said that I'd be over right away with a courier delivery?"

"Yes," She said.

I was experienced in this job, so I checked up with her a second time: "Please state your address and the full name of the person taking the delivery." As she gave her reply, I rushed to grab a pen, jotted this down, and promised the speediest of responses. In such a situation, I should naturally work with the utmost speed. People like her, with what appears to be an unhurried personality, are pretty fair to deal with; the hurried ones won't even ask about the black and white, won't discuss who's wrong and who's right before they bring the complaint to your company and drag your life into a mess. Then, even if it becomes clear on some other day just whom the responsibility lies with for this mistake, you've already lost your perfect image in the eyes of your boss. You've already got a smear on you. Not really worth it, huh?

张单子都有人签收,这说明什么呢,说明我没有出差错。我给那个妇女回了个电话,告诉她,她的那个地址,确实有快件,货物也确实已经投递了,因为有人签收了。她立即"咦"了一声,说,签收?不可能,我们家白天除了我,没别人的。我说,我这里白纸黑字,这是百无抵赖的。她又说,奇了怪,那是谁?谁签收的?我看了看那个名字,签得龙飞凤舞,我勉强看出来了,告诉她,是某某某。她愣了一会,说,某某某?某某某是谁?我说,就是你家签收的人呀。怕她不明白,我又重新说清楚一点,就是说,我把货物投递到你家,你可能不在家,但是你家有另一个人签收了。那妇女说,不对呀,我根本就不认得你说的这个某某某,她不是我们家的人,你投错了。她的口气倒是一直蛮平静蛮客气的,可客气有什么用,她再客气我也要把快件投给她呀,可是快件到哪里去了呢?我的脑袋"轰"的一下大了,我赶紧冷静下来,让脑袋缩回去,仔细想了一想可能发生的错误在哪里。既然签收的

The receipts for deliveries from two days back had long been collected at the company, and, rushing against time. It was there I returned to check up on the papers. Hunting out the receipts, I went through them one by one. Absolutely nothing was left out. Every single piece of paper had been signed by someone. This proved that I myself was not in error. I made my return call to the lady, telling her that there was indeed a delivery made to her address, and that the goods had already been delivered, since the order had been signed for. She responded with a sudden cry—

"Aha,"... Then she went on, "It's been signed for? Impossible! There's no one here during the day apart from me."

"Well," I said, "it is written in black and white, so there's no denying the delivery."

"So odd! Who was it? Who signed for it?" I took a look at the name, scribbled down like mad so that I had to strain my eyes to make it out. I told her so-and-so's name. She stalled for a moment before asking just who this so-and-so was.

"The person who signed at your home." I said. Afraid that she still couldn't understand, I clarified the situation once more—"This is to say, I delivered the goods to your home, and it's possible that you weren't in, but there was someone else who signed."

"It can't be," She said—she didn't know this so-and-so-"she's not a member of our family. You delivered to the wrong place." Her tone throughout was quite calm and polite—but what was the use of being polite? After all, no matter how polite she was, I would still have to make the delivery, but where had that parcel got to? I felt as if my head were going to explode, but I cooled myself down quickly

人名错了,首先,我当然想到了地址。我还是有些经验的,我再和那妇女核对地址,果然,地址错了一个字,洪湖花园,成了洪福花园,我经验丰富,一下就知道,这是方言口音问题,因为发音中的和 h 和 f 分不清的原因。

我的心情就更宽松了,我首先想到的是,那不是我的责任,那是寄件人的责任,怪不着我,当然,也同样不能怪收件人。我赶紧安慰她说,好了,你别着急,我知道问题在哪里了,我投到寄件人提供的错误地址上去了,这事好办,我再到那儿跑一趟,拿回来,再给你送去就是。那妇女说,也太粗心了,地址都会写错。我当然知道她说的不是我,我放心下来,赶紧着往那个错误的地址去。

这时候我仍然一点也不着急,写错地址的事情太多了,写错人名的也很多,许许多多的错误,只有你想不到的,没有他们犯不出的。有一次我打电话问收件人,你是某某街某某号某某小区

and forced the feeling to die down. Then I gave careful thought to where the possible error might lie. Considering that the wrong person signed for it, it would be obvious to check the address first. I was experienced at this after all, and yet, again, I checked the facts with the lady. That was it!—a single-character had been mistaken in the address—Honghu Gardens had become Hongfu Gardens. With my rich experience I knew straightaway that this is a problem with the local dialect—people confuse h's with f's in their pronunciation.

I was feeling far more relaxed now. Firstly, I thought, this was not my responsibility—that lay with the person who sent the parcel. The blame wouldn't be falling on me; naturally, blame in this way couldn't fall on the intended recipient, either. So I made haste to conciliate her:

"Alright! No need for you to panic. I know where the problem is. I made the delivery to a wrong address provided by the person who sent your parcel. This is easy to sort out. I'll run over there and bring it back and then send it over to you."

"How thoughtless, making a mistake when they wrote the address!" She said. Of course I knew that she was not talking about me, so I calmed myself down again and hurried over to the mistaken address.

At that moment I was still quite unhurried. It was only too common for an address to be written down wrong. Instances of wrongly spelt names also abound, and there are a great number of other errors—some you wouldn't think of, but never any they won't make. There was this one, for instance, when I made a call to a recipient, asking:

某幢楼某零某室吗？对方说是的呀，我正在家等着快递呢。我就送过去了，那个人也高兴地签收了。可是很快有人来电话讨要这个快件，我说已经准确投递了，而且签收了，但是他并没有收到，更没有签收，这真是奇了怪。这事情后来经过长时间的反复纠缠，搅得我们大家都不知所以了，最后才发现，这个快件根本就投错了一个城市，两个城市竟然有两个同名的小区，不仅小区同名，连街名和门牌号都是一样的，你以为这样的事不会发生吗，它真的会发生。

更多的是写错收件人电话的。你打到那个错误的电话上，人家好说话的，告诉你打错了；不好说话的，还"操你妈"。你能和他对"操"吗？当然不能。

总之事情就是这样的，无论是正确的寄件人和收件人还是错误的寄件人和收件人，他们都是你上帝，只不过这些看得见的上帝和那个真正的看不见的上帝才不一样呢。有一次我手机出了故障，用不起来了，我知道情况紧急，赶紧去维修，可是就那么短

"Are you apartment so-and-so, Block Y, District Z, on such-and-such a number, on such-and-such a street?"

"That's me!" came the voice from the other end. "I'm right at home waiting for your delivery." So I couriered along, and the person happily signed. Yet soon after, a call came demanding the very same goods. I said that it had already been delivered as requested and signed for, but the man hadn't received anything, far less signed anything, which truly was odd. After repeated rounds of wrangling, dragging on over a great period of time, which stirred us all up to the point of not knowing what on earth to do, we finally realized that the delivery had been made to completely the wrong city! Imagine there were two cities which somehow had districts with the same name, and not only that, within those districts were identical street names and numberings on the doors. You'd think there's no way such a thing could happen, but it really does.

More often it's a case of a phone number of the intended recipient being written down incorrectly. When you call that wrong-number, amicable folk will tell you that you have dialed the wrong number, but dislikeable folk will tell you to "go fuck yourself". Can you return the compliment and tell them to "go fuck themselves" too? Of course not.

Whatever, the general situation is like this: it doesn't matter if the sender and recipient are those actually intended or written down wrongly, they are, each and every one, your God—it's just that these visible Gods are of a different kind from the true, invisible One. Once I had a problem with my phone. It just wouldn't work. I knew the situation was urgent, so I rushed off to get it repaired.

短一个小时时间,有客户就已经投诉到公司了,说我关机,一个送快递的怎么能关机呢?强盗逻辑呀,难道送快递的就不能有一点特殊情况吗,万一我路上遭遇车祸昏死过去了呢——我呸。我还是别遭遇车祸吧。无论你遭遇什么祸,人家都是上帝,你都是上帝的仆人。

现在我到了洪福花园的那幢楼,上了那个几零几,敲门,门开了,一个陌生的妇女出现在我面前,有些茫然地看着我。尽管很可能我前天刚刚见过她,但我仍然觉得她陌生,我不可能记住每一个收件人的面孔,这很正常,我如果有那样的超常的记忆力,恐怕我也不必再风里来雨里去送快递,我干脆毛遂自荐到情报部门当间谍算了。

不过她的脸陌生不陌生倒也无所谓,我又不是来找她本人的,我是来讨回送错了的货物的。我直截了当跟她说明了情况,我一边说,她一边摇头,摇到最后,她说,你搞错了,我没有收你送来的快件。我说,我是前天来你这儿投递的,是你自己签收的。

However, in the short space of time in between, in just one hour, a client had already made a complaint to the company—my phone was off, the client said, and how could a courier have his phone off? This was "robber's logic". Could it not happen that we couriers might get involved in some unexpected situations—what if I fell victim to a car accident en route and passed out? Damn it! It'd probably be better not to get involved in car accidents. Anyway, regardless of any misfortunes you encounter, they are God, and you are God's servant.

Now I was at that block in Hongfu Gardens. I ascended to the floor, knocked on the door of the room, and it opened to reveal an unfamiliar woman, looking at me somewhat confusedly. Even if I was supposed to have seen her but two days ago, I still felt like she was a stranger now. I couldn't recall the face of everybody I made a delivery to, so this was very normal. And, anyway, if I had such an exceptional memory I probably wouldn't have to weather all this wind and rain doing such a job; I'd recommend myself as a spy to the intelligence services.

But it didn't matter whether or not this woman was a stranger to me, and I wouldn't come to ask for her in particular. I was here to ask her to return a parcel that had been delivered in error, and I made a clean breast of it with her. As I spoke, she shook her head. Having shaken her head right through to the end of my speech, she said:

"You've got it wrong. I didn't receive any parcels delivered by you."

"I came over here two days ago and handed you a delivery," I said, "and you signed it yourself." Although I suspected she was a stranger, I still had to get the upper hand over her at first; there

虽然我觉得她是个陌生人，但我一定得先强加于她，否则——没有否则，事实就应该是这样的。她疑问说，你投快件给我，我收的？你见过我吗？我怎么没有见过你？我不好说见过她，但也不敢说没见过她，我换了个思路问她，那你，平时有网购、电视购物这些吗？她说，有呀，经常有，我经常收快递，不过，不是你送来的。只要她承认收过就好，我这才拿出单子来，递给她看，我说，你看，这地址，是你的吧？她看了看地址，有些奇怪地说，咦，地址确实是我的，但是收件人不是我呀。不等我再发难，她又进一步看出了问题的实质，跟我说，不仅收件人不是我，签收的人也不是我，别说名字不是我，笔迹也不是我的呀。

我满以为这样一个小错误，只要再到错误的地址上跑一趟，负负得正，就能解决了，哪知情况复杂起来了，我的脑袋又大起来。她倒是蛮善解人意的，跟我说，是的呀，现在送快递麻烦的，很容易搞错，现在的人都是粗枝大叶的。看来她真是深知我的难处，她又主动建议说，你要是不相信，你拿纸出来，我签个名你

was no alternative. Things had to go this way.

"You made a delivery here, and I received it?" she asked, doubtfully. "Did you see me? How it comes I didn't see you?"

It wouldn't be wise to say that I had seen her, but I dare not deny either. I switched into a different way of questioning: "Well then," I asked, "do you do a lot of internet and TV shopping?"

"Yes," she said, "I receive courier deliveries often, but not from you."

Things were okay as long as she admitted that she had received the parcel, and so, at this point, I took out my receipt and handed it to her: "Take a look," I said, "isn't this your address?" She took a look, and said, in a slightly surprised tone, "*Ai*... it truly is my address. But it wasn't me who received the delivery." Without waiting for me to bring up more questions, she then took a step forward in pointing out the true crux of the problem. "Not just that I am not the one who received the delivery," she said, "I didn't sign for it either. Neither the name, nor the writing, is mine."

I was totally confident that this little mistake would be solved by rushing back to the mistaken address and putting things straight—how could I have known that the situation would grow so complicated? My head began to explode once again. Fortunately she was quite understanding.

"Yes." She said, "Nowadays it's not easy being a courier. It's very easy to make mistakes, and we've all become so careless." It appeared that she was keenly aware of the fix I was in, thus coming up with an idea. "If you don't believe me, you take out some paper and I'll sign the name for you to compare, so you can see whether or

比比看，看那单子上到底是不是我的字。我也没有其他的法子，只能这样做了，显得我很不相信人，很小鸡肚肠，但是你们不知道，干我们这行的，不得不这样，不然你稍稍马虎一点，赔得你倾家荡产。即便是货到付款的那一类，不需你赔钱，也得让你赔时赔力赔声誉，总之你得赔点什么。

她在我提供的纸上，写下了她的名字，我只瞄了一眼，心里就认了，我手里的运送单，肯定不是她签收的。她见我没说话，以为我看不出来，又认真地指点着她的笔迹跟我说，你看，这笔迹，完全不一样，再说了，我要是签了，我为什么要抵赖呢，没必要吧。虽然我一眼就看出来不是她的字，但我还是不甘心，我不能甘心，我一甘心，这事情就没有余地，没有退路了。我又换了个思路，再问她，会不会你不在家，是你家里人签的？她说，我家里人白天都不会在家的，再说了，我家里也没有人叫这个名字的呀。她看我一脸的疑惑，又说，你快递的什么东西呀，贵重物品吗？我说，好像不是贵重物品，没有保价，是某某电视购物

not the writing's mine."

Having no other means of my own, I can only go along with this, though I knew it would make me come off as a deeply suspicious and mean person. But you wouldn't know: when you do this line of work, you have no choice but to be this way. Otherwise you'll pay for a split-second of carelessness with your own bankruptcy. Even for a cash-on-delivery order, you may not lose money if it goes wrong, but it will invariably cost you something—time, efforts or your good name. At the end of the day, you have to pay in something.

She wrote her name down on the paper, and I was certain, even after a quick glance, that the courier's receipt in my hand was never signed by her. Seeing that I was not saying anything and, believing that I couldn't make the distinction, she spoke to me with her fingers pointing earnestly at her signature:

"See for yourself. This writing is totally different. And anyway, if I had signed it, why would I want to deny it? There's no point in doing that."

Although I could tell with a mere glance that the writing on my receipt was not hers, I remained unsatisfied. One cannot be so easily satisfied. As soon as you feel satisfied, then there is no room left to negotiate—there is no way out. I changed tact once more, and asked: "Could it be that you weren't at home, and this was signed by someone in your family?"

"No one from my family would be around during the day," she said, "and anyway, there's nobody with that name here." She looked at my face, now wrapped in bewilderment, and then asked,

的拖把。她说,那就更不可能有人冒领了,冒领个拖把干什么?值吗?我说,可是,可是那把拖把会到哪里去了呢?她态度一直很好,可我仍在怀疑她,她终于也有点不高兴了,开始批评我说,你自己也有问题的,单子上的收件人明明叫张三,你却让李四签收,连个"代"字也不写。我不能同意她的说法,公司规定也没有说一定要本人签收,家人是完全可以代收的,再说了,如果有人存心冒领,写个"代"字有屁用。

我就真的奇了怪。虽然说起来,送快递的奇怪事情很多的,但是因为我这个人生性谨慎,也知道保住饭碗不易,所以一般是不会出差错的。这一回问题到底出在哪里呢?我整理了一下思路,先是寄件人把小区的名字写错了,我当然是按照寄件人写的地址去投递,这第一步,我没有错;第二步,电话没有错,我也通过电话,收件人本人也接到过电话,等待我送货去的,这第二步我也没错;第三步,我到了寄件人给的错误地址那里,人家确实正在等着快递呢,就签收了,虽然不是收件人本人的名字,但反正他们是一个屋

"What was it you were delivering? Something valuable?"

"It would appear not." I said, "It was not insured—just a mop bought off the television."

"Well then," she said, "there's no way someone would have posed to get hold of that. What's the point in doing so for a mop? Is it worth it?"

"But," I said, "but, where can the mop have got to?" She had been quite nice all along. Yet I still had my doubts about her, and finally she started to show some displeasure. She took me to task: "You've got a bit of a problem yourself. The recipient on your paper is obviously Tom, and there you go giving it to Dick or Harry to sign and receive. You don't even bother to put down on the receipt that one did this in another's stead."

I couldn't agree with her argument. Our company doesn't stipulate that the delivery has to be signed by the person it is addressed to—it is perfectly suitable for family members to receive an item in his or her stead. But whatever, if someone's set his mind on posing to take a delivery, there's about as much use as a fart in demanding that to be written down.

So odd!—when you think about it. Although the courier service sees many strange things, I myself am cautious by nature, and I know that it's tough to hold on to your rice bowl, so generally, I just won't make mistakes. Where on earth could the problem lie in this instance? I took a second to organize my thoughts. First of all, the sender wrote the district name wrong. Then, naturally, I made my delivery in accordance with the given address. This was Stage One, and I had made no mistakes here. Stage Two: no mistakes

檐下的，应该不会错，这第三步，我仍然没有错。

我没有错，拖把就不会有错，但是那把正确的拖把它到底到哪里去了呢？

我再调动起以往的经验教训，仔细想了一下，是我走错了楼层吗？应该到五楼的，结果潜意识里我想偷懒，就少爬了一层，到了四楼？或者，我走错了一幢楼，把三幢看成了二幢，这也是有可能的，或者，我根本就没有来过这个小区，我到的是另一个小区？

反正你们知道的，小区和小区之间，楼和楼之间，楼层和楼层之间，真是很相像的。

这个想法一出来，立刻把我自己吓了一跳，正如我在梦里看到的，一幢一幢的楼，一个一个的小区，都是一样的，但是我是按图索骥的，难道我手里拿着一个地址，会走到另一个地址去吗？我如果没有去过那个小区，我怎么会记得那个小区呢，难道是在梦里去的？

with the phone-number, I got the connection and the recipient picked up the phone, waiting for me to come with my delivery. So, no mistakes with Stage Two. Stage Three: I headed off to the wrong address as provided by our sender, where there was, in fact, somebody waiting for a courier. And so this guy signed. Although the name he gave was not that of the actual recipient, they still lived under the same roof, so there couldn't be any mistakes here. This was Stage Three, and I was still blameless.

If I had made no mistakes, then there would be no error in delivery. So where could the mop actually have got to?

Again I tried to stir up some previous experience or training, and I had another hard think. Perhaps I had gone to the wrong floor? Maybe I had meant to go to the fifth, but with an unconscious slipping into laziness, had left out a floor and ended up on the fourth? Otherwise, I could have gone into the wrong building, taken block-number-three for block-number-two—that was possible, as well. Or perhaps I had not actually come to the right district, but some other one?

As you, after all, are well aware by now-everything is very similar from district-to-district, from block-to-block and from floor-to-floor.

Now, when this thought came to me, all of a sudden I was scared out of my wits. It was just like what I had been seeing in my dreams, one district after another, all the same. But I followed the instructions to the letter, so could it really happen that I had taken one address and wandered over to another one? And if I had never been to that district, how could it be that I had this memory of it?

难道梦里的事情比现实更清楚?

我不敢说"不可能"。

什么都是有可能的。

只是现在没有任何证明来证明我到底是犯了哪一项错误。

我回忆起前天送快件的情形,忽然灵光闪现,我想起来了,我在那个小区,曾经遇到了一个熟人,我们还站在小区的路上说了一会儿话。

我只要找到这个人,事情就迎刃而解了。

可事实上,我离迎刃而解还差得远呢。

我本来是个不着急的人,所以我难得犯错,一个难得犯错的人,一旦犯了错,肯定比经常犯错的人要着急,我就是这样。

我现在有点着急了,倒不是因为丢了一个拖把,而是因为我的工作责任心和我的记性,这两者比起来,后者更重要,如果连两三天前发生的事情都不能记起来,岂不要让我吓出一身冷汗来。

我着急呀,一着急,就把我在小区里碰见的那个熟人的名字

Could it be that I'd gone there in my dream?

Could it be that those events in my dream are truer than what have gone on in reality?

I wouldn't dare to say that it was impossible.

Anything is possible.

It was just that, as things stood now, there was not a single piece of evidence to prove which mistake I had made...

I thought back to the scene, two days back, when I made the delivery, and it occurred to me in a flash. I had an encounter with a familiar face in that district, and we even had a conversation on the road...

All I've got to do is to find that person and the pieces will fall into place.

Though, in reality, we're a long way from any of the pieces slotting in.

I've always been a patient person, so it's rare for me to make mistakes. But anybody who makes mistakes rarely will act more impatiently than one frequently in error when he does make a mess of things. And I am of this type.

I was slightly impatient now, not because of some lost mop, but rather on account of my sense of responsibility for the job, and my memory. Between the two, the latter is more important—if I cannot remember some event of two or three days back, how can I help but my whole body breaks out in a cold sweat?

I was impatient! Once I got impatient, the name behind that familiar face I encountered got forgotten. I made a great effort to recall the name, striving to fish out the concrete identity of this man

给忘记了。我努力地回想，努力地在自己的混乱的脑海里捞出他的确定的身份来。

他到底是谁？

家人？同学？朋友？同事？亲戚？邻居？

还好，像我这样的屌丝男，关系密切的人也不算多。我先在手机通讯录里找了一下，用他们的名字对照我记忆中那个人的长相，想启发一下自己。开始的时候，我看着每一个名字，都觉得像，但再看看，又觉得每一个都不是。

然后我又不惧麻烦地一一地把有可能的人都问了一遍，有人听不懂，不理我，凡听懂了的，都特奇怪，说，什么小区？听都没听说过。我到那里干什么？你怀疑我包二奶吗？也有的说，你什么意思，今天又不是愚人节，就算今天是愚人节，你的把戏一点也不好玩。还有一个更甚，说，你在跟踪我？谁让你干的？你不说我也知道，是谁谁谁让你干的。我一听，这不快要出人命了吗，赶紧打住吧。

from my jumbled brains.

Who the hell was he?

A family member? A classmate? A friend? A colleague? A relative? A neighbour?

I suppose it's alright, since a loser like me won't have too many people that he's close to. First of all, I searched through the directory on my phone, matching their names with the appearance of that person in my memory, hoping that this would enlighten me. At first every name that passed my eyes seemed to resemble that person, but, looking again, I thought that none of them really fitted at all.

With no fear for the trouble it would bring, I then asked around—inquiring of everyone, one after another, who might turn out to be that person. Some just couldn't understand and ignored me, and some who seemed to understand thought it was all quite odd:

"What district? Never heard of it."

"What would I be doing going there? Do you think I'm having some bit on the side?"

"What are you driving at?" some others would ask, "It's not April Fool's. And even if it were, couldn't you make the joke a little funnier?"

One went even further: "Are you stalking me? Who put you up to this? I know who has made you do this even if you don't tell me. It must so-and-so." Hearing this, I was afraid that these efforts might end up with someone getting killed—best put a stop to it!

As things developed in this vein, I became even more

如此这般，我心里就更着急了，再一着急，不好了，连那个和我在小区里说话的人长什么样子我都忘记了，我们在哪里说了什么，更是一点印象也没有了。我急呀，我怕这个明明出现过的人一下子又无影无踪了，就像从来没有一样。

见我抓狂了，我一同事提醒我说，你去看看小区的摄像吧，只要你们站的位置合适，也许会把你和那个人录下来的。我大喜过望，赶紧跑到小区，可是那物业上说，这个不能随便给人看的，要有警察来，或者至少要有警方出具的证明。这也难不倒我，我再找人吧。联系上警方，警方问我，什么事要看录像？我说，我送快递的，丢了一把拖把。警方以为我跟他们开玩笑，把我训了一顿。我不怕他们训我，打我也不要紧，我再央求他们，又把事情细细地说了，拖把虽然事小，但是丢饭碗的大事。结果果然博得了他们的同情。其中更有一个警察，特别理解我，说，你们也挺不容易的，现在要快递的太多了，我老婆就上了瘾，天天买，甚至都不开包，或者一开包就丢开了，又去买，害人哪。

impatient. Any further, and it would go pretty pear-shaped. By now I had even forgotten the appearance of the person who had talked to me in the district. And I was even more at a loose-end as to what we had actually talked about. I was burning with impatience—I was afraid that this person, undoubtedly not a ghost, would disappear into thin air, as if he had never existed.

Seeing that I was clutching at straws, a colleague gave a timely reminder: "Go and have a look at the district's security video. As long as you were standing in the right place, they might have recorded you and that person." This advice made me happier than any I could have hoped for, and I scampered off to the district. But the management said the security video recording was not just for anyone to watch. You had to have the police come, or at the very least you had to have some documentation provided by the police.

But setbacks would not get the better of me at this stage. May as well go and find someone to help! I contacted the police, who asked me what business I did that I had to look at the recording.

"Well," I said, "I'm a courier and I lost my mop."

The police thought I was joking with them, and I got a real scolding. I was not afraid of getting an earful, not even a few swings. So I pled with them once more, and explained what had happened in precise detail. Losing a mop might be a small matter, but losing your rice bowl, that was a big problem. And finally, I won the expected sympathy.

"You couriers haven't got it easy by any means," said one of the police-officers who seemed to particularly understand me. "Nowadays there really are too many deliveries made. My wife's

我靠着警方的这点同情心，终于可以看小区的录像了。小区物业也挺热心的，帮着我一会儿快进，一会儿快退，找到我所说的那个时间段，再慢慢看。我的个天，果然有我，我还真的是进了这个小区的。我看到我电瓶车上绑了如此之多的快件箱子，自己都把自己吓一跳，要是看到的是别人，我一定会替他担心的，这轻轻飘飘的车子，能载这么多的货物吗？

但那确实就是我干的事情。只是平时我骑着车子在前面走，那许许多多的货物堆在我身后，我看不见它们。

跟着我的身影再往下看，我的个老天，我真的看到我在小区碰到的那个人了。

那个人是我爷爷。

你们别害怕，我爷爷死了三年了，我遇见的是三年前去世的爷爷，我都没害怕，你们更不用怕。

大家都说，在现在的这个世界上，什么都可能发生的，难保死而复生的事情就不会发生哦。

become addicted to it. She buys things every day. Sometimes she won't even open the parcel, or she'll open one and then throw it away and go and buy it again. It kills me!"

Boosted by this piece of sympathy from the police, I could now, finally, take a look at the district's video recording. Management, too, had become awfully friendly, helping me fast-forward here, rewind there, tracking down the moment of my arrival as I dictated it to them, then looking through once more, slowly... my God! There I was! So I really did come to this district. I was alarmed by myself, noticing the great number of parcels strapped around my electric moped. If it were not me, but someone else, in that video— I would be sure to feel worried for him. How could such a feather-light vehicle carry so much cargo?

But that's exactly what I have been doing, only that I cannot see what is piled up right there behind me when I'm cycling along on my electric moped.

I kept watching. Onwards I followed my movements... Lord Almighty! I was actually looking at the person I met here...

... And it was my grandfather.

You are not supposed to be afraid. My grandfather's been dead for three years—I bumped into my grandfather who departed from this world all that time ago. But if I am not afraid, there's even less reason for you to be.

Everyone says that anything can happen in today's world, so what's there to say that there won't be instances of resurrection?

My grandfather was wearing his green postman's uniform, pushing along his bicycle, on top which were strapped paper-

爷爷穿着绿色的邮递员的制服，推一辆自行车，车上也绑着大大小小的纸箱子。不过这并不奇怪，因为爷爷年轻时是邮递员，我干上快递的时候，我妈曾经骂过我，说，龙生龙，凤生凤，老鼠生子打壁洞。我干脆一不做二不休，跟我妈开了个恶心的玩笑，我说，我是爷爷生的吗？把我妈气得笑了起来。

虽然爷爷的出现没有让我觉得奇怪，但我多少还是有些不解，在小区的摄像头下面，我问爷爷，你这么老了，怎么还没退休？爷爷说，我本来是休息了，可是他们说人手不够，请我们这些早就休息了的都出来帮帮忙。我想了想，觉得这也无可厚非。所以你们别以为你们平时能够看到大街小巷的驮着快件的快递员穿来穿去，其实还有一部分你们并没有看见哦。我正这么想着，爷爷又跟我说，现在这日子真的方便，就算你从美国买个东西，几天就收到了，不像过去，等一封平信都要等上十天半月的。我说，那是，现在这速度，简直就不能叫速度了。爷爷说，那叫穿越。

parcels, big and small. However, there's nothing strange about all this—my grandfather was a postman in his younger days. In fact, when I'd started off as a courier, my mother cursed me:

"A dragon's child is a dragon, a phoenix's child is a phoenix, and the sons of mice nibble holes in walls."

I decided to hit a cruel nail on the head and so I returned the abuse with a wry joke: "So I am grandpa's boy then?" This made my mother chuckle despite her anger.

Now, although my grandfather's appearance at this point hadn't struck me as odd, there were still a few questions that I couldn't answer. Under the security camera, I spoke to my grandfather:

"You're so old. Why haven't you retired?" I asked.

"I had retired," he said, "But then they said that there weren't enough hands on deck, so those of us who'd since been allowed to take a break all came out to lend a hand."

I thought about this, and it seemed perfectly reasonable. So you really shouldn't think that those couriers you are able to see bustling around the streets and byways, laden with parcels for delivery, are the whole story—there's a portion that you yourself have not seen. This was what I was thinking, when my grandfather started to speak to me again:

"Life in these modern days is really convenient. Even if you buy something from America, you'll receive it within a few days. It's nothing like the past, when you had to wait over ten days, perhaps even half a month, just for an ordinary surface mail!"

"That's right," I said, "even the word 'speed' nowadays doesn't do it justice."

我正想夸爷爷时尚,爷爷又说了,快过年了,我想给你奶奶买个新年礼物快递过去。我吃了一惊,说,我奶奶?她不是死了二十多年了吗,她能收到吗?爷爷说,孙子哎,咱们这是赶上好日子啦,你说现在这日子,有什么事是办不成的?

说了几句,爷爷就推着自行车送快递去了。我也想得通,他年纪大了,车上装了那么多货物,他骑不起来了,只能推着走。

我回家告诉我妈,说我三天前在某某小区遇见了爷爷,我妈"呸"了我一声,骂道:"做你的大头梦吧。"

我妈这一呸,让我迷惑起来,或者说,让我惊醒过来,难道小区里发生的一切,真是我做的一个梦吗?

一直到我的手机响起来,我才确认,这会儿我醒着呢。但是我又想,真的就能够确认吗,人在梦里也会接打电话的呀,我自己就经常做打电话的梦,那真是活灵活现,按键,接听,说话,

"It's called 'shuttling through time'," said grandfather.

I was just thinking that I should congratulate him on this fashionable expression, when he started talking again, "It's almost the lunar New Year. I want to buy a present and have it delivered to your grandmother."

This really stunned me: "My grandmother?" I asked, "But hasn't she been gone for over twenty years? Could she receive your gift?"

"My grandson, nowadays all of us are leading a good life! Tell me, in these days, is there anything that we can't do?"

Having uttered these few words, grandfather started to push along his bike and make his deliveries. I could see why he did this— being advanced in years, he could not ride his bike when it was stacked with so many goods. He could only push it along as he went.

I went home and told my mother, saying how I saw grandfather three days ago in so-and-so district. She threw a "Bah!" in my direction before deriding me: "What the hell are you dreaming about?"

It was this "Bah!" that threw me into a state of confusion... or perhaps should I say that it brought me, with a start, back to consciousness? Perhaps everything that happened in that district was a dream of my creation?

I am not sure whether I am awake until my phone starts to ring. Yet, I still remain somewhat doubtful about it—people can make and receive phone calls in their dreams, and I happen to have

无一不和醒着的时候一模一样。

电话是应收拖把的那个妇女打来的,她说拖把收到了,还谢了谢我。我很惊奇,我还没找到拖把呢,她倒已经收到了,真叫人费解,这把拖把到底是哪一把拖把?是哪个好心人知道我纠结,替我把拖把补上了;或者,是另一个粗心大意的寄件人,也写错了地址,恰好错到她的地址上去了,于是别人的拖把就错递到她家去了;或者,是我爷爷心疼我,躲在哪里做了个法。

谁知道是怎么回事呢,反正拖把到了,不再有我什么事,我很快就把拖把抛到脑后了,只要不再追究我的责任,一切OK。

我回到公司,又接了一叠任务,低头一看,单子上头一个投送地址是:梦幻花园。

我就出发往梦幻花园去了。

2013 年

frequent dreams in which I'm calling someone. These are as vivid as anything in real life—pressing buttons on the keypad, picking up and listening to the other end and your own speaking—all indistinguishable from what you would do in your conscious state.

 This call is from the lady who should have received her mop. She has received it, she says, but still wishes to thank me. I am astonished. It taxes the brain to think that she has already taken delivery of it when I haven't even gone looking for the mop, and what mop of all mops is this mop anyway? Was it that some goodhearted soul sensed the mess I was in and so offered a new one, or was it that some other careless sender who had written his address down wrong, an error which happened to bring it to the lady's address, with the result that someone else's mop had been sent to her home, or was it that my grandfather who, hating to see all this trouble I'd been going through, had concealed himself somewhere and played a magician's trick?

 Who knows what it was all about? At the end of the day, the mop has arrived, and it's nothing to do with me anymore. Quickly, I push the mop to the back of my mind. As long as there is no more chasing me down as if it is my responsibility, then everything is okay.

 I return to the company, and take on another pile of consignments. Lowering my head to take a look at the strips of paper, I see one address for delivery written on the first receipt: Reverie Gardens.

 So I set out. Off towards Reverie Gardens.

2013

附录 | Appendices

评论

转型前后
——阅读范小青

王 尧

如果从一九八二年六月第一次读到《飞扬的尘土》算起,我阅读范小青小说的历史已近二十五年。在这一"时间简史"之中,范小青的小说地图不断扩大版面,而作为阅读者,我们也随之调整自己的视线。我想以这篇短文,质朴地表达我的阅读感受。

20世纪90年代中期,我曾经应约为一份报纸写过一篇关于范小青的短文。见报后我发现原稿中的一句话被编辑朋友删除了,我记得这句话的意思是:我们一方面认为范小青是著名作家,但另外一方面又很少确认她的代表作是什么?编辑删除这句话的动

Critique

Before and after Transition: Reading Fan Xiaoqing

By Wang Yao
Translated by Jesse Field

Starting from my first encounter with "Flying Dust" in June 1982, I estimate that I have close to twenty five years of history reading the fiction of Fan Xiaoqing. Throughout this "brief" history, the map of Fan Xiaoqing's fiction has kept expanding; as readers, we adjust our own perspectives in response. In this short essay, I would like to state plainly what I have learned from this reading.

Back in the mid-1990s, I once wrote a short piece on Fan Xiaoqing at the request of a newspaper. When I saw the published article, I discovered that one sentence had been deleted by the editor. I remember that the import of the sentence was to ask: we all think of Fan Xiaoqing as a famous writer, but which of her works

机非常善良，他显然是认为我这句话可能会误解成：既然不能确认范小青的代表作，那么所谓"著名作家"也就是"空头"的了。这样的删除确实是对我原文意思的误读。其实我在肯定范小青创作的那篇文章中提出此问题，一是质疑评论范小青的方式，二是说出自己阅读范小青的困惑。这一质疑和困惑在我后来的阅读中，也持续过相当长的时间。

在范小青的短篇小说《城乡简史》获得"鲁迅文学奖"后，我们开始重新追溯她的写作历史，也重新搜寻我们的阅读记忆。一个比较普遍的印象是，这几年范小青的长篇小说和短篇小说愈写愈好，出现了新的变化，特别是她的短篇小说提供了新的艺术可能性；这些看法我是非常赞成的。但同时我觉得以"断裂"的而不是"联系"的方式阅读和评价范小青有失偏颇。通俗地说，小说家的范小青并不是在这几年才长大的。在范小青的小说写作简史中，她曾经达到过怎样的高度？有没有提供过新的可能性？如果不能够思考和回答这样的问题，我们能够清晰地确定范小青小说写作转型的"起点"和"转折点"吗？

《像鸟一样飞来飞去》是范小青短篇小说的结集。这本集子与其说大致反映了范小青短篇小说写作的轨迹，毋宁说更多地呈现

stand out as most representative? The editor meant well in deleting this sentence, for he clearly felt that it could be misconstrued as lacking some widely-acclaimed representative work, there was perhaps no excuse for her fame. This is certainly a misunderstanding of what I meant. In fact, I was affirming Fan's work and also raising issues: first, my skepticism as to how we currently evaluate Fan Xiaoqing, and second, my own confusion in reading Fan's work. This skepticism and confusion were both to continue for a long time.

After Fan's short story "City Living, Country Living" won the Lu Xun Literary Prize, we started retracing the history of her writing and rummaging in our memory the experiences reading her work. One of the more common impressions was that in recent years, Fan's novels and short stories had both improved with her increased experience. Both had changed, and her short stories especially supplied new artistic potential. I couldn't approve more of such opinions. But I think it's inappropriate to read and evaluate Fan in terms of breaks instead of continuities. In plain terms, Fan the fictionist did not suddenly mature in just the last few years. Over the course of her writing history, what are the high points she has achieved? Has she ever shown new potential? If we cannot consider and answer these questions, how can we tell for sure the "starting point" and "turning point" of the transitions in Fan's fiction?

Flying In and Out, like a Bird is Fan's definitive short story collection. The book reflects to a large degree the general direction of her short stories, and we might as well argue that all of the basics of her fictional art are exhibited here as well, since traits from her short stories are closely related to those in her longer works. If we

了范小青小说艺术的基本面貌,因为这些短篇和她的长篇中的基本特征是相互关联的。当我们"飞来"读范小青晚近的作品时,还需要"飞去"读她过往的小说,所以我以为读《像鸟一样飞来飞去》这本集子,应当由后往前读,再由前往后读。如果这样巡回,我们无疑在晚近的作品中会选出《这鸟,像人一样说话》《城乡简史》《像鸟一样飞来飞去》以及《我们的战斗生活像诗篇》这些短篇;在过往的作品中选出《真娘亭》《瑞云》等作品,而介入这两者之间的是《错误路线》和《鹰扬巷》。当我们今天比较一致地确认了《城乡简史》《我们的战斗生活像诗篇》这些小说的成就时,实际上我们形成了一个评论范小青的平台,在同一个平台上,《真娘亭》《瑞云》等短篇小说以及《光圈》《顾氏传人》等中篇小说的意义也就无法遮蔽了。从小说的艺术与写作的可能性讲,《瑞云》《顾氏传人》与《城乡简史》《我们的战斗生活像诗篇》等可"等量齐观"。换言之,范小青曾经有过的高度和成就其实在一段时间里是被忽视的,或者没有得到应有的重视。这样的"追认",在我看来是必要的。

从评论界接受范小青的热情与认可程度来说,第一个高峰期

"fly in" to read her more recent works, we must also "fly out" to read her past stories. Thus I would argue that *Flying In and Out, like a Bird* is best read from back to front, and then again, from front to back. If we were to circle back in this way, we would doubtless select, from the later and recent works, "This Bird Talks like a Person", "City Living, Country Living", "Flying In and Out, like a Bird" and "Our Fighting Life Is like Poetry"; from her past works, "Zhenniang Pavilion", "Rui Yun"; and in between these two, "Wrong Road" and "Ying Yang Alley". The stories most highly rated today, "City Living, Country Living" and "Our Fighting Life Is like Poetry", have actually become a basis for evaluating Fan Xiaoqing. On this same basis, the significance of "Zhenniang Pavilion", "Rui Yun" and the novellas *Circle of Light* and *Mister Gu's Descendants* cannot be obscured. In terms of the art of fiction and the potential of writing, "Rui Yun" and *Mister Gu's Descendants* can really parallel "City Living, Country Living" and "Our Fighting Life Is like Poetry". In other words, the heights of Fan's achievement have been overlooked for a time, or have not been emphasized enough. This understanding in hindsight is necessary, in my view.

In light of the enthusiasm and approval of the critical world for Fan Xiaoqing, her first peak period must have been the later 1980s. By then, Fan had written "Rui Yun", *Circle of Light* and *Mister Gu's Descendants*, and the critics had just come up with what would be the last collective name for literature of the 1980s: "the New Realism." These critics included Fan's work within the currents of

应当是八十年代中后期。这个时间，范小青已经写出了《瑞云》《光圈》《顾氏传人》等中短篇小说，而此时，正是批评界对20世纪80年代文学进行最后一次集体命名："新写实小说"。批评界在"新写实小说"思潮中接纳并且比较高地评价了范小青当时的小说创作。这是范小青和八十年代以来的文学思潮最贴近的一次，不久以后，整个文学界似乎兵荒马乱。随着"新写实小说"的式微，在作家与思潮的关系中阐释作品价值的批评模式和文学史叙述方式遭遇到挑战。现在回头来看，如果我们只是在范小青小说中找到了"新写实小说"的特征，还是没有能够把握住范小青小说。所以，批评最初的危机和危害应当是不能贴着作家的小说说话。

而另外一个影响我们阅读和评价范小青的参照系是"吴文化"和"小巷文学"。因为陆文夫先生的巨大成就，苏州的作家几乎常常被"小巷文学"一网打尽。苏州作家写苏州自有许多相同之处，但差异其实是主要的。如果从文化身份来讲，陆文夫的主体是"文人"，而范小青则是"知青"。所以，以阅读陆文夫的方式阅读范小青同样错位。

new realism and held it in high esteem. This was the last time Fan was so closely aligned with a certain literary current since the 1980s, for not long after, the entire literary world seemed to enter a chaotic age. The decline of the new realism brought major challenges to the critical methods and historical narratives to be used to interpret the value of works and the relation between the author and intellectual currents. Looking back, if all we find in Fan's work are the traits of "new realism," we fail to grasp her work. Thus, the initial crisis and danger for criticism is probably not sticking close enough to what the author's story actually says.

Two other reference points also influence our interpretation and evaluation of Fan Xiaoqing: "Wu culture"[①] and "Alleyway Literature". Because of the enormous achievements of Mister Lu Wenfu, nearly every Suzhou writer has been tossed into the category of "Alleyway Literature". Suzhou writers writing Suzhou have much in common, but their differences are more distinct. In terms of cultural identity, Lu Wenfu is every bit the "traditional Chinese man of culture" (*wen ren*), while Fan Xiaoqing is an "educated sent-down youth" (*zhi qing*). Thus, it is similarly a mistake to read Fan Xiaoqing the way we read Lu Wenfu.

---

① Editor's note: Wu (吴) refers to a region around the Tai Lake that covers part of today's Jiangsu and Zhejiang Provinces in eastern China. And Suzhou, once the capital of Wu State—one of the most powerful kingdoms in its prime—during the Spring and Autumn Period (771-476 BC) is generally regarded as the cradle of Wu Culture, whose history can actually be traced back to the Shang Dynasty about 3,000 years ago. Wu Culture thus is acclaimed as one of China's most time-honored and distinctive regional cultures.

如果剪去其他枝蔓,范小青的小说创作有一条路径大致是稳定的。

范小青的小说始终有一种气息,这种气息来自于这个城市的根本。这个城市散发着种种旧式的气息,因而让人觉得苏州人的生活似乎总是传统的、旧式的,因为这个城市把新的东西也会做旧,把新的东西包装成传统。这种传统和旧式会在小说里演化为一种氛围、色调、情怀,苏州的小说家、诗人、散文家、画家等都带有这样的特点,因此读者会把这些文学艺术作品看成是"怀旧"之作。

应当说,长期以来范小青的小说也散发着与这座城市一致的呼吸。但如果细究起来,范小青的小说重心并不在此。如果从内容上看,范小青写的也是"新苏州",但这个"新"是以"旧"做底子的。那么在新旧之间,范小青小说中的"艺术"与"人生"在哪儿呢?

此阶段范小青的叙述仍然像一个苏州姑娘那样讲话,絮语,细腻,温情。这些构成了范小青小说的美学,这个美学是与吴文化的温文尔雅一致的。所以写的是"新苏州",但给人的感觉是"旧文化"的气息。纯净与中和之美,这样的品格与迅速到来的文

Once all the weeds are pulled out, Fan Xiaoqing's work does exhibit a path that is for the most part stable.

There has always been a certain atmosphere in Fan Xiaoqing's fiction, an atmosphere whose roots are in the city—Suzhou—itself. The atmosphere of this city remains in many ways old-fashioned, which makes people feel that the lives of Suzhou's citizens seem always to be traditional and old-fashioned, because this city makes new things old, repackages new things as traditional things. The traditional and the old-fashioned in a story evolve into a certain atmosphere, tone, feeling. Suzhou's fiction writers, poets, essayists, and painters all have this trait, for which reason readers will see such works of art and literature as "nostalgic" (*huai jiu*).

We should say that for a long time now, Fan Xiaoqing's fiction has seemed to breathe in tandem with this city. But upon closer examination, the heart of Fan's fiction lies not in this. In terms of content, Fan writes of the "new Suzhou," but this "new" is built on a foundation of the "old." Between the new and the old, then, what exactly is the "art" and "life" in Fan's fiction?

Fan Xiaoqing's storytelling in this period is like the speech of young women from Suzhou, whispering, garrulous, and warm. These form the aesthetics of her fiction, an aesthetic that is consistent with the refinement of Wu culture. Thus she may write the "new Suzhou," but the feeling it leaves on the reader is the air of "old culture." A clean, moderate beauty, but such character feels at odds with the cultural transformation that is soon to come. This is the cultural quietude of the brief period before the great transformation of old Suzhou.

化转型颇有不协调的感觉。这是旧苏州大变动之前短暂的文化上的宁静。

范小青试图挽留的是在现实生活中逐渐流失的人性，逐渐消失的人性之美，而在这种挽留之中，我们看见了历史在现实中的背影，感受了文化在生存中的辉映。也正是在这个意义上范小青的小说让人读到了一些"怀旧"的味道，这样的感觉肯定让读者疏忽了范小青的"挽留"其实是由现实而来的。这样一种写作的方式，借用范小青一篇小说的题目来说，是"文火煨肥羊"，此种境界让我想到了汪曾祺老先生。相对于 20 世纪 90 年代以后文学语境的大众化、小说的粗鄙化，范小青这类不张扬的小说也就产生不了我们平常所说的"冲击力"。人性其实迁流曼延，但不易被人察觉；艺术的意义其实不必总是变革，沉潜、冲淡、温和无论是作为一种写作态度，还是作为一种美学趣味从来都没有失去价值。我试图在这样的层面上估价范小青的《光圈》《瑞云》《顾氏传人》等作品的意义。

但是，"挽留"的方式并不是范小青的全部。她从一开始创作就表现出对现实生活的热情。范小青为数不少的长篇小说写作构

Fan Xiaoqing tries to redeem the kind of person and the beauty of human nature gradually disappearing in this modern world. In the course of that redemption, we see the parting image of history in modern reality, and feel the glints and flashes of culture in life. And just as Fan's fiction imparts the reader with the flavors of nostalgia, these feelings certainly cause the reader to overlook that Fan Xiaoqing's redemption is in fact the product of modern reality. Such a writing style is like "Stew Fat Sheep over a Slow Fire," to borrow the title of one of Fan's short stories, and yields a world that reminds me of reverend Mister Wang Zengqi. Compared with the post-1990s popularization of literary discourse and the vulgarization of fiction, the more reserved and low-profile of Fan's style cannot produce as much of the "impact" we so often talk about. Human nature is actually volatile and profuse, which is almost often imperceptible to the human eye. And artistic significance is not, in fact, invariably about flux and change-concealment, plainness, and moderation never lose their value whether we consider them an attitude of writing or a form of aesthetic interest. My evaluation of *Circle of Light*, "Rui Yun," and *Mister Gu's Descendants* is just in this light.

However, "redemption" isn't all there is to Fan Xiaoqing. Since the beginning of her career, she has shown enthusiasm for life in reality. Her many novels have formed another path for her. By the time we come to *One Hundred Days of Sunshine* and *Urban Expressions*, we can see Fan Xiaoqing has begun to "stir" within modern reality. She turns directly to reality, writing of small town

成了她的另外一条路径。到了《百日阳光》《城市表情》等，我们可以看到范小青在现实之中也躁动起来。范小青直接转入了现实，写乡镇企业写城市改造抑或其他变革，她自己也因此从小巷走到了现代大道，她的热情与努力也获得了评论界的赞许。我想，范小青从中或许会获得一定的自信。

我从来不否认范小青这类小说创作的意义与价值，但在我看来，《百日阳光》《城市表情》等长篇小说其实只是范小青的过渡之作。我们需要关注的问题不应当是范小青写了现实没有，而应当是她处理小说与现实的方式是什么？在这样的追问中，我们才能发现范小青小说艺术到了这个时候究竟有没有出现新的可能性。

她开始更多地把自己的写作和现实对接，现实中的矛盾冲突也在小说中展开。矛盾在于，范小青的长篇小说显然不是我们所看到的那些主旋律式的小说，特别是主旋律式的长篇小说。而另外一面，在《百日阳光》《城市表情》这些长篇小说中，范小青个人的特征与素质并没有充分地发挥出来，至少在我的阅读中我感觉到写这一类长篇小说其实不是范小青的长处。她也可以在这条路上走得很远，取得瞩目的成就，但是，长篇小说里那些感动我们的东西冲击我们的东西，更多的来自于现实生活本身，而范小

businesses, writing of urban renovation and other changes. She herself has gone from the small lanes to modern boulevards, and her enthusiasm and hard work have won her the praise of critics. I think she must have earned certain self-confidence from this.

I have never denied the significance and value of this category of Fan's fiction, but in my view, *One Hundred Days of Sunshine* and *Urban Expressions* both represent only a transitional stage for Fan Xiaoqing. The question we should attend to is not whether Fan is a realistic writer, but what are her methods for dealing with fiction and reality. Only by pursuing this question can we discover whether Fan's work to date has in fact yielded new potential.

She has begun doing more to connect her writing with reality, and tensions of reality have also begun to appear in her fiction. There is a contradiction in that her novels apparently do not fall into the category of "mainstream fiction" we see prevailing elsewhere. Another aspect is that *One Hundred Days of Sunshine* and *Urban Expressions* do not in fact feature the unique strength and character of Fan Xiaoqing at her fullest, and in my reading, at least, such novels are not Fan's strong suit. She may go a long way down this road and win many accolades, but the essence of a novel, that which moves us and impacts us, comes more from real lives per se, and Fan's artistic ability to handle real, modern lives in her fictions is not as outstanding as that in her novellas and short stories. At the time, I even began to suspect that her writing like this might have meant she was throwing away her strongest abilities. Old times and old places have already become history, become culture, and new times and places are emerging. How do the two go together? Between the

青处理现实生活的艺术能力，和她的中短篇小说相比，并没有特别之处。我在当时甚至产生疑问：范小青如此写作是否会丢失自己的长处？旧的时空已经成为历史，成为文化，新的时空在生长，这两者如何对接？而在这两者之间，生活，人生，人性又处于怎样的状态？

在产生这些疑问的同时，我又特别感受到范小青观察世界与人生的角度开始发生了比较大的变化，她对世事的洞察、人情的练达在这些长篇小说中得到了锤炼，她笔底下的历史与文化开始发生松动，另外一种和既往不同的素质与气息开始在字里行间涌动。她心中的时空再一次发生了错落，这是范小青文化心理变化的一个前奏。

到了这个时候，范小青已经处于十字路口。

旧的苏州没有了。吴文化也在各种文化的冲击中坐立不安。

在二〇〇六年第一期《山花》的创作谈《变》中，范小青以小说家的口吻说了她和一个城市的关系："长期以来，我一直生活在一个小城，这个小城曾经是旧式的，或者至少是让人怀旧的。我在这个城市的狭小的巷道穿行了许多年，我曾经这样写过这个

two, what is the state of life, human lives, and human nature?

At the same time I was experiencing these doubts, I especially felt that Fan's perspective on the world and human life was beginning to undergo a bigger transformation. Her perception of the world and insight into human sophistication were tested and tempered in these novels. History and culture began to loosen up under her pen, and a new character, a new air, began to surge forth from her lines. And once again, time and space in her mind suffered a dislocation. This was a prelude to the change in Fan's cultural psyche.

At this point, Fan Xiaoqing was at a crossroad.

The old Suzhou was no more. Wu culture was also unstable, at stake under assault from all kinds of other cultures.

In an interview called *"Transform"* in the first issue of 2006 of the journal *Mountain Flowers*, Fan Xiaoqing spoke in writerly tones about her relationship to the city:

For a long time, I've lived in a little city, and this little city was old-fashioned, or at the very least it inspired nostalgia in people. I have been rambling along the lanes in the city for many years. Once I wrote, "Once upon a time, on any given day, walking alone in the narrow lanes of Suzhou was a truly good thing." I speak here of "once upon a time." Almost without even knowing it, we have gone from "once upon a time" to "now." In what seems the blink of an eye, the past and the narrow lanes and the peace and the nostalgia have all transformed, from views outside the window to pictures hung on a wall. Say someone who has been living for so long in an

城市:'从前,在平常的日子里,一个人在苏州的小巷里随便地走走,真是一件很好的事情。'我在这里说的是从前。几乎是在不知不觉中,我们就从'从前'一下子到了'现在',几乎就是一眨眼的工夫,从前、小巷、安静、怀旧等等都从我们的窗景变成了我们挂在墙上的画。一个曾经长期生活在旧式的小城,并且为那一个小城写作的人,当有一天打开门户的时候,忽然发现,门窗外的景色变了,变得陌生,变得喧闹,这个人会怎么样?会东张西望到处寻找,会茫然失落手足无措,这个人你们已经知道了,就是我。"在这个变幻的时空中,范小青和所有在这个城市生活的人一样,自然而然地生出时空错置的感觉。

区域文化对一个在这种文化中长大的作家来说可能是一种宿命。范小青在《变》中说:"我从小在这里长大,每天走出门踩着的每一块砖石,不定就有成百上千年的历史,每天呼吸的空气,都是经过多少代传承的文化酝酿出来的,我就是被浸染和淹没在漫长无边的文化和历史中,所以,在许多年的写作中,我笔下的人物和事情,无论如何也离不开这种特定的色彩。"但是,这种文化已经不再凝固,它不变的一面在范小青那里已经写得很充分,它变的一面又怎样感知和呈现?往回走,往前走,对一个作家来说其实是进

old-fashioned little city, writing for that little city, one day opens the door and suddenly discovers that the view outside is totally different, alien, noisy—how would that person feel? She would search all over, confused and fumbling. You already know this person. It is me.

In this swiftly tilting time and place, Fan Xiaoqing and all who live in the city are alike in feeling quite naturally that they are misplaced.

To a writer who grew up in it, local culture is like destiny. As Fan continues in *"Transform"*:

I grew up here from an early age. Every slate that I stepped on when I went out each day might have centuries of history, and the air I breathed in a day would all have been brimming with culture passed down for many generations. I was steeped in this culture and history, with the result that the characters and events in my work never stray far from these unique colors.

But this culture is no longer wholly coagulative. Fan has written amply on the unchanging face of culture, but what to do with the changing face of it? Going forward or backward leaves the author in a dilemma. What makes writing different from other occupations is that the old is not necessarily meaningless and the new is not immediately meaningful on its own. Fan faces a dilemma: what to do when there is no way out? Going backward? That way is blocked, as the city is now transformed and made new. Is it possible? One might want to return to "once upon a time," but there is no returning. Fan realizes that there will be no more chances for Mister Zhang and Aunt Li to sit in the courtyard and enjoy the cool

退维谷。写作不同于其他行当的是,旧的不等于没有意义,新的不等于其意自明。范小青困惑了:没有去路怎么办,往回走吗,可是往回走的路也被堵住了,一个城市已经变掉了,翻新了,往回走的路还可能存在吗?想回到"从前",却怎么也回不去了。范小青意识到,她小说中的张老先生李家姆妈不再坐在天井里乘风凉,顾家的老小姐们也早已作古,鹰扬巷拆除了,变成了大街,街名叫世纪大道,一针一线缝衣裳的小裁缝瑞云,已成为一位叱咤风云的服装界女企业家。范小青说她自己"迷失了方向"。

我想一个优秀的小说家写作到一定程度之后都会困惑于怎么写小说,这种困惑很大程度上不是技术的,而是文化的,人生的。范小青在从20世纪90年代末到新世纪之初时,便处于这样的困惑阶段。回顾这么多年的文学界,我们可以看到,一类文学或者一批作家的"虚假影响",以及被批评家个人好恶夸大了一些作家的个人经验都会迷惑和影响另外一些作家的写作。通常认为作家对自己的坚持是固执的,其实不然,作家的定力也时常会被外来的因素松动。有不少作家就是在这样的情境中丢失了自我。20世纪90年代以后,在文学批评的褒贬之外,市场与读者的选择、文学评奖制度与出版制度的、主旋律文学与纯文学的纷争等以更强

breeze; the old maids of the Gu clan have long passed into the past; Ying Yang Alley has been demolished and turned into a big modern street called Century Avenue; Rui Yun, once an obscure dressmaker who used to sew clothes stitch by stitch, may have grown into a mighty entrepreneuse in garment industry. Fan Xiaoqing herself says she "has lost her sense of direction."

I think that after a certain amount of work, all excellent story tellers will become confused about how to write fiction, and this confusion is to a large extent related to culture and life, not technique. Fan Xiaoqing was in this confused stage from the late 1990s to the early 2000s. Looking back on literature during all those years, we can see the "vain and false influence" of certain trends and authors, and the personal experience of certain authors amplified by the personal tastes of certain critics, which in turn could enchant and influence other writers. We often think that writers tend to stick stubbornly to their own views, but this is not true; the certainty of a writer can at times grow slack due to external elements. Many a writer has lost their true selves in such circumstances. Since the end of the 1990s, even more powerful forces have impacted these writers besides the praise and blame of the critics: the choices of the market and readers, the system of literary awards, the publishing system, and the endless dispute between mainstream literature and pure literature. These are some of the external elements that influence Fan Xiaoqing.

The problem Fan herself faces is: Can a storyteller have opinions of her own? What are her positions and views regarding history, modernity, culture and human nature? In other words,

的力量冲击着小说家们。这是影响范小青写作的外在因素。

范小青自己面临的问题是：一个小说家究竟有没有自己的想法？她对历史、现实、文化、人性等诸多问题究竟持有怎样的立场和观察的视角？换言之，有无自己的世界观人生观？在急遽变化的社会生活中有无数的作家虽然仍然在写作，但众多的文本背后是没有"脑袋"和"心脏"的。另外的问题是，曾经有过的文化记忆和当下的个人经验如何在矛盾冲突中交融并在多大程度上能够呈现时代的特征？当这两个问题已经解决时，技术上的问题是小说家讲述故事的能力在哪里？我想，小说写作的新的可能性至少与这些问题密切相关。

既然东突西闯仍然没有出路，那么不妨"把眼光投回到活着的生活中来"。用范小青自己的话说，她笔下的人物不再是清一色的小巷遗老遗少，笔下的故事，也不仅仅是大小姐爱上了门房，二小姐一辈子守寡。于是老苏州们仍然是在的，但又出现了一些新的人物：一拨是干部，另一拨是农民工。

但是如果仅是回到活着的生活中，仅是人物的类型发生了变化，还不能说范小青已经找到了"出路"，因为在这之前的《百日

does she have her own worldview, life view? In this rapidly-changing society, many writers may still write, but their works lack "mind" and "heart". Another problem is: how can we combine the cultural memory of the past with individual experience of the present in the face of the contradiction and tension between them, expressing, at least to a goodly extent, the character of the age? If these two problems can be solved, then comes the technical question: where can a writer acquire the ability for such narratives? I think that the new possibilities of storytelling are at the very least closely related to these questions.

Fan may find no escape even if she "dashes about frantically," so she might as well "cast her eyes back to the lives of the living." In Fan's own words, her characters are no longer a uniform cast of lost souls filled with nostalgia, nor are her stories of how older sister falls in love with the doorman while second sister remains a widow the rest of her days. This anachronistic specimen of Suzhou is still around, but new characters also appear: one batch of these is the cadres, while another consists of migrant laborers.

But were it just a matter of returning to the lives of the living, or changing the spectrum of her characters, we could not claim that Fan Xiaoqing had found her "way out," because she had already been doing these things around the time of *One Hundred Days of Sunshine* and *Urban Expressions*, but it seems Fan had not continued along this path. Fan's transformation then, was not only a matter of entering the lives of the living again, but also a matter of reconstructing her understanding of time and space, of reshaping her

阳光》《城市表情》等其实已经这样做了,而范小青似乎又没有再沿途往前走。所以范小青的转型其实不仅仅是重新投入到活着的生活中来,而是她变化了自己对时空的认识,变化了自己对历史与现实复杂性的认识,变化了自己对这座城市人文结构和社会结构的认识。于是,仍然是写人生写人性,但已经不是"挽回"的方式,而是构造了冲突之中的人生场景和人性图解。相对于以往的"静",现在多了"动",相对于以往的"稳定",现在多了"变动",小说的艺术张力也因此而生。

我在早前的文章中,把范小青的变化叙述为:"据我所知,在范小青生活的这个文化圈子,以及在这之外又关注这个文化圈子的一批人当中,引为自豪或者津津乐道的是吴文化的胜处,而且通常沉湎在怀旧之绪中:我并不反对这样的文化观,但是我觉得这样的文化观往往会把'历史'与'现实'割裂开来,以凭吊静止的历史代替关注动态的现实。于此,范小青长期以来也有诸多困惑。在苏州古城逐步翻新以后,始终以'苏州'为原型城市写作的范小青这几年也逐渐从苏州小巷走出。读《女同志》,我以为范小青找到了观察一种文化和一种人生的角度……范小青在'苏州'穿行和沉潜的时间太长了,她终于意识到这座城市的'历史'

understanding of the complexity of history and modernity, of revising her understanding of the structure of the society and culture of the city. Then she continued to write about human lives and human nature, but no longer as a means of redemption; instead she created scenes of life and diagrams of human nature in the midst of conflicts. Where before she was "still", now she is "moving"; where before she was "stable"; now she is "dynamic". In this way, artistic tension in her fiction grows.

In another essay from long ago, I described the transformation of Fan Xiaoqing in this way:

As far as I know, the cultural circles in which Fan Xiaoqing lives, as well as those outsiders who pay attention to such circles, all take great pride and pleasure in the strengths of Wu culture and generally prefer to remain immersed in their feelings of nostalgia. I certainly do not oppose such a view of culture, but I do think that it often separates history from modern reality, pondering on the still and quiet past when it could be attending to dynamic modern reality. Fan has been facing much confusion and difficulty for quite a long time. As old Suzhou undergoes reconstruction and renewal, Fan Xiaoqing, whose archetypical city has always been Suzhou, is also gradually walking out of its little lanes. Reading *Women Comrades*, I feel that Fan Xiaoqing has found an angle from which to observe culture and life... Fan Xiaoqing has spent too much time wandering and indulging in Suzhou, and now at last she realizes that the history and culture of this city are no mere accessories, but rather the very air she breathes... she enters into reality in the most direct manner imaginable, without ambiguity. She uses a spirit fostered on the

和'文化'不是外套,而是她当下呼吸的空气……她以直截了当的方式而不是暧昧的态度介入'现实',又以在历史文化中滋养出的平和冲淡的精神抑制书写时的功利主义倾向。"我这里说的不仅是《女同志》的创作。

在这个意义上,我认为《女同志》是范小青最好的长篇小说,《城乡简史》《我们的战斗生活像诗篇》与《瑞云》《顾氏传人》构成了范小青转型前后的一致性和差异性。而以后的范小青究竟会在"错误路线"还是在"正确路线"上,对她来说仍然面临选择。

2008 年

philosophy of moderation and equilibrium in our historical culture to repress the utilitarian tendencies of her writing.

This comment applies to more of her work than just *Women Comrades*.

In this vein, I believe *Women Comrades* to be Fan's best novel, while "City Living, Country Living" and "Our Fighting Life Is like Poetry" and "Rui Yun" and *Mister Gu's Descendants* are examples of her previously consistent style and her later, changed style, respectively. Whether later work of Fan Xiaoqing is on the "wrong path" or the "right path" is a choice with which Fan is still faced.

2008

访谈

写作于我,更多的是享受过程中的创造、宁静和自由
——范小青访谈录

杨昊成

杨昊成: 我们知道您是苏大中文系毕业的,毕业后也留校当了一段时间的教师。但据说上大学中文系的学生,没有不想当作家的。您也属于这一类人吗?您后来成了专业作家,是否因为在教师与作家之间您更偏爱创作?如果人生可以重来,您还会选择当作家吗?抑或做出别的什么选择?

范小青: 上大学中文系的学生,很多人都有作家梦,很多人也都曾经尝试过写作——这是在我们上大学的那个时代或者更早

Interview

"It Is More the Creativity, Peace and Freedom in the Process of Writing that I Enjoy": An Interview with Fan Xiaoqing

By Yang Haocheng
Translated by Helen Wang

Yang Haocheng: We know that you graduated from the Chinese Department of Soochow University, and that you stayed on as a teacher for a while. It's said that all university students in Chinese departments want to be writers. Was this true in your case? Then you became a professional writer—was it because given the choice between being a teacher and a writer, you preferred creative writing? If you were to have your life again, would you still choose to be a writer? Or would you choose something else?

Fan Xiaoqing: Many university students in Chinese departments dream of being a writer, and many of them try their hand at writing. This was certainly true for students of my own and earlier generations. Whether it's true for students of Chinese Literature

一些的时代,现在的中文系学生怎么样,我不是太清楚。从我个人来说,作家梦确实就是从大学时代开始的,我在上大学之前,读过的书非常少,几乎少到没有,因为没有书读,进入大学后,开始大量阅读,尤其在大一大二的两年时间,几乎读遍了图书馆里的所有的文学方面的世界名著经典书籍。我想,这可能就是一个强大的推动力,同时,七十年代末八十年代的席卷全国的文学热,更是点燃梦想的火种,我是从大二开始写小说的,大三发表了小说处女作。

在教师和作家之间,我确实更偏爱写作——至少在当时离开大学、开始从事专业写作的那个时候,完全是义无反顾的。

因为从八十年代开始,我的人生始终是在写作,我几乎没有尝试过其他职业,所以难以类比,很难知道,我如果不写作,去做其他工作,是会比写作更得心应手呢,还是会很糟糕——所以,您的这个选择题,我可能选择不出来。这是否也从某一个角度说明我的人生是比较单调的。

杨昊成:您是一位勤奋而多产的作家,在这么多各种题材、类型和风格的作品中,有没有您认为可以称为自己代表作的作品?面对自己丰硕的创作成果,撇开读者的反映和专家的评论,总体

now, I don't really know. In my case, the dream of being a writer started when I was at university. Before going to university, I hadn't read many books, in fact hardly any at all, because there weren't any books available for me to read. But when I went to university, I read a huge amount, especially in the first and second years, when I read pretty much all the classics of world literature in the library. It was so inspiring. At the same time, in the late '70s and '80s, there was a nationwide craze for literature in literary circles, and that may have been the spark that lit my dream. I started writing novels in my second year, and in my third year published my debut novel.

As for choosing between teacher and writer, I prefer writing. I had no hesitation in leaving the university and starting a career as a writer.

Since the beginning of the '80s, my life has been about writing. I haven't really tried any other occupations, so it's hard to compare. If I were to do some other work instead of writing, it might be a better fit than writing, or it might be a disaster. It's hard to know. So, I can't really answer your question about choice. From that perspective, I suppose my life might appear a bit monotonous.

Yang Haocheng: You are a hardworking and prolific writer. You write about different subject matters, and in different genres and styles. Are there any works which you consider to be representative? Thinking about your rich creative output—and leaving aside comments from readers and critics—are you satisfied? Have your works achieved what you wanted them to achieve? And if not, why not?

上您自己感到满意吗？这些作品是否达到了您心中的理想？如果没有，您认为原因何在？

范小青：我的创作量确实比较大，其中也有我自己比较偏爱的作品，但是奇怪的是，我自己偏爱的东西，也经常会发生变化，所以要说代表作，也有几个风格不相同的作品。就说我的中短篇小说吧，比如八十年代的《瑞云》，九十年代末的《鹰扬巷》和后来的《城乡简史》，都可以算是代表作，但它们之间，也是有较大的差别的。

对我自己的作品，总体我是满意的——可能因为数量较大，其中总有一点点写得比较好的比较满意的东西。有一些作品已经达到了我心中的理想——只不过理想这个东西，也是会变化和发展的，也许昨天认为的理想，到了今天一看，已经不够理想了。所以，写作是一个不断追求变化、不断创新的过程——从这个层面说，我的作品可能还远没有达到我的理想，原因就是理想一直在成长。

杨昊成：您的作品，无论是长篇还是中短篇，都没有所谓宏大壮阔的叙事，大多是在一种平实的、细腻的、有时小巧的，甚至絮叨的话语流中展开，这是由于您的性格使然，还是因为您的

Fan Xiaoqing: I have written a lot, and there are some pieces that are quite special to me, but it's strange how the things I like keep changing. In terms of representative works, we could talk about different styles. If we look simply at my short stories, we could say "Rui Yun" in the 1980s, "Ying Yang Alley" in the late 1990s, and more recently "City Living, Country Living" are all representative works, but each one is quite different.

On the whole, I'm satisfied with what I've written. Maybe it's because I've written such a lot that I can always find something that I think I've written well and am happy with. There are some pieces that achieved what I wanted to achieve. But, ideals and ambitions change, and the ideals and ambitions of yesterday aren't always the same today. Writing is a process of constantly chasing change, and creating new things. Looking in this way, my works might seem a long way from my ideal, because my ideal is always developing.

Yang Haocheng: Your works—your novels, novellas and short stories—don't have big, sweeping narratives; they are mostly quite modest, delicate, sometimes clever, even "garrulous", stories that develop with the flow of language. Do you think this comes from your personality or from the fact that you are a woman?

Fan Xiaoqing: When I first started writing, I didn't pay too much attention to style, so it probably comes from there. In my first pieces, I wrote as I pleased, about whatever I liked. The subject matter of my earliest writings was mostly about old Suzhou, with that kind of quiet and peaceful background, and often the content influenced the form, and the writing had a kind of easy feel to it, like going for a gentle stroll. At the same time, I suppose this kind

女性身份所决定了的?

范小青：这和一开始创作就没有十分认真地研究过文风问题有关吧。开始的写作，就是任随自己的喜好，想怎么写就怎么写，而我早期的写作题材，多半是和老苏州有关的内容，那样一种幽静平和的背景，而很多时候形式是受内容影响的，于是就形成了比较平淡、娓娓道来的习惯，同时，这种风格，和我的性格，和我的女性身份也一定是有关系的。

杨昊成：不作惊人之语，不制造悬念，情节上也不跌宕起伏；既不让人泣，也难让人笑，这种类似拉家常的素朴的叙事风格，尤其在当今这个信息、知识和娱乐获取无限多元的社会，很难讨读者或批评家的欢心。您怎么看这个问题？我们当然可以说，一个作家绝不是为了获奖或迎合别人而写作，但如果连自己也意识到，有必要"与时俱进"时，就您而言，在坚守与"进步"——当然也未必就是进步——之间，您会选择哪一边？

范小青：这个问题也是长期以来一直困惑我的问题，也是长期以来我一直在探索、在寻求答案的问题，但实践的经验告诉我，它不会有明确的固定的答案，我更相信写作者是听从着自己内心的声音在写作，而同时，写作者求变的愿望又是伴随终身的，正

of style must also be linked to my personality and to my being a woman.

Yang Haocheng: I'm quite intrigued by your style of writing. The language offers no surprises, there's no suspense, the plot has no particular highs and lows. You don't make people laugh or cry. It's more the plain narrative style of everyday conversation. These factors make it very difficult to please readers and critics, especially given the limitless variety of information, knowledge and entertainment that is available in today's society. How do you see this issue? Of course, we can say that a writer doesn't write to win prizes or to please other people. But if you yourself are aware of this and of the need to "move with the times", would you choose to hold your ground or to "move with the times?" Of course, I'm not suggesting that you should; the choice is entirely yours.

Fan Xiaoqing: This issue has been troubling me for a long time now, and it's one I've been exploring and looking for an answer to. But practical experience tells me that there won't be a clear-cut answer. I'm more inclined to believe that writers have to listen to their inner voice. At the same time, as a writer, you have a desire for change that is with you all your life. You talk about there being a choice between holding one's ground and "moving with the times", but "moving with the times" is not necessarily progress. In fact, whenever I've made changes in my novels, there have been people who hailed them, but there also have been people who complained, or sighed with regret, or even criticized them. And at those times, I swing back and forth with self-doubt, but when I pick up my pen and start writing again, I have to listen to my inner voice. It's a case

如您所说,在坚守与"进步"之间会选择哪一边,因为有时候"进步"也未必就是进步,事实上,每当我的小说发生了一些变化的时候,总是有人说好,也有人叹惜甚至批评,这时候,我一定会动摇,会怀疑自己,但是等到我又开始动笔写作的时候,我只能听从我内心的声音:在坚守中变化,在变化中坚守。

杨昊成:说到这一点,您平时关注外界对您作品的反应吗?或者说,外界的反应会影响到您的创作吗?

范小青:当然是关注的。而且十分希望有人关注我的作品。外界的反应我会认真思考,仔细琢磨,而不是盲目听从或者盲目拒绝。凡是能够进入到我内心的,它就成了我内心的声音,我就会听从它们;凡是进不了我内心的,可能就会随风而过。

杨昊成:正如有些评论家指出的那样,您的许多作品,尤其是短篇,都有一个共同的主题——"寻找"。比如我们《中华人文》第一期发表的《梦幻快递》以及您后来发给我的几个短篇《我在哪里丢失了你》《我在小区遇见了谁》《南来北往谁是客》《右岗的茶树》《生于黄昏或清晨》等。就是本期发表的您的两个名篇《城乡简史》和《鹰扬巷》,也都是在"寻找"。您为何如此钟情于这样的主题?另外,您许多作品中的人物的身份都有着很

of changing while you hold your ground, and holding your ground while you change.

Yang Haocheng: While we're on this subject, do you pay much attention to what the outside world thinks of your work? Or, to put it another way, does what the outside world thinks have an influence over your creative writing?

Fan Xiaoqing: Of course I pay attention to this. And I very much hope that people pay attention to my work. I consider the responses of the outside world very carefully. I don't heed them or reject them blindly. Whatever enters my heart becomes part of my inner voice, and I will listen accordingly. But if something doesn't enter my heart then it will probably blow over me.

Yang Haocheng: As a number of commentaries have pointed out, many of your works, especially the short pieces, can be seen as sharing a "searching" theme. I'm thinking of "The Hallucinated Courier" (published in the first issue of *Chinese Arts and Letters*) and the pieces you sent me subsequently: "Where Did I Lose You?", "Who Did I Meet in the Neighbourhood?", "Tenant", "Tea Trees at Yougang", "Born in an Unknown Hour". And your two pieces in this issue of *Chinese Arts and Letters*—"City Living, Country Living" and "Ying Yang Alley"—are both concerned with a search. What is it that draws you to this theme? Also, in many of your works, the status of the characters is very vague, we may not know their names, or whether they are male or female, or whether a brother is older or younger, or whether they are "born at dusk or dawn". These things appear not to be important. Such characterization is quite different from traditional writing methods.

大的模糊性,姓甚名谁,是男是女,哥哥还是弟弟,"生于黄昏抑或清晨",都显得不重要。这样的人物塑造与传统手法有很大的距离。您是有意为之吗?可以算是一种后现代的努力吗?通过这一个个缺乏明确身份的人物,您是否试图想给读者传递某种文化或哲学信息?

范小青:"寻找"主题和人物身份不确定性这两个问题其实是紧密结合在一起的。在物质社会发展的过程中,新的秩序尚未正常建立,老的传统还没有完全消亡,在这新老交替的节点上,往往会产生许多悖反甚至荒诞的东西,这是现代社会,尤其是我们中国社会的一个特征。比如近来大家所知道的被要求证明"你妈是你妈"等现象,迫使人要去不断地寻找并证明本来已经非常明确的事实。许多人、许多事叫人不可理解,这就让我对这个社会产生一种疑惑:我们究竟还有没有一种比较稳定的价值标准和行为标准?人类社会理应按照一定的规则向前发展,但事实往往不是这样。我们这个社会充满了那么多不确定的东西,人人都觉得不可信:政府不可信,企业不可信,个人不可信,全民如此,这是怎么了?比如现在每当我在媒体上看到一个新闻,我首先关心的不是它的内容,而是它的真实性。微信上海量的信息也是如此,

Have you done this intentionally? Can it be seen as an attempt at postmodernism? Are you trying through this lack of status in the characterization to give readers some kind of cultural or philosophical message?

Fan Xiaoqing: Actually, the theme of "searching" and the imprecise characterization are closely linked. We are in the process of developing a material society, but the new order is not yet properly established, and the old order has not completely disappeared, so we're at a stage in between old and new, when there are lots of contradictory, even absurd, things. It's a feature of contemporary society, and particularly of our Chinese society. For example, recently everyone has experienced phenomena like being required to prove that "your mother is your mother", and being forced to go on constant searches to prove some fact that is already very clear. There are many people and many things that are impossible to understand, and they raise doubts in my mind about this society: do we still have a fairly stable standard of values and behaviour or not? Human society should move forward in accordance with certain rules, but the reality is often not like that. Our society is filled with so many uncertainties, and things that people feel cannot be trusted. We hear that the government cannot be trusted, businesses cannot be trusted, individuals cannot be trusted—how can it be that everyone feels this way? Every time I see a piece of news in the media, my first concern is not its content, but its authenticity. It's the same for most of the information posted on WeChat. There is so much doubt. The theme of "searching" is about looking for a standard of value. The imprecision in my

它们是真实的吗？非常值得怀疑。我因此就想寻找，寻找那种可以作为价值标准的理想。至于人物身份的不确定性，也与此有着密切的关系。我的小说几乎没有对人物的外观描写，因为我觉得这些人物只是某种符号，其象征意义要大于实际意义，就是这样。我近期的许多短篇都隐隐约约受这么一种思想的主导。

杨昊成：我不知道如何来归类您的小说，它们记录或描述的，似乎都是我们能感知或实际也可以经历的实实在在的真生活，可与此同时又都掺入了某些非理性甚至"魔幻"的成分，给人以亦真亦幻，游走于现实与非现实之间的感觉。这或者是艺术创作的通常做法，但我想您一定不属于所谓的"荒诞派"。这就涉及一个对合理性的"度"的把握的问题。像《右岗的茶树》中的二秀，仅仅凭老师对"玉螺茶"的一番诗意描述，就那样魂不守舍地纠结于那个人和他口中的茶，以至于老师死于意外后，非得去寻找那片埋着老师的墓地，还要在老师的家乡留下来，做一名"一抹酥胸蒸绿玉"的采茶女。我想读者读到这样的作品，许多人可能都会对故事的合理性产生疑问，尽管艺术的真实并不需要完全等同于生活的真实。好像有些评论家对《城乡简史》中的王才，因为要弄清"香薰精油"究竟为何物，就非得移居城市的

characterization is closely linked to this. My stories seldom describe the physical appearance of characters, because I feel these characters are only representatives, and that what they symbolize is greater than a character's reality. I'd say this is the dominant thinking behind the vagueness in many of my recent stories.

Yang Haocheng: I'm not sure how to place your stories. The accounts and descriptions seem to be real-life things that we can actually feel or experience for ourselves, but at the same time they seem to incorporate some non-rational, even "magical" components. This creates a feeling of being caught between reality and illusion, of not being sure whether you are on solid ground. I guess this is a common practice of artistic creation, but you certainly do not belong in the Writers of the Absurd, do you? It's all about the "degree" of rationality. Take Er Xiu from "Tea Trees at Yougang" for example. Simply by her teacher's poetic description of Yuluochun, the gunpowder tea, the enchanted girl should be so obsessed with it that after her teacher dies in an accident, she feels compelled to go and find the grave where she believes her teacher is buried, and insists on staying in the teacher's hometown to be a tea-picker. I think readers may question the reality of your stories, even though truth in art doesn't need to completely match truth in reality. And the same is true, as some critics have pointed out, of Wang Cai, the protagonist in "City Living, Country Living", who feels compelled to move himself and his family to the city, simply to find out what essential oil is.

Fan Xiaoqing: Yes, that was an issue. In fact, in "Tea Trees at Yougang" I also feel that the ending was a bit far-fetched. Just as

举动也提出了质疑。

范小青：是有这个问题。其实《右岗的茶树》我自己也觉得那样一个结果确实显得比较牵强。正如你所说，我的作品基本上还是属于现实主义，合理性当然是一个必须要认真对待的问题。《城乡简史》中的合理性也有人提出质疑，但我认为，这里边的所谓欠合理与《右岗的茶树》中的欠合理是不完全一样的。王才进城表面看来是为了那瓶"香薰精油"，其实不然，这里有个大的社会背景，那就是前些年大量农民工进城的现象。中国社会发展到这个时候，农民工进城已成必然趋势，王才即便不是为了那瓶"香薰精油"，也还是要进城的。与此相对照，《右岗的茶树》就比较勉强。如果我是一位魔幻作家或超现实主义作家，那么怎么欠合理也是合理的，然而我不是。所以我在以后的创作中对这个问题要更加慎重。

杨昊成：请您顺便谈谈本期发表的《城乡简史》《鹰扬巷》和《生于黄昏或清晨》：当初是什么东西触动您写出了这样的作品？

范小青：《城乡简史》刚才已经部分谈到了，大背景当然就是十多年前农民工大量涌入城市这个现象。农民工的到来，直接间接地都会影响到我们的生活，点点滴滴加起来，让我必然要去关

you say, my stories are basically realist, so rationality is something that must be taken seriously. The rationality of both of these stories has been called into question, but the situations are quite different. Superficially, you can say that in "City Living, Country Living", Wang Cai went to the city for a bottle of "essential oil", but in fact that wasn't the full story, because there was a huge social background to this event, namely the phenomenon of migrant workers moving to the cities. Chinese society had developed to a point that the migrant worker phenomenon was inevitable. Wang Cai would still have gone to the city, even if he hadn't gone for the "essential oil". There isn't the same sense of inevitability in "Tea Trees at Yougang". If I were a magical or surrealist writer, then a lack of rationality would be acceptable, but I'm not. I need to take more care over such things in future.

Yang Haocheng: Would you tell us a little about the stories in this issue?—"City Living, Country Living"; "Ying Yang Alley"; and "Born in an Unknown Hour"? What inspired you to write stories like these?

Fan Xiaoqing: We've already touched on "City Living, Country Living", and the background is, of course, the phenomenon of migrant workers. The influx of migrant workers to the city over a decade ago affected our lives, both directly and indirectly, and as the various effects began to accumulate, I found I had to go and focus on their lives. The basic framework of the story, including the section about the "essential oil", is fictional. As for inspiration, Ziqing is a shadow of myself, because like Ziqing, I have the habit of keeping a close eye on family expenses. Writing a story like that was a

注他们的生活。故事的基本框架以及包括"香薰精油"在内的细节，都是虚构的。要说原型，倒是其中的自清有着我自己的影子，因为我和自清一样，生活中也有记账的习惯。写这样一个故事，是一个逐渐思考和积累的过程，并不是突然地有某个事件激发了我。《鹰扬巷》的创作有一点来由。我本来就比较关注家乡苏州的风土人情，而一次偶然的机会，在史书上看到一篇关于章太炎夫人的故事，故事很简短，说的是章夫人年轻时曾是上海某女校的校花，不仅漂亮，而且很有才华。至于《鹰扬巷》中汤好婆身边的其他几位老人，原故事中是没有的，是我加进去的，麦先生前来寻她，也是虚构。我对苏州的小巷生活非常熟悉。通过这样一个故事我是想说，平凡的背后往往都曾经有过波澜。你看这么一个已到暮年的老太太，安安静静地闲坐在小巷深处，和一帮差不多年纪的老人聊着家长里短，谁会想到她曾经有过那么风光的青春年华呢！她还偏有！

杨昊成：我个人也是非常喜欢这篇东西，故事平淡，平淡而唯美。一个人可以为了一个年少时的美梦，一辈子孜孜以求，念念不忘，多好啊！

范小青：是啊，很难得。《生于黄昏或清晨》也是有所触动而

gradual, cumulative process of thinking and development; it was not the result of suddenly being inspired.

There's more of a story behind "Ying Yang Alley". I was researching the people and customs of my hometown, Suzhou, and by chance came across a story of Mrs Zhang Taiyan in a historical document. The account was very short. It said that she was once the campus queen of a girls' school in Shanghai, and that she was clever as well as beautiful. Grandma Tang is based on her. No one else was mentioned in the document. I added the other old ladies and Mr Mai, who came looking for her. They are fictional characters. I am familiar with life in the little streets of Suzhou, and I wanted to show through the story that behind very ordinary things there have often been great waves. This old lady in her twilight years, tucked away in the little lanes of Suzhou, quietly chatting with a group of people of her age... who would imagine she once had such a dazzling youth! And yet she had!

Yang Haocheng: I myself like "Ying Yang Alley" very much. The story is very simple, and at the same time very beautiful. To think that someone can hold a dream from their youth, and cherish it their entire life until it comes true, is quite special!

Fan Xiaoqing: Yes, it's rare that something like that happens. I can tell you about the inspiration behind "Born in an Unknown Hour" as well. I was in a car with some friends, and one of them said, he could tell whether the official year of one's birth was accurate or not. It was completely unexpected, and I thought about my family, in which three out of five people share the same birthday, 1st February. In fact, no one in the family was born on

写的。有一次我和几个朋友在车上,其中一个人说,他能判断出每个人现在所认定的出生年代是否准确,那样子神乎其神,一下让我想起了我们家的情况:从前我家五口人,其中三个人的生日都是二月一日。其实我们家没有一个人出生于二月一号。我们小时候,一个人的生日大概写一个就行了,错了也就错了,无所谓,不像现在这么重要,与晋升、退休等都有直接的关系。我的生日是我母亲告诉我的,是七月二十二日,而且是黄昏,因为她说,生我的时候正好是夏天的傍晚,刚好看到外面灯火亮了。但不知怎么回事,我的身份证上到现在为止依然还是写的二月一日,我也懒得去改它,因为非要搞清楚自己究竟生于哪一天,好像也没有多大意义。这样的情况还很多,并非我一个。这又让我觉得人生的荒诞和不确定性,因此就写了这么一篇小说。

杨昊成:本期《中华人文》发了您的三个短篇,其中的《城乡简史》其实我们创刊时您就给了我们,我个人是一下就看中了,只因当初我偶然在美国的一份刊物《今日中国文学》(*Chinese Literature Today*)上看到了它的英译文,担心有版权问题,所以没有及时发出来。这篇东西虽然也是反映普通草根的生活,但因小见大,从中可以看到当今中国城乡生活的变迁,具有一定的典

that day. When we were little, birthdays weren't important, any date would do. It didn't matter if your birthday was accurate or not. It's not as important as it is today, when birthdays have a direct bearing on promotion and pension, and so on. My mother told me that I was born on the 22nd of July. She said I was born at dusk, because it was a summer evening, and she had just seen the lights coming on outside. But somehow my birth date on my ID card has always been the 1st of February. I never bothered to change it, because there didn't seem to be any point in going to all the trouble of working it out exactly. I'm not the only one; there are still many cases like mine. It made me think about the absurdity and uncertainty of life, and I wrote it up as a story.

Yang Haocheng: In this issue of *Chinese Arts and Letters* we are publishing three of your short stories. In fact, one of them, "City Living, Country Living", you gave to us when we were setting up the journal. I wanted to publish it then and there, but I happened to see that an English translation had been published in an American magazine named *Chinese Literature Today*, and I needed some time to check if there were any copyright issues. This story reflects ordinary grassroots life, but through this small setting we see a much bigger picture, the evolution of city and country life in China today. It has the qualities of a classic, and there is wisdom and humour in the clever ending, which makes the reader smile with recognition. The second one, "Ying Yang Alley" is characterized by its calmness. Nothing jars. There is a long, soothing timelessness, and from the calmness emerges the beauty of life. It's rather like a beautiful essay or a poem. But, if I may be so bold, it seems that

型性,轻巧的结尾智慧而幽默,让人莞尔之余颇觉回味。《鹰扬巷》给人突出的特点是淡,淡到无痕,但是淡而隽永,悠悠的,舒缓的,平淡从容中显出生活的美好,像一篇散文诗。但恕我直言,类似这样令人难忘的作品似乎还不是很多。长期以来,人们一直强调文学作品的典型性,尤其是人物塑造上的典型性,我个人认为这永远都不过时,也不会过时;经典作品,无论是古典还是今典,之所以成为经典,就是因为它们塑造了一个个鲜活而有个性的典型人物,林黛玉、贾宝玉是这样,阿Q、孔乙己是这样;哈姆雷特、麦克白是这样,哈克贝利·芬、《老人与海》中的圣地亚哥也都莫不如此。现代、后现代之后,对形式的追求似乎成了不少作家(艺术家)的偏好,所以乔伊斯(James Joyce)的意识流,格特鲁特·斯泰因(Gertrude Stein)对重复和声音的痴迷等,都令人眼睛一亮,在长长的文学传统中,可谓别具一格,或者也不妨说,另创了一种新的传统。由此看来,典型的人物塑造和奇崛独特的写作手法,或者是确立写作者个人面貌的最常见的途径。如能做到极致,或者就成经典。您同意我这样的说法吗?您对自己众多作品中人物的典型性和写作手法有何自我评价?我想,不论承认与否,每一位作家,其心灵深处,一定怀有自己的作品有

most writing of this kind is fleeting—there are not many such memorable pieces. For a long time, people have emphasized the classical nature of literary works, and it's my personal belief that such emphasis does not date, and will not date in the future. Certain works, ancient and modern, have become classics because of their vivid and idiosyncratic characters—Lin Daiyu and Jia Baoyu, Ah Q and Kong Yiji, Hamlet and Macbeth, Huckleberry Finn and the Santiago in *The Old Man and the Sea* are all strong characters. These days, after Modernism and Post-modernism, many writers (and artists) have chosen to focus on form—and so we have, for example, James Joyce's stream of consciousness, and Gertrude Stein's obsession with repetition and sound. These works stand out; they catch our attention. We can say that they are unique in the long tradition of literature, and we can also say that they create a kind of new tradition. So it seems that great characterization and a unique writing style are the most common routes to establishing a writer's individual status, and if a writer can take these qualities to the ultimate stage, then he has a classic. Would you agree with this? In your many works, how would you evaluate your characterization and writing methods? I think that, whether they acknowledge it or not, every writer, deep down, must dream of their work standing out as a classic one day. Do you have such a dream? Do you think that any of your works might become classics?

Fan Xiaoqing: That's a very interesting question, and a very stimulating one. On the question of classics, we can ask about characterization in modern novel writing, and about the continuation of that tradition. Modern and contemporary fiction isn't always

朝一日也能被列为经典的梦想。您有这样的梦想吗?您认为您的作品中有可能诞生经典吗?

范小青:您的这个问题非常有意义,也非常有启发性。典型性的问题,典型人物的问题,在当代小说的写作中,应该怎么体现,怎么延续,这是非常重要的话题。当代小说或现代小说的写作,有时候不是写的某一个个别的人,而是通过一个无所谓是谁的人,写出当代社会现代社会的特性,比如荒诞性,比如不确定性等等。就以我自己最近几年的小说为例,小说中的人物是谁并不重要,甚至他是男是女,长什么样子,都无所谓,重要的是他的经历、他的遭遇,代表了现代社会的共同性——这就和传统的文学典型性、人物典型性相去甚远——我是否应该回归,目前来说,这也是我给我自己设置的重要问题,暂时似乎还无法解答。

作品被列为经典,肯定是每个写作者所追求的,但是最后能否被列为经典,却不是个人的能力所能达到的,就像对待获奖一样。我想,我写作,更多的是体会写作过程中的创造、宁静和自由。

杨昊成:您的作品有明显的地域性,您的家乡苏州可以说是您许多作品,尤其是早期作品的胎记。许多作家的作品都呈现出

about a particular person. Sometimes it is only through someone whose identity really doesn't matter that the absurdity and uncertainty of modern and contemporary society are conveyed. For example, in my own writing of the last few years, none of the characters in my stories are important *per se*, and sometimes I don't care if they are male or female, or what they look like. The important thing is how their personal history and experiences represent the commonality of contemporary society. This is a far cry from traditional classical literature and characterization. I often wonder whether I should return to a stronger characterization—it's an important question, but, for the time being, I don't seem to be able to answer it.

As for one's work standing out as a classic, I'm sure that's what every writer desires. But, as with winning prizes, such an achievement is not solely dependent on an individual's ability. For me, it is more the creativity, peace and freedom in the process of writing that I enjoy.

Yang Haocheng: In your works there is a very clear sense of place, and Suzhou, your hometown, is rather like a birthmark on many of your works, particularly your early works. This is true for many writers: for example, Thomas Hardy, Mark Twain and William Faulkner, and our own Mo Yan, Jia Pingwa and Wang Shuo. Do you think you have written all there is to say about Suzhou? You made your name writing about people and matters in Suzhou, and now, when you look back, do you think that the strong sense of place made you a success, or limited you?

Fan Xiaoqing: As you say, Suzhou is like a visible birthmark on

这一特点，比如哈代、马克·吐温、福克纳；我们的莫言、贾平凹、王朔也是这样。您觉得苏州的这种地域性被您写到位了吗？您最初是以写家乡苏州的人和事成名的，回过头去看，您认为这种地域性究竟是成就了您，还是限制了您？

范小青： 如您所说，我早期的作品中，苏州的胎记比较鲜明，写的苏州人、苏州地、苏州事，甚至用的语言也都是苏州方言，这种写作，在一定的时间内是成就了我的，至少大家知道你是在写苏州的，后来的作品则渐渐地减少了这种外在的胎记，可能是我不想被地域束缚得太紧，想放松一点。但是，即使外在的胎记减少了，内在的精神风貌应该还是苏式的，至少是苏南式的。比如说，即使我写一个农民工，他也是一个在苏州打工而不是在北方某个城市打工的农民工，一方水土养成的写作特点，是很难彻底改变的。

作为我的家乡，苏州的地域性我是远远没有写到位的，所以，也许，经过多年以后，我可能又回到地域性的写作。

杨昊成： 我不是作家，但我敢肯定，写作和任何一个行当一样，做好是很不容易的。就您而言，写作最大的难处是什么？或者说，面对写作，您最大的苦恼是什么？

my early works. I wrote about the people of Suzhou, about Suzhou as a place, about things that happened in Suzhou, and I wrote using the local language of Suzhou. That kind of writing, at that time, did bring me success. At least, everyone knew I was writing about Suzhou. In my later works I gradually tried to make the birthmark less visible, perhaps because I didn't want to be so tightly bound by place, and wanted to loosen the hold a bit. But, even if the birthmark is less apparent, the spirit is still that of Suzhou, at least that of southern Jiangsu. For example, if I write about a migrant worker, he'll be working in Suzhou rather than in a northern city. Once the local water and earth has nourished your writing style, it's very difficult to change it completely. Suzhou's my hometown. Have I written all there is to say about it? Actually, I'm a long way from that, so maybe, in a few more years, I might go back to writing about it.

Yang Haocheng: I'm not a writer, but I dare say, that writing is like any other profession, in that it's not easy to excel. What is the hardest aspect of writing for you? Or, maybe I should say, when you are writing, what troubles you the most?

Fan Xiaoqing: It's still a question of creating new things. Writers can't always be repeating themselves otherwise they and their readers will get bored. I've produced rather a lot, which is both a good thing and a bad thing. But I have come to realize now that a huge output might be more of a problem than a blessing. If you write a lot at a particular time, it's likely that those pieces may be very similar. For example, I've recently been interested in absurdity and uncertainty, but if I write a lot all in one go, a single

范小青：还是一个创新的问题。作家不能老是重复自己，尤其在一些细节上，否则自己和读者都会觉得无趣。我的创作量比较大，这既是好事，也是坏事，现在看来可能还是问题更多一些。同时期的作品容易写得雷同。比如我近阶段比较关心荒诞性和不确定性，结果就会一口气写好多，单篇看，觉得还不错，如果每篇都这样，人家就会说"都差不多嘛"。所以，像我这样一个算是比较多产的作家，如何拉开作品与作品之间的距离，不重复自己，既是我写作中时常会遭遇的苦恼，也是我以后必须要解决的问题。好在我现在已经开始放慢节奏了，慢慢地一篇篇地磨，争取不让人产生厌倦。

杨昊成：您好像说过自己崇尚"中和"之美，这或者也决定了您的作品不会有大起大落或大喜大悲。但社会有光明与黑暗，人生有苦难与欢乐；"中和"作为一种人生态度也许是很高的境界，但就艺术创作而言，是否会给人以不上不下、不温不火、不优不劣的"中庸"之感？揭露黑暗与苦难，相对于叙写欢乐与光明，难道不更具有张力吗？

范小青：我同意你的观点。艺术需要有冲击力，需要有力量，否则难以打动读者。但我的写作一向比较追求内敛，希望淡而有

piece might seem quite good, but a lot of similar pieces will cause people to complain "they're all the same". So, for writers like me with a high output, the key questions are how to draw a distance between works, and how not to repeat oneself. These are both frustrations I have when I am writing, and problems that I must resolve. Fortunately, I've now started to slow down a bit, and grind away slowly at each piece, doing my best so that people won't get tired of them.

Yang Haocheng: You've spoken previously of your love for the beauty of "moderation", and how this guides your writing. There are no great ups and downs in your stories, nor great joy or great despair. But in society there is light and dark, and in life there is suffering and joy. "Moderation" as a life attitude may be a lofty spiritual realm for one to attain, but in artistic creation, it might give people a feeling of "mediocrity", neither high nor low, neither hot nor cold, neither good nor bad. Have you ever considered that exposing darkness and suffering as compared to the narrative of joy and light might lend more tension to your writing?

Fan Xiaoqing: I agree with your point of view. Art needs to have impact, it needs strength, otherwise it's difficult to move readers. But my writing is rather restrained; I'm hoping for a light taste, it's my personal preference, if you like. Often, at critical moments, I can't resist putting pen to paper, but then I'll suddenly pull myself back, and stop. There are always some people who feel my writing lacks passion, but I like it this way, and believe that it is no less valid a state of being. I write like this intentionally. Many critics have also said that my works leave them feeling unsatisfied at

味,这或者也可以说就是我个人的喜好。在关键的时候我往往不忍下手,突然就会收一下,打住。人家总觉得差一把火,但我自己很欣赏,认为不失为一种境界。我是有意为之。许多评论家也都提到,我的不少作品,到最后总觉得差那么一口气。当然,这口气能否提起来,一要看我有没有足够的能力,二也要看我是否愿意,如果提起来后的效果并不是我想要的,那我还是不提的好。

杨昊成:本期《中华人文》发表的王尧的评论文章谈到了您的"转型",我想这多半是评论家给您前后作品的定位。您同意这样的定位吗?您是否就是在有意识地做这样的"转型"?是什么东西促使您做这样的"转型"?您自己对"转型"的结果有何评判?

范小青:关于"转型",我应该是认同的。当然这个"转型"是在自觉与不自觉之间发生的,并不是说我今天想转就转的。有时写着写着,回头一看,发现已经跟前期的东西有所不同了。我现在的生活跟以前有很大的不同,烦琐的行政工作,决定了我不可能像以前那样从容写作,《鹰扬巷》那样的作品再也写不出来了,往往是一上午开会,下午赶紧忙里偷闲写点东西,因此写作速度和文字节奏就都变得比较快。所以我想,这个"转型"应该跟我的生活有关,另外当然也跟年龄有关。至于"转型"后的结

the end. Of course, whether I can provide them with a satisfactory end or not, the first question is whether I have that writing ability, and the second is whether I am willing to change the way I write. If I change and do not like the result, then I think it's better not to change.

Yang Haocheng: This issue of *Chinese Arts and Letters* has a critical essay by Wang Yao on your "transition". This is more or less a definition of your writing by critics. Do you agree with what he says? Have you made a conscious "transition"? And if so, what prompted you to make it? And how do you rate the results of the "transition"?

Fan Xiaoqing: I have to acknowledge that there has been a "transition". Of course, it has taken place subconsciously. It was not a case of deciding that one day there would be a transition, and so it happened. Sometimes, when I am writing away, I look back, and discover that there is something different from before. My life now is very different from before. The heavy but tedious administrative work determines that I cannot write as leisurely as I used to. I can no longer write pieces like "Ying Yang Alley". Often I will be at a meeting all morning, and in the afternoon I will snatch whatever time I can to write, and because of this, the speed and rhythm of my writing have become faster. I think the "transition" must be linked with my life, and also, of course, with age. As for the results of the "transition", it's not easy for me to judge. I can only say that before, as a professional writer, my life was quite calm and leisurely, my writing was unhurried, and I was relatively more at ease and at home writing on those subject matters about Suzhou.

果,我自己不大好评判,只能说以前当专业作家的时候,生活比较闲散宁静,写作比较从容,而驾驭苏州题材相对而言也比较得心应手;如今因为工作的关系,不仅写作速度较快,写出来的东西也比较紧。我自己当然还是比较喜欢《鹰扬巷》那样的作品,但前后作品的效果究竟如何,还是由读者去评判吧。

杨昊成:对于写作,前提当然是热爱,但接下来具体的写作,有些人认为有赖于经历和阅历,有些人则认为需要天才。钱锺书的写作,无论是学术还是创作,几乎全凭他的博览群书;莎士比亚不怎么读书,却成为前无古人、后难来者的伟大作家。您属于哪一类?您如何看待阅读与写作的关系?请谈谈您的读书生活。

范小青:我的阅读不算很多,我的写作,更多的是靠着对生活的感悟、对生活的敏锐感觉和捕捉生活中的文学特质。但是我认为阅读一定是写作的最强大的后援。我的阅读分两个大的阶段,早期是大量阅读文学作品,后来就是杂书了,或者干脆就是写作参考书,而我的读书习惯,就是不强求自己读,比如听到别人在谈论什么书好,而我手边却一时无法找到这本书,我一般不会千方百计去找来读。我觉得人和书是有缘分的,有缘的书到了你手

Today, because of work commitments, my writing is faster, and the pieces I write are tighter. Personally, I still prefer pieces like "Ying Yang Alley", but as for judging my works before and after "transition", perhaps we should let the reader decide.

Yang Haocheng: In writing, we talk about the passion to write coming first, and then about the actual writing. Some people believe that writing comes from personal experience and wide reading; others believe that one must have a gift or talent to be a writer. Qian Zhongshu's writing, both his academic and creative writing, drew for a large part upon his phenomenal breadth of reading. Shakespeare didn't read much, and yet he earned himself a place in history as a great writer. Which camp do you belong to? What connections between reading and writing do you see? Would you tell us a little about your own reading?

Fan Xiaoqing: I don't read a huge amount, and my writing draws mostly on how I perceive life, on my sharp observation of life and on capturing the literary qualities of life. But I believe that reading provides the most power for writing. I would say there have been two stages of reading in my life. When I was younger, I focused on literary works. But later I turned to reading a greater variety of books, sometimes simply as reference for my own creative writing. My reading habit is not to force myself to read. For example, if I hear someone discussing a good book, but I can't get hold of a copy easily, then I won't go to a huge amount of trouble to get one. I think there's an element of fate in people and books coming together. If fate brings the book into my hands, then I'll read it.

边，就读。

杨昊成：您是一位职业作家，但无法回避的一个事实是，您又是江苏作协的主席。作家要求对外直面人生，对内直面自己的灵魂，换一个说法就是，作家要真。可是我们都心知肚明，一个纯粹的作家与一个作协领导之间，绝对是有许多难以一致和协调的尴尬的，因为我们的作协跟国外那种俱乐部性质的作协完全属于两种性质。您是如何在这两种角色之间协调自己而胜任愉快的？或者，您其实过的是一种 double life（双重生活）？在您具体写作的过程中，是否自觉不自觉地感觉到有某种无形的力在控制着您？如果让您做出选择，您更愿意忠于写作，还是更愿意忠于体制的规约？

范小青：杨教授，这个问题能否不作答了？

杨昊成：应该说，您的生活基本和知识阶层和官场有关，但有趣的是，您的作品在题材选择上却多半倾向于普通百姓。一般说来，作家驾驭自己熟悉的人物及其生活显然要容易一些，而您却反其道而行之，是否出于某种特殊的考虑？是有意在规避什么东西吗？

范小青：我出生在城市，但后来跟着父母到了农村，那是刚

Yang Haocheng: You're a professional writer, but you cannot deny the fact that you're also the Chair of Jiangsu Writers Association. As a writer, on the outside, you'll have to face the world, and inside, you'll have to face your own soul. To put it another way, a writer looks for truth. We all know that being a pure writer and the head of a writers association involves many awkward contradictions that are difficult to reconcile. Our Writers Association is an official organization, quite different from the club-like nature of writers' associations overseas. You are required to be both writer and official—two very different beasts. How do you find a happy balance between the two? Or, do you live a kind of double life? Perhaps, when you are writing, you feel an invisible force controlling you? If you had to choose, would you prefer to be loyal to your writing, or loyal to the institution's regulations?

Fan Xiaoqing: Professor Yang, how can one answer that question?

Yang Haocheng: We could say that your life is basically in academia and officialdom, but what's interesting is that your choice of subject leans more towards ordinary people. It's usually the case that it's much easier for authors to manage characters who have lives familiar to their own, but you do the opposite! Is it a conscious decision? Or perhaps you are trying to avoid something?

Fan Xiaoqing: I was born in Suzhou. Then I moved with my parents to the countryside when I was twelve and just starting junior high school. It's a very sensitive age, when you sort of do and don't understand things. I was full of curiosity. I was plunged into the countryside. I went to the local school, and when I finished school in the county town at eighteen, I was sent down to the countryside

上初中的时候,正是敏感的年龄,对一切似懂非懂,充满了好奇。农村的一切突然间出现在了我的面前,我在农村中学上学,在县城读完高中后自己又插队到了农村。六年中跟农村孩子、跟农民的近距离的接触,给我留下了难忘的印象,我既熟悉他们,时过境迁后也很愿意写他们。后来上大学、留校当老师、做专业作家,则开始了别样的人生。但我的生活总的说来并无多少起伏,对于一个专业作家来说,这构成了一种局限。为了丰富自己的经历,为写作提供足够的素材,我便有意识地回到自己的家乡苏州的市民中去,还在居委会、在区政府等挂职,这就开始了一批反映普通市民生活的小说创作。至于你说到的反映知识阶层和官场的小说,前者确实很少;后者虽然不多,但还是有,包括《女同志》在内的三个长篇,就分别写了官场女干部、乡镇干部和城市干部。我为什么不写知识分子呢?我想原因可能是因为这些人和事靠我太近了。生活比艺术更丰富。作为作家,我太了解他们,了解他们就像了解我自己一样,因此提起笔来容易写得太实,一不小心就让人对号入座。而改造他们另外创造吧,还不如真实的人和事丰富和丰满;生活中的他们更加精彩。比如我写某个文化单位,肯定是一写出来,人家就知道你是怎么回事,就去对号入座了。

again. Six years of school with country children, and of close contact with country people, left a deep impression on me. I knew them, and later on I wanted to write about them. Then I went to university, and stayed on as a teacher and professional writer, and I began a different kind of life. But on the whole, there have been very few ups and downs in my life, and for a professional writer, this constitutes something of a limitation. In order to enrich my experience, and to have enough source-material for writing, I consciously went back to the people of my hometown, and worked for the local residents' committee, and for the local government, and I started to do some creative writing that reflected the lives of ordinary citizens.

You mentioned reflecting academia and officialdom in fiction. I've barely touched on academia in my writing, and have written only a few pieces that concern officialdom, but there are some, including *Women Comrades* and two other long pieces in which I wrote about a few female cadres in officialdom, cadres in a small town and cadres in the city. Why don't I write about academics? I think the reason may be because the people and their concerns are too close to my own. Life is richer than art. As a writer, I understand them too well. Understanding academics is like understanding myself, so if I write about them it's very likely that I would write too realistically, and you have to be careful or you'll have people trying to find their own places in your fiction. You can try transforming them by inventing extra things, but it wouldn't be as rich or as vivid as those people and their concerns in real life. For example, if I write about a particular cultural organization, people will immediately know where

杨昊成： 您是说写这些人有一定的冒险性？怕惹麻烦？

范小青： 倒也不是，不完全是。我是怕生活的真实压倒了艺术的创造。艺术来源于生活，但艺术与生活之间毕竟还是有距离的，也必须要有距离。比如我的农村题材的小说，并不是我当年刚离开农村时就写出来的，而是过了二三十年之后才写的，那时经过沉淀和过滤，我可以写了，也懂得如何去写自己曾经生活过的农村。对于知识分子，我想也会做这样的处理：只要我有能力，我将来一定会写到他们的。

杨昊成： 前天上午，哈佛大学英文系的一位博士生到我家采访我，她的导师是我们《中华人文》的顾问之一，向她推荐了我。我们谈到中国文化和文学走出去的问题。我说，中国作家要真正走出去，为世界所认可，很难，可谓"路漫漫其修远兮"。因此，不论官方还是作家们自己，都不能盲目地乐观。希望当然是有的，要素有三：首先所推作家必须具有真正的实力，像鲁迅那样，半个多世纪以来，其魅力经久不衰；其次是媒介，具体说就是外语，外语要好，而且能最大限度地再现原作的精髓；三是持续不断地努力，译介一次不行，译介某一面还不够，必须以重量级的作品，反复而立体地冲击读者的视觉，才能给人留下深刻的印象，收到

I'm coming from, and they'll try to find their own places.

Yang Haocheng: Are you saying that it would be dangerous to write about those people? Are you afraid of getting into trouble?

Fan Xiaoqing: Not really. I'm just scared that the reality of life might overwhelm the artistic creation. Life is the source of art, but there is a distance between art and life, and it's essential that there is this distance. For example, my stories about the countryside were not written immediately after I left there, but twenty or thirty years later, when there had been time for that material to settle and filter through. By then, I understood how to write about the life I had lived in the countryside. As for academia, I think it will be much the same, and if one day I have the ability to write about academics, then I will.

Yang Haocheng: The day before yesterday, a PhD student from the English Department at Harvard came to visit me at home. Her supervisor is one of the advisors to *Chinese Arts and Letters*, and had recommended that her student contact me. We talked about Chinese culture and Chinese literature going out into the world, so the world can know about it, and how difficult it is. "The road will be long. Our climb will be steep." Neither officialdom nor individual writers can afford to take it for granted. Of course, there is hope, and we have three main considerations in mind in how to achieve our ambition. First, the authors being promoted must have staying power, like Lu Xun, whose appeal hasn't diminished over the last half century. Second, we must promote them in foreign language media, which must be of good quality and must succeed in conveying the essence of the original. Third, we must consolidate our efforts:

理想的效果。以您作为作家和省作协主席的双重身份,您怎么看中国文学走出去?莫言获诺奖对您有触动吗?据您所知或所感,对您认识的其他一线作家有触动吗?

范小青:您说的这三个要素我完全赞同,尤其是第二第三这两个方面,我们迫切需要能够真正地"最大限度地再现原作精髓"的外语支持,还需要"反复而立体地冲击读者的视觉"的不断努力,而您现在所做的正是这样的努力,在这里我想我应该要代表江苏作协和江苏的作家们,向您和您的团队表示最崇高的敬意和最真挚的感谢!莫言获诺奖,更证明了您的这个观点。作为具有实力但又十分内敛低调的大部分中国作家来说,真的十分需要推动力。

2015 年

a single translation is not enough, nor is the translation of one single aspect; we need to take our strongest works and promote them in a range of media repeatedly, and thereby make an impact, a very deep impression. In your roles as writer and Chair of Jiangsu Writers Association, how do you see Chinese literature going out into the world? What kind of impact did Mo Yan's winning of the Nobel Prize have on you? And on any other writers that you know?

Fan Xiaoqing: I completely agree with you on these three points, especially on the second and third ones. It is absolutely right that foreign language editions "must succeed in conveying the essence of the original" and that we must strive to deliver them repeatedly and in different media, so that the impact will be felt. This is what you are doing now, and in this respect, on behalf of Jiangsu Writers Association, and Jiangsu writers generally, I'd like to express our greatest respect and sincere gratitude to you and your team! Mo Yan's winning the Nobel Prize certainly validates this point of view. For powerful yet modest introverts, as the majority of Chinese writers are, this is so necessary and truly inspirational.

2015